TERRORISM

TERRORISM

Roots, Impact, Responses

Edited by
LAWRENCE HOWARD

PRAEGER

New York
Westport, Connecticut
London

Library of Congress Cataloging-in-Publication Data

Terrorism : roots, impact, responses / edited by Lawrence Howard.
   p. cm.
   "This book grew out of the proceedings of a lecture series on
terrorism sponsored by the Global Peace and Conflict Studies (GPACS)
Program at the University of California, Irvine"—Pref.
   Includes bibliographical references and index.
   ISBN 0–275–94020–9 (alk. paper)
   1. Terrorism.   I. Howard, Lawrence, 1945–
HV6431.T497   1992
303.6'25—dc20   91–37252

British Library Cataloguing in Publication Data is available.

Library of Congress Catalog Card Number: 91–37252
ISBN: 0–275–94020–9

First published in 1992

Praeger Publishers, One Madison Avenue, New York, NY 10010
An imprint of Greenwood Publishing Group, Inc.

Printed in the United States of America

The paper used in this book complies with the
Permanent Paper Standard issued by the National
Information Standards Organization (Z39.48–1984).

10 9 8 7 6 5 4 3 2 1

Copyright Acknowledgment

The chapter by Abraham H. Miller was previously published in *Terrorism and Political
Violence* 2, no. 3 (Autumn 1990). It is reprinted here with the kind permission of Frank Cass
and Company, Ltd., Gainsborough House, London E11 1RS, England.

This book is dedicated to Thomas and Elizabeth Tierney,
whose generosity and vision brought it into being.
With the efforts of people like these,
the world will not wait long for peace.

Contents

Contents

Preface

This book grew out of the proceedings of a lecture series on terrorism sponsored by the Global Peace and Conflict Studies (GPACS) Program at the University of California, Irvine (UCI), funded by a generous gift from the family of Thomas and Elizabeth Tierney.

All essays written for this volume were presented as public lectures at the university during the academic year 1989–1990 and have been revised substantially since then. Our intention was to bring together some of the world's most distinguished experts on terrorism to share their insight and engage in dialogue with the university community on this vital topic of personal and international security.

All contributors were asked to address the causal background (the roots) of terrorism and the impact on various audiences and institutions and to suggest responses that they believe should form the bases of public policy. To the extent possible, transcripts were exchanged among these experts to encourage dialogue. The mix of professional expertise—ranging from 19th century history, Middle Eastern culture, political science and psychology—and the topics surveyed makes this collection both rich and timely.

Several scholars, some of whom wrote chapters for this volume, provided invaluable advice and support during the various stages of this project. I owe special thanks to Christon Archer of the University of Calgary; Brian Jenkins of Kroll Associates; David C. Rapoport of UCLA; and Keith Nelson and Riley Newman, my colleagues in the GPACS Program at UCI. I also wish to thank Russ Dalton, Raul Fernandez, Karl Hufbauer, Greg Kavka, and Margot Norris for their helpful comments on chapters. Finally, I owe a special debt to Paul Wilkinson of the University of St. Andrews, Scotland. These scholars all gave freely of their time and encouragement in bringing this project to fruition.

While I am deeply in their debt for their assistance, all errors, of course, are mine.

I also owe enormous thanks to my editor at Greenwood Press, James Sabin, who never failed to return my harried calls with patience, humor, and always helpful advice, and to my production editor, Nita Romer, who saved my fish from the fire more times than I can count.

Finally, I wish to express my appreciation to Susan D'Antonio for her assistance in editing; to Bonnie L'Allier for her prompt transcriptions; to Bobbye Powers and Magda Agramonte for printing, copying and mailing correspondence to everyone from my scribbled notes without a flaw; to Cheryl Larsson and Ziggy Bates for turning separate floppies organized every which way into a coherent and beautiful manuscript. And finally, to Daniel C. Tsoug, the Social Sciences Bibliographer, for all his assistance in correcting dreadful citations and in compiling the index. To all of you I extend my deepest thanks.

TERRORISM

Introduction

Lawrence Howard

I feel no desire for vengeance. I feel no desire for retribution. I don't
see them as positive; I don't see them as meaningful. I find these things
self-maiming and I do not intend maiming myself.
      Brian Keenan, held hostage 52 months in Lebanon, August 24, 1990

The phenomenon of terrorism has become a major concern of the American
public. The Reagan administration elevated it to the foremost foreign policy
problem of the nation.[1] The American and Canadian publics consider terrorism to be a greater threat to their personal safety than driving on the
freeways and working at their jobs, worse even than the risk of nuclear war.
However, these same people are much more at risk from their jobs and their
daily commute than they are from terrorist attacks—by orders of magnitude.[2]
In the past two decades fewer than 500 Americans have been killed in incidents of international terrorism.[3] Gary Sick, formerly staffing the Iran desk
of the National Security Council in the Carter administration, reports that in
1985 a total of twenty-three U.S. citizens died in terrorist incidents around
the world, one quarter of the number killed that year by lightning.[4] Terrorism,
abhorrent as it is, is largely a symbolic threat to America.

America also continues to be relatively free of the threat of domestic
terrorism[5] and the draconian anti-terrorist measures that many states endure.
The obligatory stroll through the airport metal-detectors is as close as most
Americans come to encountering the reality of an anti-terrorist regime. Yet
we are obsessed with terrorism. One result of the Gulf War has been the
wholesale cancellation of airplane travel plans and even terrorist acts *by*
Americans.[6] The fact that the public is so gripped by terrorism actually may
serve to reinforce it: if one of its purposes is to rivet the public's attention,

terrorism may be said to be actually "working." The question of whether we as a people should give terrorism this sort of legitimacy is one I hope the reader will keep in mind while reading these chapters.

Terrorism does pose serious questions for democratic societies. This is not the question of terrorism undermining the legitimacy of the government of the United States by provoking a breakdown of the social order. "On balance," notes Martha Crenshaw, "terrorism assists in the demise of regimes already distressed."[7] What is more worrisome is that the threat of terrorism may work to shift the balance of power in the regime away from institutions of democratic participation and civil liberties toward the military and the police. It is hard to imagine a better *shibboleth* to rally the forces of repression than terrorism.

How a democracy should respond to terrorism is explored in the chapter by Brian Michael Jenkins, formerly the senior policy analyst on terrorism for the RAND Corporation, who has advised the U.S. government about terrorism for over seventeen years. He uses the opportunity of this chapter to step back from the immediate policy recommendations to reflect on the larger questions terrorism poses for democratic societies.

Jenkins considers the planting of bombs on aircraft to be the major security threat terrorism poses to the United States today. Whereas in the past terrorism on aircraft principally involved seizure of the plane for hostage-holding, more recently bombings have become the principle method of terrorist attacks on aircraft. This change in tactics has made terrorism a more deadly affair: both the number of attacks and the mortality per attack had shown an increasing trend.[8] Jenkins describes the increasing prevalence of insurgent terrorism and explores the mindset of individuals and groups that engage in or may well turn to terrorism.

Despite his warning, and despite his judgment that terrorism will continue to be a feature of the modern world, Jenkins does not think this threat is worth undermining the distinctive features of democratic government. In his mind, our democratic institutions are themselves a bulwark against terrorism,[9] and neither the public's right to travel nor to read uncensored news should be sacrificed in a campaign against terrorism:

If we were forced to change the rules that govern the news media for terrorists, we would have suffered a grave defeat, the terrorists would have won a great victory. So it will remain a vulnerability which they can exploit. But I wouldn't ground aircraft to prevent hijackings, and I wouldn't shut down the media to prevent terrorism.

While many[10] argue that an effective campaign against terrorism requires strengthening the powers of the police to arrest suspects, of the courts to expedite sentencing, and of the president to prosecute pocket campaigns against states suspected of harboring terrorist activities, Jenkins is much less excitable. Except for situations where hostages may be recovered, he argues that giving the president extraordinary powers to attack terrorist bases or retaliate against states sponsoring terrorism accomplishes little good. Indeed, it can be wholly counterproductive when it reinspires the hatred that would provoke further terrorism. When the president believes military force is necessary to retaliate against terrorists or the states sponsoring their activities, he should seek a formal declaration of war from Congress. Such a formal commitment by the United States constrains and legitimizes us in exactly the way terrorists are not.

The phenomenon of terrorism is commonly thought to be a recent event in modern postwar history, often associated in the public's mind with radical Palestinians or members of fundamentalist Islamic groups who wreak spiteful acts of terror against the innocent to fulfill the commands of the Koran. The chapters by Christon Archer and Khalid Duran raise challenges for these commonplaces by, separately, showing that many of the abhorrent features of terrorism occurred in earlier periods far from the Middle East and that the terrorism arising in Muslim countries does not reflect the injunctions of Islam as much as the history of colonialism and the cynical behavior of modern governments—some of them allied with the United States.

Archer, a historian of colonial Mexico at the University of Calgary, shows that terrorism had a long and bloody role in the war leading up to Mexican independence. Exhibited here are many of the trends of insurgency and counterinsurgency campaigns of the modern era. There were the root factors of colonial occupation, rising unemployment and inflation, the unequal distribution of land and privileges among different ethnic groups, and even a messianic religious movement. The pattern of military suppression by the Spanish to keep New Spain and the pattern of the insurrection foreshadow the Algerian war of independence and the French and American experience in Indo-China.

The military forces of royalist Spain, operating from key cities and struggling to keep open lines of supply and communication between fortified outposts, never lost a major military campaign against the insurgent forces, who held vast areas of the countryside. These insurgents ranged from true nationalists to bands of criminals who seized hostages for ransom. Some insurgent mobs committed heinous murders. As the military became frustrated with pacification, they turned more and more to draconian means of suppression: from destroying homes of suspected bandits (a policy employed today in the Israeli occupation of the West Bank) to outright campaigns of mass executions and scorched earth waged against whole regions. But these efforts failed. As the efficacy of the royalist army diminished along with its morale, the cost to Spain mounted, and she granted Mexico independence. The seeds of violence sown in Mexican society were to continue to flower for decades.

Khalid Duran, an international scholar of Islamic culture at the Foreign Policy Research Institute, points out that the modern image of a terrorist as a Muslim fanatic is a stereotype that obscures the salient fact that such violence

is specifically forbidden in the Koran. Islamic terrorism is a complex contemporary phenomenon whose roots lie in the anti-colonial struggles still
unresolved in the Middle East, in the disparity of wealth between Middle
Eastern states, and in the simmering problem of Palestine. But most of all
such terrorism is the result of the actions of authoritarian states which cynically
wrap themselves in the sanctification of Islam. Professor Duran argues that
the principal inspiration for Middle Eastern terrorism is neither Islam nor
the struggle of the PLO against Israel but European fascism and communism
and the successful campaigns of Jewish terrorists against British rule in
Palestine.

He argues further that the state-sanctioned terrorism, of which Washington
accuses Libya or Syria, pales before the terrorist network organized world-
wide from revolutionary Iran. But this violence, principally directed against
Western targets, is still less than that carried out by the Pakistani Intelligence
Service, the principal conduit for U.S. funds to the Afghan resistance fighting
the Soviet-installed government in Kabul. The irony is that the victims of this
terror have been for the most part Western-oriented members of the Afghan
resistance movement, killed because they resisted both the pro-Pakistani
fundamentalists as well as the Soviet occupation of their country. Pakistan's
motives are neither religious nor altruistic, but geopolitical: to gain control
over Afghanistan so as to be better placed for the next war with India. This
chapter calls for a serious reexamination of the fundamentals of U.S. anti-
terrorism policy.

Martha Crenshaw of Wesleyan University examines the psychological factors
that permit people to engage in the indiscriminate violence that so evokes
the public's outrage at terrorism. Professor Crenshaw argues that insurgent
terrorists deliberately choose outrageous acts of violence precisely because
they violate the norms of civilized behavior. To understand this sort of choice
requires a strategic analysis to exhibit the rational choice of an organization;
for these are political acts carried out by political groups.

She argues that a political analysis, by itself, is inadequate to explain why
some groups like ETA (Euskadi ta Askataguna or Basque Fatherland and
Liberty Movement), the terrorist group purporting to speak for the Basques
who were suppressed during the Franco regime in Spain, continue to engage
in terrorism long after political suppression has ended. Although the parliamentary government that replaced Franco has been trying to negotiate an
end to the conflict, the terrorist campaign continues.[11] Crenshaw argues that
to understand how this occurs requires a psychological analysis to assess the
role of personal and group-psychological determinants of violence. A willingness to commit violent actions propels impatient, revenge-seeking individuals onto the world stage, an elevation that both enhances their status
within their clandestine group and, also, makes them spokespersons for
causes that would normally eschew them. Coupling psychological with strategic analyses can explain the different tactics various groups employ, from

planting bombs to the taking of hostages, and a wise response requires an assessment of the particular mix of factors that serves to hold the group together and those that may be manipulated to help dissolve it.

Engaging in an Entebbe-like rescue of hostages or the capture of the *Achille Lauro* hijackers can be a prudent use of military force. However, like Jenkins, Crenshaw argues that retaliation against terrorist bases or against their suspected patron states has not shown itself to be particularly effective against terrorism and may only reinvigorate the motivation of the terrorists themselves. Sober good sense and not hysteria is required to respond effectively to terrorism.

Nehemia Friedland, a social psychologist at Tel Aviv University, takes this argument a step further when he argues that a political framework for understanding insurgent terrorism can be rigorously constructed from social psychological axioms. Psychological explanations based on personal psychopathology are inadequate to account for the occurrence of terrorism. Individual propensities must be examined in the context of intergroup conflict between groups of greatly different power. Friedland modifies the frustration-aggression explanations of John Dollard and Ted Robert Gurr to develop a quasi-formal decision-making model to describe when the violence of a group reflects the participation of violence-prone individuals and when it reflects a reaction to iniquitous social conditions. Such a model should predict, if the data may be obtained, when individuals with a personal tendency toward violence can sway a group toward acts of terrorism and when their presence would not matter. This very powerful, well-argued concept could help resolve important anomalies in the literature—such as the continuing Basque violence and why young, educated West Europeans, often of upper-middle class backgrounds, can feel impelled to commit acts of terrorism for the sake of oppressed groups of completely different social status from themselves.

These social psychological factors mediating terrorism are facilitated by external factors of the ready access to modern weapons, the ease of worldwide transportation and, finally, the access to the electronic media. Friedland argues that "the greatest contribution to the heightened potential effectiveness of terrorism is due to the current technical capabilities and orientation of the news media. . . . Taking advantage of the capabilities and operating philosophy of the media, practitioners of terrorism have become highly 'cost effective.' "

Alex Schmid of the University of Leiden expands on this theme by arguing that terrorism is violence focused on the media and enhanced by it. Terrorist acts are "pseudo-events" performed to attract the media's eye and bring their perpetrators to the world stage. Schmid thinks that "the media inspire and encourage terrorism, that they are the oxygen which terrorists need to stay alive." From the time of Herostratus, who set the temple of Artemis ablaze to immortalize his name, people have attempted violent acts to gain notoriety for themselves or public attention for their cause. The electronic media, in their demand for gripping images, play into the hands of these people. With excruciating care Schmid describes flagrant cases of media abuse in which family members of hostages are cruelly hounded for a story while a loved one is still at risk, or in which hostages have been killed by their captors after the media have identified them as people of importance. The issue is not simply one of thoughtless reporting. It is rather the larger issue of whether, if terrorist acts are performed to catch the media's attention, some form of media censorship is required. Professor Schmid thinks the media should practice a measure of self censorship: "Between a blackout and saturation coverage there is room for a reasonable compromise. I believe that some form of restraint, agreed upon between the editors of all major media, would not be in conflict with the First Amendment of the U.S. Constitution."

How big a step is it from self-imposed restraint to public censorship? How much is a democracy giving up by taking this step? Should democratic states under siege try to separate terrorists from their "oxygen?" Is suppression of press freedom a wise tradeoff for state security? Two democratic countries that have chosen censorship to deal with terrorism are the United Kingdom and the Republic of Ireland.

In 1974 the Republic of Ireland's Minister of Posts and Telegraphs banned members of organizations deemed "terrorist" from speaking on television. Subsequently, the British government did the same with the passage of the Prevention of Terrorism Act of 1974. The immediate cause of this legislative action was a spate of IRA bombings in England itself. The intent of the legislation was to protect the democratic way of life from the actions of a violent minority. Abraham Miller of the University of Cincinnati shows how a democratic government under siege can persecute the innocent in a frantic attempt to defend itself against terrorism and how free and persistent media were alone capable of rectifying this wrong.

Miller describes the case of the Guildford Four who were convicted of bombings that killed seven and injured forty-two during a campaign conducted by the Provisional IRA in England. In the resulting climate of outrage and fear, four young people and seven others (including the invalid father of one) were sentenced to long terms of imprisonment on the bases of perjury and forced confessions despite implausible features of the culprits, a paucity of physical evidence, and charges of police torture. Their cases were rejected by the Court of Appeals even after IRA operatives captured red-handed in another crime demonstrated in court that they had made these attacks! The eleven people languished in jail for fifteen years, the invalid father dying there.

Ultimately, the electronic media became the court of last appeal. Stories on this case were run on television, carefully so as to avoid censorship. But they had the effect of reopening this case by keeping the facts of the mistrial before the public's eye until the authorities were forced to reexamine the convictions. A democracy under siege, fearful of its loss of authority, weighed the value of public order against the civil liberties of individuals and chose in favor of the state, mistakenly believing that this was the effective way to combat terrorism. The resulting forced confessions, destruction of evidence, and outright fabrication of other "evidence" by the police coupled with an unwillingness of the judicial system to believe the extent of police misconduct produced one of the worst miscarriages of justice in the history of English law.[12] Miller concludes:

Ultimately, however, such tactics contribute little to the preservation of democracy. Instead they call into question the very legitimacy of the system and make it appear that the system has resorted to its own brand of violence to deal with its political frustration as the terrorists have used violence to deal with their political grievances.

What are the future prospects for terrorism world-wide? Bruce Hoffman, a researcher in the Behavioral Science Department of the RAND Corporation, thinks terrorism and insurgent violence spring from common roots, and the United States faces a "revolution in warfare that it is unprepared for." While Europe has undergone remarkable political change with little resort to force, terrorism and insurgent violence are becoming more ubiquitous in the Third-World and more violent in their effects. This is in part because terrorism has been shown to "work." The access to the world stage gained by the all but unknown Palestinian cause after the 1972 attack on Israeli athletes at the Munich Olympics is a lesson not lost on other groups struggling for social change. Other reasons for a continuing prospect of violence include the dissemination of high technology weapons—from *Semtex* to SAMS—the presence of unresolved political conflicts, and the growing economic hopelessness and political frustration of vast numbers of people world-wide. The third and fourth generations of Palestinians are now growing up in refugee camps in Lebanon, where they are preyed on by murderous militias and bombed by foreign aircraft. In the slums of Lima, children as young as fourteen join the *Sendero Luminoso* ("The Shining Path") as the only believable option to crushing poverty. While some think it specious to locate the roots of terrorism in the festering conditions of the third world,[13] Hoffman sees the pressure of these factors tending toward more extreme and more diverse violence, violence euphemistically described as "low intensity conflict."

Despite locating the roots of terrorism in the iniquitous societies of the third world, Hoffman counsels a greater use of military force to respond to terrorist incidents than do other contributors. The United States must hold the state-patrons of insurgent groups responsible for the terrorism wrought with their support. Since the actual bases of the terrorists that would attack our interests are usually neither permanent nor centralized, the United States has "no choice" but to attack targets in the patron state.

Attacks should be crafted in such a way as to send a powerful message, not to create martyrs and therefore prove counterproductive in the long run. Operations that strike at a terrorists state-patron's economic infrastructure—oil fields and refineries, for example—or that disrupt internal and external telecommunications or black out entire cities by damaging power transmitters and substations will have a more salutary impact than those that kill innocent civilians. They will also help the United States escape at least some international criticism.

The embarrassment caused to the United States by the bombing of a "command post" in Baghdad that sheltered hundreds of civilians during the Gulf War underscores this point.[14]

However, the estimate of 170,000 infant deaths in Iraq due to the collapse of hospitals and sewage systems this summer as a direct result of such "crafted" targeting calls even this policy into question.[15] This preponderance of civilian deaths is one of the reasons that the Vatican refused to declare this campaign a "just war."[16] Although the military briefers declared these to be "collateral" or unintended deaths during the campaign, comments by Pentagon officials since then reveal these components essential to a modern state to have been deliberately targeted, at least in part, to send a message to the Iraqi citizenry. In the words of one Air Force officer, "The definition of innocents gets to be a little bit unclear. . . . They do live there, and ultimately the people have some control over what goes on in their country."[17] The similarity of such thinking to that of terrorists who randomly place bombs to compel an enraged citizenry to assail their government should give us serious pause. It is to the credit of Dr. Hoffman that he distances himself from such barbarism: "Although dramatic reprisal operations without specific objectives may assuage the American public's frustration, they have little, if any, effect on the terrorists." The wisdom of the policy of retaliation remains to be shown.

Hoffman's account of this situation is grim reading at best. It points up the policy-maker's pressure to act. Yet we cannot close our minds to these issues of oppression, disenfranchisement, and poverty, hoping they will go away. To take an ostrich-like approach will surely lead to being rudely wakened by further outrageous acts of terrorism, for these crimes are designed to grab the attention. The climate of hysteria leads to strident demands to lash out at someone. Such hysteria can compromise the values of a democratic order— witness the abuses of the Guildford Four case. They serve to create still more hatred and vengeance and weaken the possibility of legitimizing a world order committed to values we do hold dear: human rights, economic justice, and political access.

This concern is echoed by Professor Paul Wilkinson of St. Andrews University in "Observations on the Relationship of Freedom and Terrorism." Surveying the momentous events of 1989 and 1990 culminating in the reunification of Germany, free elections in Eastern Europe, and the collapse of the Warsaw Pact, Professor Wilkinson sees a deeply rooted human impulse toward political freedom that has succeeded in some instances in the face of repression by the state and has, itself, been characterized by the total eschewal of terrorism. Wilkinson reasons that we should not neglect the magnetic drawing power of democratic institutions: the Western democracies served as beacon-lights for this process. The former Soviet Union itself went through this revolution, reversing a seventy year course of one-party rule and dissolving the process. A consequence of this liberalization of Eastern Europe will be the vulnerability to insurgent terrorism that these new democratic governments suffer. It is a vulnerability unique to democratic government and one that should not be compromised to suppress terrorism.

In a second chapter, "Can the European Community Develop a Concerted Policy on Terrorism?" Professor Wilkinson examines the impact of the lowering of borders that will come as the European Community proceeds toward economic and political integration in 1992. He argues that although there has been considerable care taken with establishing accords on integrating the economies of the European nations, little work has been accomplished in creating a common policy towards terrorism. The events of this year should serve to remind us that Europe is not free of terrorism.[18]

Professor Wilkinson argues that the European Community would strengthen security for all members by establishing a common European legal policy toward terrorism. The establishment of a common legal regime would bolster individual states in the face of terrorist intimidation. Much of the criticism raised against the utility of international law as a tool to deal with terrorism is that it is impotent because such law is hopelessly politicized over definitional issues and bereft of any mechanisms of enforcement.[19] This leaves states with little resort but to engage in divisive expeditions such as the Reagan bombing campaign against Libya, which may well have provoked the attack on the Pan Am Flight 103 which killed 271 persons at Lockerbie, Scotland.[20]

The European Community already shares much closer legal commonality than the world as a whole, including a shared terrorist threat, functioning courts such as the European Court of Human Rights, and a continuing commitment toward economic and political integration. The suggestions developed here will go a long way toward establishing a seamless regime of law to combat these kinds of crimes. The efforts of the European Community will serve as a model for the international regime of law that may well be our best hope for finally containing terrorism. This is an encouraging and inspiring chapter on which to close this collection.

NOTES

1. Robert Oakley (formerly Ambassador at Large for Counter-Terrorism at the Department of State), "International Terrorism," *Foreign Affairs* 65, no. 3 (1987): 611.

2. Ronald D. Crenlinsten, "Terrorism, Counter-terrorism and Democracy: The Assessment of National Security Threats," *Terrorism and Political Violence* 1, no. 2 (April 1989): 242.

3. Cited in the chapter by Alex Schmid of this volume.

4. Gary Sick, "Further Into a Trap" (op-ed), *The New York Times*, 27 April 1986.

5. This is not to say that the United States is free of domestic terrorism, as the chapters by Jenkins, Hoffman, and Wilkinson show. See also Bruce Hoffman, *Recent Trends and Future Prospects of Terrorism in the United States* (Santa Monica, CA: The RAND Corporation, R-3618, May 1988) for a recent review.

6. See Bob Drogin and Charles P. Wallace, "As Terrorist Acts Multiply, Iraqis are Expelled," *Los Angeles Times*, 22 January 1991 for some of these. They include the account of a fifteen-year-old Florida boy who threw a pipe bomb at the home of an Indian family he believed to be Iraqi. *The New York Times* of 10 February 1991 also reports the arrest of three men who blew up chemical storage tanks in Virginia to collect insurance while hoping the Iraqis would be blamed.

7. Martha Crenshaw, *Terrorism, Legitimacy, and Power: The Consequences of Political Violence* (Middletown, CT: Wesleyan University, 1982), 8.

8. Fortunately, even this worrisome climb has begun to decline. The U.S. State Department reported: "The continuing decline in the number of international terrorist incidents during 1990 is encouraging. From a peak of 856 in 1988, the number of incidents decreased to 455 in 1990." See *Patterns of Global Terrorism: 1990* (Washington, D.C.: United States Department of State Publications, April 1990), iii.

9. A view also articulated by Wilkinson in his chapter "Observations on Terrorism and Freedom."

10. See Robert Kupperman and Jeff Kamen, *Final Warning: Averting Disaster in the New Age of Terrorism* (New York: Doubleday, 1989); Claire Sterling, *The Terror Network: The Secret War of International Terrorism* (New York: Holt, Rinehart, and Winston, 1981); Benjamin Netanyahu, *Terrorism: How the West Can Win* (New York: Farrar, Straus, Giroux, 1986), and *Fighting Back: Winning the War Against Terrorism*, ed. Neil Livingston and Terrell E. Arnold (Lexington, Mass.: Lexington Books, 1986) for some representative examples of this approach to the problem.

11. Robert P. Clark, "Negotiating with Insurgents: Obstacles to Peace in the Basque Country," *Terrorism and Political Violence* 2, no.4 (Winter 1990), 490.

12. As this volume goes to press, six Northern Irishmen sentenced in a parallel case, known as the Birmingham Six, have likewise been released from English prisons for similarly tainted convictions. Craig R. Whitney, "British Free 6 Jailed in '74 Blasts," *The New York Times*, 15 March 1991.

13. Benjamin Netanyahu articulates this position in *Terrorism: How the West Can Win*, 204:

The root cause of terrorism is not in grievances but in a disposition toward unbridled violence. This can be traced to a world view which asserts that certain ideological and religious goals justify, indeed demand, the shedding of all moral inhibitions. In this context, the observation that the root cause of terrorism is terrorists is more than a tautology.

14. Alessandra Stanley, "Iraq Says U.S. Killed Hundreds of Civilians at Shelter, But Allies Call it Military Post," *The New York Times*, 14 February 1991.

15. Nina Burleigh, "Watching Children Starve to Death: An Exclusive Look at the Suffering Inside Iraq's Devastated Hospitals," *Time* 10 June 1991: 56. This number

exceeds by almost twice the number of Iraqi military deaths estimated by the Department of Defense. See Patrick E. Tyler, "Iraq's War Toll Estimated by U.S." *The New York Times* 5 June 1991.

16. Clyde Haberman, "Pope Denounces the Gulf War As 'Darkness' Over Mankind," *The New York Times*, 1 April 1991.

17. Barton Gellman, "Storming Damage in the Persian Gulf: U.S. Strategy Against Iraq Went Beyond Strictly Military Targets," *The Washington Post National Weekly Edition*, 8–14 July 1991: 6.

18. IRA attacks in London and renewed RAF killings in Germany. See Jenkins' chapter, this volume.

19. See useful criticisms of international legal measures dealing with terrorism in Grant Wardlaw, *Political Terrorism: Theory, Tactics, and Counter-Measures*, 2nd ed. (New York: Cambridge University Press, 1989) and in Abraham D. Sofaer, "Terrorism and the Law," *Foreign Affairs* 64, no. 5 (Summer 1986): 901–22.

20. Robin Wright and Ronald L. Ostrow, "Pan Am 103 Clue Leads to Libyans," *Los Angeles Times*, 24 June 1991. The United States has now formally charged Libyan agents with this crime. See Andrew Rosenthal, "U.S. accuses Libya as 2 are charged in Pan Am Bombing," *The New York Times* 15 November 1991. Critics argue that this indictment should not be taken to exonerate Iran, which also had a motive to seek retaliation for the accidental downing of Iranian Air Flight 655 by the U.S. cruiser Vincennes on July 3, 1988, killing all 290 persons abroad. Much evidence has pointed to the Popular Front For the Liberation of Palestine-General Command (PFLP-GC), a contract terrorist group operating out of Syria, as the agent of the Lockerbie attack. See Steven Emerson and Brian Duffy, *The Fall of PAN AM 103: Inside the Lockerbie Investigation* (New York: G. P. Putman's Sons, 1990) for a readable account of this evidence. Critics within the Israeli and the American governments are convinced that the Iranians and Syrians were involved and that the United States is whitewashing their role. See Clyde Haberman, "Israelis Remain Convinced Syrians Downed Flight 103," *The New York Times*, 21 November 1991 and David Johnston, "Pan Am Bombing Case Still Open, U.S. Aides Say," *The New York Times*, 26 November, 1991. Several reasons could be at work here: the desire to keep Syria in the Middle East Peace process, to secure continued Iranian cooperation in releasing hostages in Lebanon, or to demonize the Libyan government before the U.S. presidential elections. Clearly the final chapter on this tragedy has yet to be written.

1

Terrorism: A Contemporary Problem with Age-old Dilemmas

Brian Michael Jenkins

In this chapter, I want to review some of the larger issues of terrorism, the ones that are out of the policy briefings given to government officials. I want to underscore the caveats, the uncertainties, and some of the fundamental questions raised by terrorism for a democratic society. Many of these are discussed in the academic literature and will be examined in subsequent chapters. I hope to bring some of these uncertainties and questions before the public because, in our form of government, it is the public who is ultimately responsible for our policy. Given the importance of the problem, and the hysteria and demagoguery present in much of this literature, the public deserves better.

The philosophical questions are the most fascinating part of the subject of terrorism. They are the ones requiring the most careful reflection. Not how many guns the IRA has or how many pounds of *Semtex* it takes to blow up an embassy, but questions like, how far may one go in the name of a cause? Do the ends ever justify means? Is terrorism morally evil, or is it simply a problematic form of violence? Does providing for the common defense, as called for in the Constitution, extend to the threat of terrorism? Indeed, what responsibility does a government have to its citizens when they are held hostage abroad or they are killed by a bomb placed to maximize random casualties? Should we ever bargain for hostages? Should we ever use military force as an instrument of anti-terrorism policy, or should the organized, state-sanctioned taking of human life and the destruction of property be reserved for only the most serious threats to our national survival? All of these questions are laced through the topic of terrorism.

What exactly do we mean by terrorism? It is imperative to begin with the problem of definition because terrorism is a politically and emotionally loaded subject and the term is applied indiscriminately to all sorts of acts of violence. The word itself is unescapably pejorative and is often used as a political weapon. But for the purpose of objective research, as opposed to the purposes of propaganda, some definition must be applied.

It is possible to define terrorism objectively as long as we define it in terms of the quality of the act, and not in terms of the identity of the perpetrator nor the nature of the cause. This removes us from the dilemma of "one man's terrorist, is another man's freedom-fighter." Of course, choosing to define terrorism in this way is itself a value judgment. It is a backhanded way of saying that ends do not justify means.

Many would dispute this, arguing that if a cause is just, we cannot call actions in pursuit of that cause terrorism.[1] We must look not only at the actions but at the perpetrators and their goals. I reject that sort of definition. It leads to a kind of sophistry that we must avoid.

In an attempt to approach the subject objectively, our definition of a terrorist act must meet several criteria. A terrorist act is first of all an ordinary crime. As such it is defined by prohibition and proscription. All civilized societies, even primitive societies, have laws against murder, kidnapping, and the willful destruction of property. To be sure, we permit those we refer to as "privileged combatants" to break those rules in warfare. A soldier can kill in combat, and he is not designated a murderer; he is privileged to break the rules. However, even in warfare, certain restraints on the behavior of military personnel are expected: the laws of war. These are codified in international law like the Geneva Convention. Many acts of terrorism would break even these minimal limits to human violence. Those laws, for example, prohibit the taking of hostages and prohibit the deliberate application of violence against noncombatants. They define parties and territory that will be outside the conflict. On any normative grounds, terrorist acts would be crimes.

Secondly, an act of terrorism is, as we define it, carried out by an organized group. We are not talking about the actions of a lunatic who hears God whispering in his ear that the world is a wicked place and must be destroyed, who walks into a former place of employment or onto a school campus and begins shooting people. We mean actions carried out by groups for political ends.[2]

Thirdly, terrorism refers to actions that are intended to produce fear and alarm. This is critical. All acts of violence produce fear and alarm as a by-product, but in the case of terrorism, it is not a byproduct—it *is* the objective. Being confronted by a mugger who demands your wallet may be a terrifying experience, but a mugger is not a terrorist; he is interested in your wallet. A terrorist, on the other hand, is interested in the psychological effects of his violence on the people watching the event. There is, therefore, the awareness of a difference between the victims of terrorist violence and the target audience of that violence. This distinction between the victims of terrorist violence and the targets of that violence sometimes manifests itself in extraordinary ways.[3]

This problem of definition is particularly evident in international terrorism—that is, terrorist actions in which foreign targets are attacked, borders are crossed, or airliners or other international lines of commerce are attacked. The lack of a generally accepted definition of terrorism has been a barrier to international cooperation against this form of terrorism.

Slowly, however, a rough consensus on the meaning of terrorism is emerging without any international agreement on the precise definition. In the fall of 1985, members of the United Nations General Assembly unanimously condemned terrorism.[4] That was a new development because the UN had never been able to agree on what they meant by terrorism. The General Assembly said in its statement that terrorism included but was not limited to acts described in five international treaties. They referred to conventions, which deal with the hijacking of aircraft, and other criminal actions aboard aircraft[5] and to the treaty that deals with protecting diplomats.[6] Not surprisingly, despite being unable to agree on the definition of terrorism, all of the diplomats in the world have been able to agree that diplomats ought not to be a target of terrorism, whatever it is. Another treaty addresses the taking of hostages.[7] None of those treaties specifically defines terrorism, but together they cover about half of all of the incidents currently considered to fall within the category of international terrorism. So, in fact, a kind of rough definition is emerging, and those efforts to increase international cooperation plus a tremendous investment in security have had some modest results.[8]

International terrorism is, actually, an American concern. It reflects the unique terrorist problem of the United States. Although we have an appalling crime rate in this country, we fortunately have very little politically-motivated violence or domestic terrorism. But abroad the United States is the first target of terrorism. This is the price we pay for presence and influence in the world, and it is that aspect of terrorism that bothers us most as a nation, causes public outrage, and creates the dilemmas for our political leadership.

If terrorism is the organized execution of crimes of violence carried out by groups to evoke fear in a larger audience for some political purpose, what brings this about? What are the roots of terrorist violence? What motivates terrorists?

It is hard to demonstrate that there are more grievances in the world today than there were twenty, fifty, or one hundred years ago. Ethnic conflict and religious extremism are not new in the world. Fanaticism is not an invention of our time. What has changed is not the number of grievances but the ecology of violence, the environment in which the most fervent believers operate.

For one thing, weapons and explosives are more widely available than ever before, constituting a dangerous form of political pollution. Weapons have become a commodity traded freely like oil or wheat.[9] Secondly, we now live in a world of global mobility. Geographical boundaries mean nothing to terrorists, who can just get on a jet. Finally, we live in a society of mass communication in which terrorists, by creating dramatic acts, can demand a global audience. This latter aspect of the current environment deserves further comment.

An important part of the ecological change that has affected modern political violence is the fact that we live in a world where radio, television, and communication satellites provide instantaneous access to a global audience. This communication technology gives us great benefits in terms of the flow of information, but it also represents a vulnerability that terrorists exploit. There is no question that by creating dramatic incidents of violence they gain what an infantryman would call "the advantage of terrain." In this case, it is the terrain of the electronic media, especially television, much more than the medium of print. However, while terrorists exploit the kind of immediacy and visual impact you get from television, this initial tactical advantage has not translated into a strategic weapon.

Terrorists complain about the media coverage they receive.[10] Television focuses on the human drama: lives hanging in the balance, pistols pointed at people's heads, tearful family members. Those are the very things that get terrorists on television yet, paradoxically, prevent their message, whatever it is, from getting through. How many of us know more today about the grievances of the Shi'ites in Lebanon than we knew before the kidnappings in that country? How many of us know more about the cause of any of these groups that have used terrorism?

The problem is not simply that the media carry only the images and not the message. Part of it is that terrorists themselves tend to be dreadful communicators. Although they are fairly effective at getting to center stage, when they get there, they usually don't know what to do. One has only to try reading terrorist communiques to appreciate this point. The Red Brigades, for example, used to issue strategic directives, sometimes hundreds of single-spaced pages long, filled with mind-numbing prose. Even if terrorists didn't have bombs or pistols, they could still bore you to death.

What trends can we discern in international terrorism? About 20 percent of international terrorism originates in the Middle East, coming from Palestinian groups, Shi'ite factions and other Lebanon-based groups, or arising from still other Middle East conflicts. Terrorist violence by Middle Eastern groups also tends to be lethal. Therefore, although it accounts for only 20 percent of the incidents, it accounts for over 35 percent of the fatalities and certainly most of the international crises that stem from terrorism. We can expect it to persist, unless one believes that in the foreseeable future there will be a solution to the Palestinian issue capable of satisfying even the most hardline elements, a resolution to the anarchy in Lebanon satisfactory to all of the factions,[11] and a solution to all the other conflicts in the Middle East that have contributed to terrorism. This list suggests to me that Middle Eastern terrorism will persist.

Another 15 percent of the total volume of international terrorism comes from the spillover of guerrilla wars being waged in the Third World. Tamil separatists bomb Sri Lankan planes killing foreigners; Sikh separatists machine-gun a bus; Shining Path guerrillas bomb a market place in Peru; the *mujahidin* lob a rocket into Kabul killing whoever is around. Most of these guerrilla struggles have been going on for a decade and some of them for several decades; they seem likely to persist as will their readiness to engage in terrorism.

An additional 15 percent of international terrorism comes from ideologically and ethnically motivated groups in Europe. Ideologically motivated terrorism, such as that carried out by the Red Brigades in Italy, the Red Army Faction in Germany, or Action Directe in France, has in fact declined but not disappeared.[12] Furthermore, ethnic violence such as that carried out by the IRA or the Spanish Basque separatists persists as well. As authoritarian rule has lifted in Eastern Europe, old ethnic hatreds have poured out in terrorist acts and armed clashes in several countries. It seems to be easier to drop an ideology than it is to change or let go of an ethnic identity.

Several new threats loom on the horizon. One that evokes great concern in the United States is the possibility that the U.S.-led war on drug traffickers in the producing countries of Latin America will provoke a terrorist response directed not only against the Colombian government, as we have already seen, but against the United States itself.[13] This possibility will become more likely if the United States is successful in apprehending and extraditing some of the major drug traffickers.

We also see a potential for terrorist violence on the part of dissident student movements in Asia—South Korea and Burma—as well as among Chinese emigrants from the People's Republic of China. I do not wish to imply that those who oppose these governments are terrorists, but rather that within the broadly based movements of resistance to those governments, the frustration that will almost certainly arise could begin to be expressed in more violent ways, particularly because it cannot be openly expressed in these countries themselves.

We are also likely to see growing terrorist violence in the (former) Soviet Union. The Russians are greatly concerned about this, which may explain why they are now talking to the United States about possible cooperation between the two countries in combatting terrorism.[14] They fear that the kind of violent Islamic fundamentalism that has swept through the Middle East will arise in the Soviet Union itself, which has a population of 50 million Muslims. In some areas the people already display portraits of Khomeini, and acts of terrorist violence have occurred. This has led to concern that ongoing conflicts within the Soviet Union involving Armenians, Azerbaijanis,

Uzbeks, and Ukrainians will become more violent. They do not know how to deal with these things. As they became increasingly frightened, they become more willing to reevaluate their traditional position on the issue of terrorism and more willing to cooperate with the United States in combatting it. The possibilities of cooperation between the Soviet Union and the United States are, however, limited. The problems of the two countries are not symmetrical. The Soviets could help us by reducing the support they provide to some of the groups, but it is not readily apparent how we could help them in dealing with rebellious Uzbeks or Azerbaijanis even if we wanted to.

In addition to the issues mentioned so far, there are a number of additional causes—not ideological conflicts or ethnic quarrels but very specific issues— that have in recent years manifested themselves in violence. The issue is the means. Concern for animal rights has become a source of increasing violence on the part of a handful of people; and the anti-abortion movement, the anti- nuclear movement, and the anti-biogenetic engineering movement have all pro- duced shooters and bombers. These are fervently held causes, the proponents of which are very righteous. They feel that their moral position demands that they take extreme measures, and that sometimes is the recipe for violence.

The three most popular categories of terrorist targets have always been (1) diplomatic facilities, (2) airplanes, airline ticket offices and airports, and (3) business concerns. Together, these have been the targets of about three- quarters of the attacks. Over the past 20 years, however, hijackings have grad- ually, albeit painfully, decreased. The number of direct attacks on airline facil- ities has also gone down, evidence that airport security procedures have made it somewhat more difficult to carry out this sort of action. Attacks on diplomatic fa- cilities have also gone down, but attacks on corporations and corporate execu- tives, intrinsically easier, more vulnerable targets, have increased.[15]

Bombing is one of the most alarming trends we face. As the number of ter- rorist incidents increased over the past twenty years—it reached a high point in 1985—it also has become bloodier. There are more incidents with fatalities and more incidents with multiple fatalities from indiscriminate violence as ter- rorists set off car bombs on city streets, plant bombs aboard airliners, or deto- nate them in public places. All these actions are calculated to kill in quantity. Indeed, an increasingly favorite target category is civilian bystanders—that is, peo- ple, not diplomats or businessmen but simply people who are in the wrong place at the wrong time when a bomb goes off.[16] They are killed just to make a point— to draw frightened attention to a terrorist cause.

Aside from bombs dropped from airplanes in a major-power war, bombs on airplanes constitute probably the major security challenge we face today. This is due to the enormous lethality of a single incident, since destroying the plane in the air kills everyone aboard. Overall, in the last two decades there have been more than fifty attempts to plant bombs aboard airliners; these have resulted in at least twelve crashes, with the total number of deaths reaching approximately 1,300. That constitutes about 10 percent of all the airline fatalities that occurred during that period.

The trend in targets reflects the fact that terrorists seldom take risks. They prefer easy targets. We see this in their movement away from attacking diplomats and airlines, which are now more heavily protected, to other softer targets such as bombing public places, which cannot be protected. So, too, the targets of hijacking and kidnapping now are persons involved in humanitarian aid activities, missionaries, and journalists—those who generally travel with little or no protection.

Over the years, there has been little change in terrorist tactics. Terrorists continue to operate with a limited repertoire. They have little reason to innovate because they can solve almost all of their problems by simply shifting targets. We have learned that our security measures enable us to push the terrorist threat around, but we are not able to reduce the volume of terrorism. We protect one set of targets, and the terrorists attack another.

If terrorist targets do not change a lot, their current weapons will suffice. However, there are technical causes of concern. Terrorists may acquire and use hand-held precision guided surface-to-air missiles.[17] They may employ remotely piloted or driven vehicles.[18] They seem unlikely to use weapons of mass destruction such as biological or nuclear weapons.[19] I am less confident than I was in the past that terrorists will not use chemical weapons for two reasons: first, more nations are acquiring chemical arsenals; second, chemical weapons have been used recently in warfare without generating the level of international outrage that one would have expected. Since World War I there has been a taboo against chemical weapons; now that taboo has been broken by the use of chemical agents in the Iran–Iraq War (including against the Kurds), and it has not cost the perpetrators very much in terms of condemnation or sanctions.[20] This does not mean that terrorists are about to enter the realm of mass destruction, but the chance that they might attempt something with a chemical weapon has definitely increased.

What sort of responses may democratic states make to terrorism? One approach is the application of technology. The x-ray machine baggage is passed through and the magnetic detector people walk through have demonstrably helped to curb hijackings by making it harder to bring handguns or grenades on board planes.[21] However, these only detect metal objects. To detect plastic handguns and explosives stuffed into luggage, newer and more exotic technology is called for.[22]

Several new technologies have, in fact, become available that promise to improve airplane safety. One works on the basis of thermal neutron analysis (TNA). A piece of luggage is passed through a cloud of neutrons and the gamma scanner can be read, showing whether or not there is a heavy concentration of certain chemical elements that would be consistent with a bomb. This technology, however, cannot be used on humans. Although this technology is expensive, six machines are currently deployed.

Another new device is a "chemical sniffer" or vapor detector, a device that can detect minute quantities of chemical substances either from bags or from people who pass through a phone-booth-like box. Air is flushed around the passenger or the suitcase and analyzed in the detection device to reveal whether or not the passenger is carrying specific substances. A third device is the backscatter x-ray, which, coupled with conventional x-ray machines, can detect materials with low atomic numbers in high density, such as plastic explosives. The deployment of these technologies could have prevented the bombing of Pan Am Flight 103, which killed 270 people at Lockerbie, Scotland.[23]

The problem with all of the new detection systems is that they are extraordinarily costly, and they are slow. The fastest luggage detection system currently in use handles about ten bags per minute (six seconds per bag). At that speed, loading 747s at a busy airport could delay flights hours. Another problem is the false-alarm rate. If the device goes off and tells you that you may have a bomb, what are you going to do? The parcel must be manually inspected. A further problem comes from the fact that neutron activation devices contain a radioactive source. If a bomb goes off inside the machine, the result could be a radioactively contaminated facility. The FAA has offered research grants of $12 million in 1989 to work on these problems and develop related technologies to make air travel more secure. Technology will not be a final solution to political or socio-psychological problems, but the widespread use of x-ray and metal-detector technology may well have served to inhibit terrorist hijackings of aircraft and we shall see more of this technology and the delays it involves at airports.[24]

In a simulation on terrorism conducted several years ago, participants were presented with a terrorist crisis and were forced, as a president or a prime minister would be, to choose a course of action. Those who chose one course of action were punished for their choice. Those who chose the other course were also punished. Neither set of participants knew what happened to those who chose the other path. The participants were then presented with the second move in the terrorism scenario and were obliged to choose again. The interesting thing is that almost everyone did again what he or she did the first time. Hardly anyone switched. This highlights that there are sharp differences in individual attitudes about how terrorism should be dealt with, and these differences reflect strongly held beliefs that even adverse results don't easily affect. I wish to suggest that examining our attitudes may be an appropriate response to dealing with terrorism.

According to the polls, most Americans view terrorism as a serious threat to the nation. In fact, perceptions of the threat wildly exceed the actual danger. People see terrorism as a source of personal danger, even though their chance of being caught in a terrorist incident is one in millions.

The same kind of visceral emotional reaction that terrorism provokes in the public affects our political leaders as well. We can imagine the dilemma of a political leader in this country who is confronted with a terrorist crisis and is trying to do both what he thinks is right and what he thinks will be supported by the American people. Our high-ranking officials are people of power who can discuss in detached intellectual terms nuclear strategies that could determine the fate of millions of people. They can address the possibility of destruction of whole nations in a cool analytical fashion. But when it comes to terrorism, fists hit palms or slam into podiums. They adopt the bellicose rhetoric that is perhaps more appropriate for a televised wrestling match. This is not mere posturing; they are reflecting what they feel deep down. However, while we can understand the sentiment, we must question the utility of such an emotional response.

When government officials send me drafts of their speeches to review, I usually start by cutting out all of the words like "cowardly," "barbarity," and "atrocity." While these adjectives may be correct, speeches made by high-ranking officials should be free of that kind of emotionally loaded language. We should try to be more phlegmatic when we respond to avoid the trap set by our terrorist adversaries of engaging them in rhetorical battles. They enjoy this. In their view, they are having a direct dialogue with the United States of America, drawing lines of death, daring us. Such rhetoric also creates within the American public expectations for action that often cannot be satisfied.

It similarly reinforces terrorism when people change travel plans out of fear of being aboard an airplane that would be attacked. People frequently call me up and ask what airline they should select to ensure a safe trip overseas. I tell them to drive very carefully on the way to the airport. Statistically, you are in far greater danger on the freeway than you are on any airline, many times over.

What about hostages? Should the United States ever bargain for hostages? Our official policy since 1973 is that we will not make concessions to terrorists. This policy has virtues: it is unambiguous and may have a deterrent value, although there is no way to demonstrate that. It is not, however, a principle like liberty, *habeas corpus*, or the right to a fair trial. These are the bases of democratic government. The policy of not making concessions is a pragmatic rule to be tested by its effect in given circumstances. Two presidents of the United States have been badly wounded by their handling of hostage crises. Failing to rescue or negotiate the release of the hostages in Teheran may have cost President Carter the 1980 election. When President Reagan's men were discovered secretly selling arms to Iran as part of a deal to release the hostages held in Lebanon, it resulted in an enormous amount of damage to U.S. credibility and embarrassment to the administration because it ran counter to the "no concessions" policy. In my view, we ought not to become so mesmerized by an incantation that we cease thinking creatively in hostage situations.

The holding of hostages in Lebanon illustrates this need for creativity. In most kidnappings, the hostage-takers seize hostages and then try to convert them into some outcome—political concessions or money. In Lebanon, just keeping the hostages confers the benefits. Since there is no government in

Lebanon, holding hostages provides prestige to the captors and makes them
a factor to be reckoned with. Every nation operating in the region has to take
into account what consequences an action they take might have for the hostages. Holding hostages also provides protection against Israeli retaliation,
Syrian military pressure, or even the possibility of American military
retaliation.

One other factor that is important in the case of Shi'ite groups believed
to be holding the Western hostages is that these groups get a lot of support
from Iran. Iran, in turn, has used its influence over the hostage-takers to
obtain concessions for itself. The hostage-takers know that holding hostages
is one way to ensure continued Iranian support: the Iranians cannot cut off
the money because then they won't be able to use their influence to their
advantage. Prestige, power, protection, payoff, and continued patronage all
contribute to the holding of hostages; there are, alas, few incentives to giving
them up. That is why we need as flexible and as creative policies toward
freeing the hostages as are consistent with our principles.

This brings up the issue of American values. Terrorism is an affront to our
values. It is something we choose to combat because we choose to uphold
these values. In my view, American values rightfully operate by constraining
our actions—even fighting terrorists. We have rules that are important for
us; it makes no difference that the other side does not abide by these rules.
We cannot in the course of combatting terrorism adopt tactics that are indistinguishable from those employed by the terrorists.

We will see terrorism in some form at the end of the century—a depressing
prospect—but does this constitute a threat to national security severe enough
to suspend the constitutional right of citizens or the right of Congress to
declare war? Does our common defense extend to security against terrorism?
Or can we do no more than issue travel advisories warning Americans which
regions of the globe to stay out of? These are difficult questions.

Terrorism is not a threat to our national survival, offensive as it is. Is then
military force an appropriate response to terrorist attacks? It is important to
distinguish hostage rescue from retaliation for a terrorist's attack. When there
is a realistic opportunity to rescue hostages, even if it involves the use of
military force against the captors, that opportunity should be taken. Retaliation
is different. I don't believe that a military response is appropriate for dealing
with most terrorist incidents for several reasons. If the situation is serious
enough and you have the evidence, then military force is permissible. However, in most instances military force is not appropriate. Terrorists offer few
targets for conventional military operations. They control no territory and
have no cities or populations to protect. States that sponsor terrorism are
more vulnerable to military violence, but we must have evidence that connects
the state to that act of terrorism—and that is hard to get. For example, the
Japanese Red Army leader shows up in Tripoli and vows to take revenge for
the bombing of Libya; attacks follow in Europe. They may have a base in

Lebanon or maybe in Damascus.[25] What do you attack? In any case, we ought not to use military force as a meaningless pyrotechnic display in order to satisfy domestic political pressure to be seen doing something.

The raid on Libya in April of 1986 to avenge a bombing of a West German discotheque that killed an off-duty U.S. serviceman is a case in point. Solid evidence linking Libya to the attack only recently emerged from the newly opened files of the East German secret police.[26] The Libyan government was involved. Unfortunately, the raid did not lower the incidents of terrorist violence; the attacks on U.S. and British targets actually increased then fell to exactly the same level as before.[27] The use of military force in retaliation is of questionable utility. Israel has used military force to combat terrorism for the past twenty years, but to what end? Can it be shown that Israel has greater freedom from terrorism than before?

We have to be realistic about what we can accomplish with military force. In the case of terrorism, we rarely have the proof of involvement or sponsorship, a target, and the possibility of doing something about it. These concerns are a reaffirmation of the rules that constrain us. If one of those rare occasions occurs when we have proof of terrorist action and an appropriate target, it is my view—and I write this as a former soldier reflecting on my experience in Viet Nam—that we should take the evidence to Capitol Hill, lay it before the Congress, and seek a formal declaration of war. Such a formal declaration of war may be an antique in today's world, but it is an expression of the will of the American people through their elected representatives. If the American people do not decide to commit American lives and fortune to this cause, so be it. Such a formal declaration legitimatizes us in the way that terrorists are not.

Similarly, we have to be realistic about what we can accomplish in a place like Colombia. While it is necessary for us to provide support to the Colombian government, which is on the front line against the drug traffickers, at the same time this can be a dangerous diversion from the real issue. President Bush has spoken about education, prevention, treatment and rehabilitation. It will take years to achieve visible results in those areas. But Americans are not terribly patient, nor do they want to make the hard decisions of deciding what the consensus around drugs should be. Therefore, "going after the cartel" in Colombia appeals to people because it provides at least the illusion of immediate progress.

The fact is that many cartels exist in Colombia, as well as a lot of entrepreneurial activity in the cocaine traffic; thousands of people are involved. From an economic standpoint, cocaine in this country is like fried chicken. We consume a lot of chicken; there are thousands of retail outlets selling fried chicken; and there are hundreds of farms growing millions of chickens to satisfy the nation's appetite. Many of the outlets are franchises. But if we were to eliminate the Kentucky Colonel or some other major outfit, there would still be a lot of chicken grown, sold, and eaten in this country. It is the same situation with cocaine: Basically, it's a domestic consumption problem. And there is no consensus on this. Public opinion polls show that Americans support the war on drugs as long as you define "drugs" as crack and cocaine. They may support sending the military off into the jungle to fight drugs, but they are uncertain that they want random drug testing, increased right of search and seizure, or the automatic suspension of the drivers' license for an offense. These civil liberties issues require hard choices that adventures in Colombia take us away from.

Finally a note on the electronic media. Some have said that if we provided access for terrorist groups to express their causes, they wouldn't be bombing and shooting. This is nonsense. Terrorists operate most vigorously in those societies that provide the greatest opportunity to communicate via the press. They could write letters to editors, demonstrate, hold marches, or run for elected office. It is not the want of opportunity; it is the fact that either they are dismal communicators or nobody is particularly interested in their message that leads them to express themselves in the only way they can—with a pistol or a stick of dynamite. Several chapters in this volume discuss the opposite effects of media coverage: its role of broadcasting the terrorist's message of fear and alarm; and its role in revealing governmental mistakes in prosecuting suspected terrorists.[28] Can the one function be limited without curtailing the other? That is another of these deeper issues that a democratic society must weigh.

The media do bring the violence to us, the intended audience, sometimes irresponsibly. They are becoming more cautious, but we cannot be too optimistic about this. The media now have a lot of guidelines that apply when they cover terrorism, but once reporters are given a juicy terrorist incident, they are off and running with the cameras. It is a problem requiring a serious choice. In my judgment, while I understand the reasons for censorship, changing the rules that govern the news media for terrorists would defeat the purpose of the media, and terrorists would have won a great victory. Our democratic society will retain a vulnerability that terrorists can exploit; however, it is a vulnerability that marks us *as* democratic. So I wouldn't ground aircraft to prevent hijackings, and I wouldn't shut down the media to prevent terrorism.

In summary, terrorism will probably continue to be with us. It raises issues not solely about tactics, weapons, targets, or individual terrorist groups, the nature of their causes, or their individual psychology. Terrorism brings up the basic questions, the hard questions, of democratic rule. The following chapters in this volume have been written by an impressive array of scholars, persons who truly deserve to be called experts. As you read them, I would like you to keep in mind the questions I have raised. It is not important whether you agree or disagree with the answers I have provided. Ask yourself how you might answer those questions. Then, when you have had time to reflect, ask yourself if you have changed any of those views.

NOTES

1. For example, Conor Cruise O'Brian argues, "If a minority is denied all partic- ipation in democratic process and thus deprived of any peaceful means of improving its situation, then . . . *it would be inappropriate to describe as terrorists those who use political violence on behalf of such a minority.*" "Terrorism under Democratic Con- ditions: The Case of the IRA," in *Terrorism, Legitimacy, and Power*, ed. Martha Cren- shaw (Middletown, CT: Wesleyan University Press), 94 (emphasis mine).

2. The contemporary reappearance of religiously inspired terrorism might seem to contradict this, for an increasing number of terrorist incidents are carried out in God's name. Still it is groups that organize to do the work, and often the political motivation and the personal inspiration are mixed. See David C. Rapoport, "Messianic Sanctions for Terror," *Comparative Politics* 20, no. 2 (January 1988). Also see the chapters by Khalid Duran, Martha Crenshaw, and Neimiah Friedland in this volume.

3. In the course of my research, I have interviewed many former hostages. Fre- quently they talk about conversations they have had with their terrorist captors in which the terrorists say something like, "If our demands are not met, we will kill you. We hope you won't take this personally." This extraordinary statement tells us much about the terrorists' mindset. Their intent is reaching this overarching audience out there—the capitalists, the proletariate, the faithful, or the oppressors. This separation of their act from its purpose allows them to kill cruelly. Yet except for the dialogue, this situation is really not so different from that of the soldier in combat who does his best to kill an enemy against whom he has no personal grudge.

4. *UN General Assembly Resolution 140/61* condemned "unequivocally as criminal all acts, methods and practices of terrorism by whomever and wherever perpetrated including those which endanger friendly relations among states and their security." The universal recognition of the criminality of these acts was a significant step.

5. These include the *Tokyo Convention on Offenses and Certain Other Acts Com- mitted on Board Aircraft* (1963), which requires all signatory states to make every effort to restore control of the aircraft to the commander to complete its flight, the *Hague Convention on Unlawful Seizure of Aircraft* (1970), and the *Montreal Con- vention for the Suppression of Unlawful Acts Against the Safety of Civil Aviation* (1971), which extends international law to cover sabotage and attacks on airports as acts deserving of several penalties.

6. *The Convention on the Prevention and Punishment of Crimes Against Inter- nationally Protected Persons Including Diplomatic Agents* (Adopted by the UN As- sembly in 1973).

7. *International Convention Against the Taking of Hostages* (1979).

8. See Paul Wilkinson's chapter, "Can The European Community Develop a Con- certed Policy on Terrorism?" in this volume for a useful discussion of building an international legal regime on terrorism in Europe.

9. A not-insignificant number of the weapons available have been supplied to various insurgent groups by the United States—the Afghan *mujahidin*, the Nicaraguan *contras* among others—and then have been sold or directly provided to terrorist groups. The Eastern Bloc countries also have enjoyed this sometimes lucrative means of gaining influence on the cheap.

10. I find the case of the Sikh terrorist group that threatened to kill Indian journalists

who referred to them as "terrorists" revealing and grimly ironic. "India Journalists Drop 'Terrorist,' " *The Boston Globe*, 25 November 1990.

11. With the Syrian imposed hegemony over Lebanon, imposed while the West was occupied with prosecuting the Gulf War, this may change. The government is attempting to disarm the factions.

12. The Red Army Faction claimed credit for assassinating the official charged with the task of integrating the moribund East German economy into the thriving Western one at the cost of much hardship in the East. This was the first terrorist killing in Germany since integration. See Stephen Kinzer, "Red Army Faction Is Suspected in German Killing," *The New York Times*, 3 April 1991.

13. Robert Kupperman and Jeff Kamen raise this spectre in *Final Warning: Averting Disaster in the New Age of Terrorism* (New York: Doubleday, 1989).

14. See Brian Michael Jenkins, *The Possibility of Soviet-American Cooperation Against Terrorism* (Santa Monica, CA: The RAND Corporation, P–7541, March 1989) for the report of a joint U.S. and Soviet conference on this problem.

15. For example, The Red Army Faction killed the chairman of the Deutsch Bank with a sophisticated bomb triggered by his car breaking a light switch. "Murderous Terrorism in Bonn," *Los Angeles Times*, 1 December 1989.

16. The IRA bombing of the Victoria and Paddington railroad stations in London killed one man and wounded forty during rush hour, breaking an almost seven-year period free of such civilian attacks in England. See William E. Schmidt, "2 Rail Terminals in Central London Hit by I.R.A. Bombs," *The New York Times*, 19 February 1991. This followed by eleven days a mortar attack on 10 Downing Street where the Cabinet was meeting.

17. Approximately 5,000 Stinger and British Blowpipe shoulder-mounted missiles were supplied to the *mujahidin* forces fighting the Soviet occupation in Afghanistan. But "an estimated 40 percent of the weapons destined for the war effort via the CIA's arms pipeline ... have 'leaked' into Pakistan." Mahnaz Ispahani, *Pakistan: Dimensions of Insecurity, Adelphi Papers 246* (London: Brassey's for the International Institute of Strategic Studies, Winter 1989/1990), 27. Similarly, Soviet-built SAM–7s have recently been used by the FMLN in El Salvador against government aircraft. "Salvador Says Rebel Missile Downed Plane," *The New York Times*, 25 November 1990.

18. The IRA has begun the grisly practice of strapping suspected collaborators into vehicles packed with explosives and ordering them (by holding their family at gunpoint) to drive into British Army compounds where the bomb is detonated. Steven Prokesch, "7 Killed as I.R.A. Forces 3 Men to Drive Bombs to Security Posts," *The New York Times*, 25 October 1990.

19. Brian Michael Jenkins, *The Likelihood of Nuclear Terrorism* (Santa Monica: The RAND Corporation, P–7119, July 1985).

20. Iran and Iraq are both signatories of the 1925 Geneva Protocol forbidding the use of chemical weapons. Although Iraq first introduced their use in 1983–1984 against Iranian assaults reminiscent of the First World War, Iran came to use them as well. See David Segal, "The Iran–Iraq War: A Military Analysis," *Foreign Affairs* 66, no. 5 (Summer, 1988): 955–56.

21. Walter Enders, Todd Sandler, and Jon Cauley, "UN Conventions, Technology and Retaliation in the Fight Against Terrorism," *Terrorism and Political Violence* 2, no. 1 (Spring 1990): 83–105.

22. An alternative and less costly solution would be to require manufacturers of

plastic handguns to have a computer chip imbedded during manufacture that identifies the gun and serial number from several feet away. "Showdown Takes Shape Over Plastic Weapons," *Christian Science Monitor*, 13 November 1987.

23. See "Relatives of Pan Am 103 Victims Call for Improved Bomb Detection Techniques," *Aviation Week & Space Technology*, 23 July 1990: 85.

24. Breck W. Hendeson, "Experts Say Total Security Program Needed to Counter Terrorist Threat," *Aviation Week & Space Technology*, 20 November 1989: 67.

25. Steven R. Weisman, "Japanese on Guard After Threats By Old Terrorist Group Over War," *The New York Times*, 29 January 1991.

26. Craig R. Whitney, "Bonn's Top Anti-Terrorist is Slightly Hurt in Bombing," *The New York Times*, 28 July 1990.

27. Enders, Sandler, and Cauley, "UN Conventions, Technology and Retaliation," 100–102.

28. Alex Schmid argues the case for limiting the press coverage of terrorist events; Abraham Miller presents the dangers of "capping the lens." Both should be read together.

2

The Cutting Edge: The Historical Relationship between Insurgency, Counterinsurgency, and Terrorism during Mexican Independence, 1810–1821

Christon I. Archer

> It is difficult to pinpoint the incident that made terrorism appear to be a worthy subject for academics.[1]

A few years ago the study of terrorism was an academic pursuit. Today it is almost an industry. Students of terrorism who approach the Library of Congress classification "HV" must shudder with awe, apprehension, and excitement at the stacks of recent books—mostly bound in red, black, or red and black—that almost cry out to them for immediate attention. Even without the slightest knowledge of the subject, a casual perusal of the shelves informs passersby that something happened in the 1970s to unleash a torrent of research and writing. The titles fit their subject: *Brothers in Blood: The International Terrorist Network*,[2] *Counterattack: The West's Battle Against the Terrorists*,[3] *Responding to the Terrorist Threat: Security and Crisis Management*,[4] or *Terrorism: How the West Can Win*.[5] And these books only scratch the surface. Early studies of terrorism informed readers that there were no adequate bibliographies. Now there are many. Unfortunately, a large percentage of these books are predictable to the point of being tiresome and superficial. There are standard chapters on the Palestinians, the Irish Republican Army, the Shi'ites, and the role of the Soviet Union in international terrorism (scratch that subject and perhaps replace it with state terrorism directed against dissenting republics within the U.S.S.R.). A closer examination of the headings produces some violent and depressing headings: "How to Fight Fire with Fire," "How to Cope," "How to Find an 'Achilles' Heel," "Private Enterprise Against the Terrorists." Indeed, no self-respecting security guard

or chauffeur would want to return to work after reading some of this material
and learning "...there is no such thing as 100% safety."[6]

As terrorists grabbed headlines around the world, academics set about to
study their origins, motivations, and how to implement controls against them.
Political scientists, sociologists, and even some historians found a gold mine.
Their readership comprised of students, tourists, business persons, travelers,
pedestrians, or sometimes even those who stayed in their homes, learned to
fear the horrors of kidnappings, indiscriminate bomb blasts, hijackings of
commercial aircraft, or other hideous attacks that seem to have slithered out
of their nightmares. After all, the newspapers are full of headlines such as
"Colombia Terror Grows, The Press Becomes the Prey,"[7] or "Sunni Muslim
Chief Killed in Lebanon: 21 Others are Slain and 100 Wounded in Car Bombing."[8] The actual stories contain detail that makes the blood run cold: "their
bodies showed signs of severe torture," "no one claimed responsibility for
the explosion," or "a State Department spokesman said that the United States
was revolted by the cold-blooded killing." Few can forget the television
images of the Italian cruise ship *Achille Lauro* showing bloodstains of the
barbaric murder of Leon Klinghoffer; the search for wreckage of the Air India
747; the massacre of Pan American passengers over Lockerbie, Scotland; the
horrors of Lebanon; indiscriminate Iraqi rocket attacks against Israeli suburbs;
or one of thousands of different incidents involving terrorist actions from
around the world.

The public wanted answers, and academics stepped forward to provide
books and more books. Today each major terrorist massacre receives its
scribes who attempt to unravel the plots; to identify whether or not Tehran,
Tripoli, Damascus, or Baghdad played a role; and to explain the actions of
nations and groups involved. Prolific writers such as Christopher Dobson
and Ronald Payne turn out popular works illustrated with pictures showing
"the results of an IRA car bomb attack," "the bodies of the Household Cavalry
horses ambushed by an IRA bomb," and "kidnapped Soviet diplomats with
pistols held to their heads."[9] They present readers who want to know with
color plates showing the terrorist weapons of choice, the Kalashnikov, the
Skorpion VZ 61, the Beretta Model 12 Sub-machine-gun, and pistols such as
the Makarov along with their muzzle velocities, maximum effective range,
and other specifications. On the heavier end, they illustrate weapons such as
the SAM–7 Strela (Arrow), the RPG–7 Portable Rocket-launcher, and several
hand grenades. One supposes that it is useful to know that the RGD–5 Anti-
personnel grenade is colored apple green with Cyrillic written on its body.[10]
These are books designed for technology buffs and readers who want to
know about terrorist hardware, but who seldom devote sufficient thought to
the underlying causes of terrorism. In other words, the symptoms of terrorism
as represented by atrocities receive much more attention than the complex
historical factors that gave rise to the varieties of terrorist activities.

This essay examines the roots and uses of terror by insurgents and coun-

terinsurgents during the revolutionary struggle that occurred in Mexico during the decade of warfare leading to national independence (1810–1821).
Although scholars such as Richard Clutterbuck,[11] Walter Laqueur,[12] Alf Andrew
Heggoy,[13] Alistair Horne,[14] David Galula,[15] and Ranajit Guha,[16] to mention just
a few, have examined aspects of this subject in different regions of the world
mostly in the context of twentieth-century movements, the independence
wars of Mexico present an interesting and hitherto unknown case study
involving what would be described today as insurgent terrorism and state
terrorism in the context of a war of national liberation. What began in 1810
as an inchoate regional rebellion led by a village priest, Father Miguel Hidalgo,
developed rapidly into broad-based insurgency and class war. Mexican society
was fractured by racial and social tensions so that rebellion exacerbated
existing cleavages and led to the use of terror by both insurgents and counterinsurgents. At the local and regional levels, Mexico had a long tradition
of violence and rebellion that surfaced periodically and whipped an enraged
town, district, or province into resistance against the Spanish regime.[17] In
addition, millenarian and messianic elements plus rumors of impending cat-
aclysm made terrorist violence possible once events mobilized these beliefs
into actions.[18] Agrarian factors intruded as Mexican regions experienced subsistence crises and there were struggles for available resources of arable land.
Finally, the Spanish regime in Mexico responded to rebellion and insurgency
with a counterinsurgency system, applied by the royalist army, that answered
insurgent terrorism with terror of its own.

Mexico was riven with cleavages between elements of the populace—
Mexican-born Spaniards against European Spaniards, mestizos against other
racial mixtures, and fear of the more or less mute Indian population that
held the potential for revolutionary violence. At the same time, within parts
of the society and across its fault lines, rumors became the triggers or mo-
bilizers of rebel action and of deep fears that would lead to acts of terror.
Lacking connections with the populace, the regime in Mexico City responded
to perceived threats with draconian force. Although many different incidents
occurred, the 1801 movement of the mysterious Mariano of Tepic illustrates
how rumors led inevitably toward violence. Appearing literally out of nowhere, Mariano spoke of convening a great assembly of the Indian population
of Northwest Mexico at which a native king linked with the pre-Hispanic state
of Tlaxcala was to appear or to be elected. Reports indicated that Indians
from different regions of the country had established communications and
begun to raise an armed force of 30,000 men. They projected a diabolical
plan for the feast day of the Virgin of Guadalupe that would announce the
beginning of a violent rebellion against the Spanish regime. Explosives-laden
tapers placed on the altars at the shrine of Guadalupe near Mexico City were
to blow up and to destroy the building. In the confusion, insurgent forces
were to attack the viceroy's palace, which was said to have been mined at
the corners.[19]

Believing that these stories portended a terrible uprising that was about to take place, army units and marines fell upon what was in fact a peaceful assembly of Indians who had gathered near the town of Tepic, Nayarit. Although some panic-stricken people died in their efforts to escape the melee, later investigations established that there had been no intent to rebel. Those who had gathered had done so out of curiosity expecting to meet an important leader—perhaps even the king of Spain.[20] The mysterious Mariano was nothing more than a crank whose message aroused curiosity and interest among the populace rather than dangerous rebellion.

Given this example and many others that appear in the documents of the period, it is clear rumors propagated fears among the different segments of the Mexican population that made each group suspect others of harboring plans for genocide. European Spaniards feared the Mexican creoles, who expressed equal anxieties that atrocities were planned against their class. The Indians and mestizo populace exchanged stories that foreshadowed even greater calamities. Much of their information originated with parish priests who articulated dark superstitions present in Mexican society.

Although historians still debate the causes of the 1810 rebellion, they agree that crop failures, population growth, and competition for the limited resources of land had much to do with what occurred in the Bajío provinces to the north and west of the capital.[21] Rising food prices, scarcity of staples, and growing unemployment exacerbated concerns among regional administrators that rural people might employ violence to withhold food from the towns and cities. Combined with unrest originating from these factors, Indians, mestizos, and other groups fed upon rumors that portended catastrophes of near supernatural proportions. Frightened by the unknown, communities searched for ways to protect their lives, properties, customs, and religion. The creole curates appear to have preyed on these fears, and they passed on their own concerns that Spain and the Spanish minority in Mexico might surrender the country to the heretical English or the Godless French revolutionaries. In their sermons, these priests invoked a primitive religious mission and whipped up a level of hysteria that would permit the most violent acts against anyone perceived to be the enemy. These curates and priests assumed temporal power and created militant factions that recruited support from other sectors of provincial society. In some respects, comparisons can be made between these religious-political leaders and the Islamic fundamentalists of the 1980s.

By 1810, the Bajío provinces were tinder boxes ready to explode into violence. The curates and village leaders blamed Spanish land owners, miners, merchants, petty bureaucrats, hacienda administrators, and the Mexico City regime as the agents of their misfortunes. Dazzled by their own self-righteousness and filled with a mix of sometimes preposterous messianic visions, the curates used their pulpits to whip up frenzy. This was anathema for creoles who believed that Mexico could attain eventual autonomy or independence under a constitution similar to that of the United States. Although Father Miguel Hidalgo emerged as generalissimo, his real strength lay in the fact that many other curates, friars, Indian governors, and disaffected Mexicans shared the anger needed to launch both rebellion and genocide against the Spanish minority.

The uprising that began on September 16, 1810, was no ordinary rebellion. It was rage that blended elements of messianism with distinctly half-baked ideas concerning reform and revolution. Almost spontaneously, Hidalgo found himself heading an ungovernable horde that swept through the fertile agricultural and mining districts north and west of Mexico City devouring villages and towns, looting the haciendas owned by their oppressors, and planting the seeds of violence that led to terror. Others who did not join Hidalgo's main force directly set off in different directions to raise their own insurgent bands. At Atlacomulco, near Toluca, a mob of Indians fell upon a disliked Spanish merchant and killed him with stones, knives, and clubs.[22] At San Miguelito, north of the capital, the Indian population butchered seven Spaniards and then exhibited their bloody garments as trophies.[23] To prevent the defenders of loyal towns from contemplating armed resistance, rebel forces marched European Spanish hostages in their vanguard exposed to gunfire.[24] In cities such as Guanajuato and Valladolid (Morelia), the insurgents killed hundreds of European Spaniards, who were marched into the countryside and slaughtered in cold blood. In 1814 a royalist reconnaissance force near rebel Acapulco found "a lake of blood" containing the decapitated bodies of twenty-one Spanish soldiers who had been captured by the rebels. Five other royalist prisoners of war had been murdered the same way in the hospital, and twenty-four mutilated bodies were found in nearby ravines.[25] A few days later at the village of Coyuca, royalist soldiers came across the corpses of 100 decapitated victims—most of whom had been cut down in a church where they sought sanctuary. The unexpected arrival of the royalist army saved another 400 prisoners from receiving the same fate.[26]

The ferocity of the rebellion and its special terror directed against the European Spaniards dismayed the regime in Mexico City and almost all commanders of the army of New Spain. Like other observers, the army chiefs looked on with incredulity as the massed Indian forces struck against towns and cities. The popularity of the uprising was undeniable as was its capacity to recruit new support. For army officers trained in conventional warfare to defend Mexico against external enemies, the rebellion came as a horrible shock. While Mexicans sometimes rebelled spontaneously against unpopular taxes or corrupt administrators, there was no precedent for the premeditated terror directed against the European Spaniards. The real difference between previous uprisings and the Hidalgo Rebellion was that the curates and others who led the Indian masses managed to coalesce a mass movement based upon hatred, fear, and superstitions. The fact that a minority of Mexican creoles and some provincial militia battalions joined the rebellion added an element of legitimacy.

Even beyond the main rebel concentrations led by Hidalgo and his subordinates, new centers of rebellion appeared as soon as word spread. It took fewer than five days for information to reach the northern mining town of Zacatecas. At Guanajuato, San Miguel, Valladolid (Morelia), and elsewhere, well-armed urban garrisons could not withstand the assaults or the psychological threats of rebels who often lacked firearms or other modern weapons. At atmosphere of *terror pánico* drove European Spaniards and other members of the elite to flee their homes, lands, businesses, and investments. For the rebels, this general flight corroborated popular views that the European Spanish minority was as evil as suspected. By October 1810 groups of exhausted European refugees searched for safety in the royalist cities of central Mexico or escaped to the coasts. Many huddled at rural haciendas and in small villages in a sad state that one friar described as "frightened and indecisive."[27] In some districts, the movement of refugees loaded down with numerous possessions interfered with military mobilizations. Some haciendas sold off their best mounts and were left with a few broken down nags that were unfit for army service.[28] In many communities, the panic of fugitive Spaniards infected and undermined local confidence to create a spirit of defeatism. Clearly, terror instilled by the rebels worked to destabilize the Spanish European elite of Mexico.

The commander of the royalist Army of the Center, Félix Calleja, expressed frustration with his fellow Spaniards, who in his view exhibited "a lack of patriotism and criminal indifference" when it came to overcoming panic to assist the royalist military. Reports from the cities of Guanajuato and Valladolid about the mass executions of Europeans served the purpose of further lowering morale, and information about atrocities from Indian communities had the same impact. At the town of Zapotlán el Grande, the populace massacred all whites whether they were European or American creoles.[29] A European himself, Calleja accepted the view that the rebellion stemmed in large part from the "inextinguishable hatreds" that Mexicans of the lower classes felt toward Spaniards. In his opinion, this enmity could be suppressed only through the application of a plan to terrorize the population. "But," asked Calleja, "Who will impose this terror?" Noting that creole and mestizo soldiers shouldered the major burdens of fighting insurgency, he stated: "Do the Europeans want half a dozen men to sacrifice themselves each night on patrols, running the risk of assassination while they [the Spaniards] live in luxury, occupied only with their personal affairs? And all the while they grumble and gossip about the army."[30] To inspire confidence in the royalist cause, Calleja asked the Spaniards to overcome their personal fears and to enlist in a special military force of 700 to 800 men.

Although Calleja had served in Mexico since the 1790s, some other officers experienced the Napoleonic invasions of Iberia and the disastrous defeats of the Spanish army from 1808 to 1810. Aware of Spanish guerrilla techniques and harsh French counterinsurgency responses,[31] commanders such as Brigadier José de la Cruz, who arrived in Mexico in 1810, added new dimensions to the Mexican struggle. From the beginning of his career in Mexico, which spanned the decade of war, Cruz believed that the regime would have to introduce methods of counter-terror to detach insurgents from their cause and deter those who had not yet joined the rebellion.[32] To replace rebel terror with state terror, Cruz executed many insurgents following brief summary trials and displayed their bloody corpses at crossroads and hung them up near the entry gates to towns. After burning several towns and haciendas to the ground, he bragged to Viceroy Francisco Venegas, "Now I have caused suffering among this infamous race and I am going to terrorize them completely."[33] At the town of Huichapan, he commenced his terror campaign by executing sixteen men, displaying their bodies as "a healthful example," and sentencing another thirty-six men to long terms of forced labor in the presidios. When he had reduced the population to a state of what he described as "horrendous fear," Cruz moved to the second stage of his program which was to confiscate all horses and other draft animals, provisions, and implements until "there is not a knife to cut bread."[34]

After 1810 the royalist counterinsurgency and counterterrorist forces had to respond to the emergence of literally hundreds of guerrilla bands that raided commerce and communications, attacked haciendas and mines, and looted undefended towns. In some isolated regions that were peripheral to the royalist defense system, the insurgents formed *focos* (centers) that retained autonomy except when organized army operations dispersed them into new districts. Based in the most inaccessible mountain, forest, island and jungle zones where they created quite sophisticated fortifications, these guerrillas dominated the routes inland from Veracruz, the tropical lowlands (*tierra caliente*) of the Pacific coast, and the mountains of Guanajuato. They set up rudimentary administrations, charged taxes to any who wished safe passage, welcomed disaffected members of society who wished to fight against Spain, and made guerrilla warfare a permanent feature in Mexico. Other guerrilla bands maintained an existence on the fringe between insurgency designed to promote the grand purpose of independence and common criminal or bandit activities. These groups are best described as guerrilla-bandits or insurgent-bandits.[35] Some were little different than the terrorist bands spawned by modern insurgencies. They kidnapped victims for ransom, held hostages, and murdered opposition leaders.

In Mexico as was common in the modern wars of national liberation in China, Algeria, Vietnam, Afghanistan, and in a number of African nations, conventional military forces usually dominated the battlefield. During the decade of warfare, the royalist armies commanded by Calleja, Cruz, and other royalist officers never really lost a major engagement. At the battles of Aculco,

Guanajuato, and Calderón, as well as in countless less important clashes and in many difficult sieges of insurgent fortifications that continued up to 1821, royalist forces enjoyed the advantages of much better weaponry and logistics. When the royalist army arrived in strength,'the insurgents simply abandoned territory and temporarily relinquished their control over regions to seek refuge in mountains, jungles, and isolated districts where travel was extremely difficult for conventional forces.

As in most guerrilla wars, the royalists found ways to defeat urban insurgency. The army occupied the towns and cities, but had to stretch its resources to protect corridors of communications between these centers. The problem was how to extend royalist power over these vital links and then to deal with the even more difficult task of clearing insurgents from the countryside, where they enjoyed entrenched civilian support. In more recent counterinsurgency wars, three basic stages usually emerge in a military response to guerrilla tactics: first, the application of harsh policies, including terror, is used to separate the populace from the insurgents; second, the army extends gradual control over guerrilla zones combined with a variety of different approaches to strengthen defenses at the district and community levels; and third, the regime introduces less violent policies designed to win back the hearts and minds of the people.[36] In Indo-China and Algeria, the French developed a system of dividing insurgent territory into operational squares (*quadrillage*) and then used available forces to crush trapped guerrillas (*ratissage* or raking). Unit commanders established bases and then launched rapid assaults (*tourbillon*) against the centers of guerrilla power. As the French commanders soon discovered, the danger in this approach was that too many of the operational troops became tied up in static garrison duty—leaving too few soldiers to operate in the field against the guerrillas.[37] This was a chronic problem for the royalist army of New Spain.

In Mexico, the war presented Spanish royalist officers with the complex problem of how to introduce effective counterinsurgency. Although there was nothing in the way of established theory other than the ideas that some officers carried with them from their experiences in Spain against Napoleon's armies, Mexican counterinsurgency followed the three stage approach mentioned above. The enormous size and ferocity of the rebellions led by Hidalgo, José María Morelos, and other insurgent commanders convinced Viceroy Venegas, Calleja, Cruz, and other senior commanders to adopt counterinsurgency terror to crush the pro-insurgent sympathies and to break the morale of the mass of the population.[38] When insurgent bands interdicted vital commerce between Mexico City and the strategic distribution center of Querétaro, Brigadier Cruz adopted a French model to scourge the rural countryside dispatching highly mobile flying detachments (*destacamentos volantes*) to "make harsh and repeated justice." More recently, the Air Cavalry in Vietnam and Russian helicopter forces in Afghanistan played the same role in applying summary terror from the air.[39] In Mexico, suspected rebels detained by the flying detachments received hasty trials, faced firing squads, and their bloody remains were exhibited as brutal object lessons at crossroads, on gates to towns, and in village squares. In addition, these cavalry units confiscated and sold off livestock, destroyed forges, burned crops, and carried off all possible weapons down to kitchen knives.[40] During 1811, the royalist commander Colonel José de Andrade swept through the towns between Mexico City and Querétaro, confiscating, burning, and leaving the roadsides hung with insurgent *canalla* (scum) who had been executed after "quick and succinct trials." When he was in a benign mood, Andrade permitted the grieving families to take down and bury the corpses after three days exposure. He supported his flying detachments from confiscated property, forced loans and taxes, and arbitrary donations extracted in exchange for possible royalist amnesties.[41]

Both Cruz and Andrade razed entire towns and villages to terrorize the populace and sever ties with guerrilla bands that withdrew beyond the easy reach of the military.[42] Although the district commanders saw nothing particularly immoral about the application of "blood and fire" policies, Calleja realized that the army should exercise some measure of prudence in applying terror so that the insurgents would have some hope of attaining amnesties. After practical experience in the field, Calleja understood that terror alone was not an effective solution to insurgency and he wished to leave open opportunities for reconciliation. Viceroy Venegas concurred with Calleja's reservations about town-burning, arguing that such generalized punishment injured both the innocent and the guilty. Rather than terrorizing people into compliance, they became even more implacable enemies of the regime.[43]

In reaching these views, the Mexican royalist commanders encountered the conundrum faced by many modern counterinsurgents. The question was how far to go with counterinsurgency terror and what to do when the insurgents responded with their own forms of terrorism? In Mexico, insolent or particularly intractable towns that harbored guerrilla bands exhausted the limited patience of royalist army commanders. Some towns, such as San Miguel el Grande and Guanajuato, sat on the fence between the royalists and the insurgents, supporting whichever side happened to hold preeminence for the moment. In order to separate the population from what he termed "lethargy," Calleja threatened to torch both towns as an object lesson for other communities.[44] Following the sieges of insurgent-held Zitácuaro and Cuautla Amilpas, Calleja did adopt counterinsurgency terrorism temporarily when he ordered both towns burned to the ground to eradicate "the fantasm of impregnability" from the insurgent forces.[45]

In the first phase of counterinsurgency, the Mexican royalists used other methods to inculcate fear. Neighbors of insurgents who failed to make denunciations, neglected to report absences from the community, or did not pay attention to other unusual activities faced severe punishments for criminal activity. The instructions for the commanders of flying detachments described methods about how to get the most out of their interrogations. They were to question witnesses separately and, where possible, to place pressure on young boys who often produced information in exchange for money or under threats of corporal punishment. Army interrogators were to identify who was absent from the district and might have joined the insurgents, which residents owned horses and mules, and where these animals and others might be hidden. The penalty for withholding information about the smallest detail ranged from ten years sentence in a forced labor presidio to execution. Boys who refused to cooperate were punished with as many as fifty lashes. If proof emerged that members of a family provided clandestine support for relatives who had joined the insurgents, they suffered confiscation of their property and their houses were burned to the ground.[46] Needless to say, some district commanders employed different types of torture to obtain information.

Notwithstanding the continuing inclinations of royalist commanders to apply terror against the insurgents, the flying detachments and draconian punishments did not result in long-term solutions. As early as 1811 Calleja realized that the fragmented nature of insurgency and use of guerrilla warfare inevitably would exhaust the royalist army. The answer appeared to lie in the creation of district and town defense forces that could pacify the country, defend fortified blockhouses unassailable by lightly armed insurgents, and chase down insurgent-bandit gangs. While this move to the second stage of counterinsurgency may have been premature in 1811, the result was to introduce a process of decentralizing the command structure to meet the insurgents on their own ground.[47] Once the system of regional commands and local forces was in place, Calleja felt that the regular army could concentrate on the guerrilla *focos*, protect commerce and mining, and reopen communications. In coordination with district militias, the provincial army chiefs would take responsibility for pursuing any insurgent bands that coalesced in their regions.[48] Here was a quite accurate portrayal of *quadrillage* and *ratissage* as practiced a century and a half later by the French army against the Algerian insurgents.

Despite the development of a counterinsurgency plan, Calleja and other commanders discovered that the operational forces of the royalist army soon divided into small divisions and sedentary garrisons. Once this occurred, the insurgents were given space to coalesce guerrilla bands that might obtain numerical superiority over the royalists in a given district. Throughout the decade of war, senior officers warned the viceroys of the need to consolidate small divisions and garrison forces. In 1812 Calleja recommended the formation of two permanent operational armies—one in the north and the other in the south. Each force would operate from a permanent headquarters equipped with recruiting depots, shops to repair arms, clothing factories to make uniforms, arsenals, foundries, and military hospitals. Each army would assign 400 to 500 soldiers monthly to convoy commerce and silver shipments from the mines. Troops from these main depots could be assigned to the regional divisions and districts as required by the level of insurgency. The northern force would coordinate its divisions, urban militias, and rural units to keep open communications between Querétaro, Guadalajara, Valladolid (Morelia), Zacatecas, and the capital. The southern force would protect the strategic routes to the port of Veracruz. The two armies were to prevent insurgent forces from coalescing their small banks into larger formations.[49]

Such an ambitious counterinsurgency program required resources that were not available in Mexico. After the fall of Cuautla Amilpas in 1812, the insurgent forces fragmented into a multitude of guerrilla bands, which made the task of the royalist army much more difficult. The royalists had to divide and subdivide regiments, battalions, and even companies into many small divisions that often were separated from each other. The guerrilla bands cut communications, paralysed commerce, halted mine operations, and entered unprotected communities to commit terrorist attacks on government administrators, Spanish residents, and any Mexicans who supported the royalist cause. They disrupted the regional economies and reduced tax income so much that some provincial treasuries could not afford to pay the garrison troops. When this occurred, soldiers either deserted or began to prey upon civilians, and their officers engaged in a variety of illegal activities. In 1813 when Calleja replaced Venegas as viceroy, he attempted to implement at least a part of his plan to create operational forces that could assist the regional divisions. Calleja discovered that essential counterinsurgency forces such as the cavalry and dragoon Regiments of México, España, San Luis, and San Carlos and the Corps of Lancers were subdivided into many different garrisons so that in many areas only a squadron or two were available to respond to attacks. Once separated from their regimental command structure, officers could not keep track of pay, replacements, equipment, and horses. Gradually, the troops lost their discipline and became ineffective.[50]

Unfortunately for the royalists, the realities of counterinsurgency warfare and the costs prevented the full implementation of Calleja's strategy. In 1816 the Sub-Inspector General of the army, Brigadier Fernando Miyares y Mancebo, requested additional regiments from Spain to replace European troops worn out by Mexican service. He noted that over time it was quite common for Mexican royalist army divisions of 1,000 to 1,200 men to be formed from as many as eleven different units. From a military point of view, Miyares described this as "monstrous" because subdivided regiments and battalions deteriorated to the point that they were next to useless. Officers could not respond to training, inspections, or record-keeping. Unlike the colonels and staff adjutants who dedicated their time to administering a unified regiment or battalion, those officers who commanded mixed divisions lacked adequate personnel or a special interest in the welfare of their soldiers. Knowing that audits and inspections seldom if ever took place, officers charged excessive sums to their regimental treasuries, collected pay for absent soldiers, and engaged in other illegal activities.[51]

The major reason for dividing and subdividing royalist forces lay in the chronic inability of the regime to put sufficient resources into the war. While concentration of forces permitted the army to regain full control over communications in some provinces, this left at least two regional centers of insurgency: the mountain zones of Veracruz province and the vast area south of Valladolid (Morelia) and Guadalajara stretching to the Pacific coast. To defend against raids and to protect strategically important trade routes, the army divisions guarded lines of fortified blockhouses manned by regular soldiers and local militiamen. Given the mobility of the guerrillas, the army established military roads (*caminos militares*) protected by forts that connected Veracruz with Mexico City and then radiated outward from the capital to the mining towns, agricultural centers, and provincial cities.

In 1816 when Viceroy Juan Ruíz de Apodaca arrived in Mexico to replace Calleja, he introduced different responses to insurgency that represented the third stage in which the regime reduced its dependence upon counterinsurgency terrorism and sought to regain the hearts and minds of the insurgents. After almost seven years of warfare, both insurgents and counterinsurgents had reached the point of total exhaustion. Until 1816, Spain dispatched sufficient expeditionary forces to maintain at least some enthusiasm for the counterinsurgency system. Insurgent defeats at the sieges of inaccessible fortifications at the Island of Mezcala in Lake Chapala, Cóporo, Sombrero, Juajilla, Jonacatlán, Palmillas, and elsewhere appeared to offer evidence that the royalists could win the war. On the other hand, from 1816 to 1821, the imperial government could not continue to dispatch fresh European units to lead the Mexican royalist army. Royalist officers and soldiers who had served more or less continuously since the outbreak of rebellion in 1810 clamored to be retired, and whether Mexican or Spanish they often deserted and disappeared. In an army that did not have a rotation or leave policy, permanent war meant permanent mobilization. Soldiers aged, fell ill in tropical postings, and their families suffered hardships when the army treasury failed to provide subsistence allowances and pay. Garrison troops ceased to chase guerrilla bands, preferring to remain in the comparative safety of their urban barracks. They developed a "blockhouse mentality" or static defensive thinking and accepted the fact of insurgent dominance over much of the rural countryside outside of their fortified towns.

The positive side to this stagnation of counterinsurgency was that exhaustion reduced the level of terrorist intimidation on both sides. Viceroy Apodaca introduced programs to offer amnesties and other benefits to insurgents who would give up their cause to joint the royalists. In some regions this approach resulted in the surrender of significant insurgent forces which were permitted to change sides under their officers and to be incorporated directly into the royalist forces as loyal militias. Often these instant royalists were sent back into the mountains to convince other guerrilla bands about the futility of continued resistance. In January 1820, Apodaca issued

1,408 amnesties to insurgents from the old rebel strongholds of Valladolid and Guanajuato.[52] In a typical case, one of the Ortiz brothers, who claimed the insurgent title of Comandante General of San Luis Potosí, accepted amnesty and a less lofty royalist commission as captain of militias. Apodaca assigned him to command fifty former insurgents and dispatched the force to hunt down bandits in the mountains of Guanajuato.[53]

The widespread use of amnestied insurgents to protect resettled villages populated by similarly amnestied former insurgents posed future dangers for the royalist army and for the regime. After years of combat without victory, Apodaca's blandishments and offers of instant respectability caused some insurgent commanders to accept resettlement in fortified communities. Described as sanguinary bandits and terrorists one day, they were transformed into patriotic royalists the day after. If conditions changed, amnestied rebels lapsed back into insurgency and banditry. Lack of administrative records and poor communications permitted some individuals to rejoin insurgent and bandit gangs as many as five or six times without facing execution. Untrained in any occupation other than insurgent or guerrilla-bandit, after years of warfare many men were not particularly concerned about which side they served.[54] When captured their testimony exhibited little in the way of fervor of commitment to any specific cause. For example, in 1820 Cristóval Flórez, a thirty-year-old mestizo insurgent from Tulancingo, received amnesty and accepted a post in the royalist militias. Although married and employed as an agricultural laborer, Flórez had begun his career in 1816 as a courier and spy with the guerrilla band of Vicente Guerrero. When Tulancingo fell to the royalist army, Flórez accepted the altered situation and attached himself to a gang of thieves that operated in surrounding districts. They hid out in the mountains and ravines waiting to rob travelers of their possessions. Flórez continued this occupation until 1819, when royalist militiamen captured him at a ranch where he had hidden. Escorted to the town of Acatlán, he jumped at the opportunity to join the royalists and accept resettlement in a rural agricultural community. Finding this lifestyle boring, Flórez fled once again to the mountains, where he reentered the bandit life. Captured yet again— fortunately without weapons in his hands—Flórez submitted an earnest petition requesting that he be allowed to serve as a royalist militiaman.[55]

Despite this misplaced generosity toward a hardened insurgent, there were limits to the amnesty program. In 1819 Agustín Santiago, magistrate of the village of Mecapalapa near Pantepec, led his community in a surprise ambush of a royalist army detachment. Only a few months earlier, Santiago and his people had requested and received a blanket royalist amnesty pardoning them for previous insurgency. After this blatant provocation, the local royalist commander sentenced Santiago to face a royalist firing squad.[56]

Although it was not outwardly obvious, at the beginning of 1821 the Mexican population was exhausted by the lengthy conflict and unwilling to pay the high costs of continuous mobilizations. Throughout the country, controversy raged about changes in Spain that resulted in the reimplementation of the Spanish Constitution of 1812, and public debates now took place about the merits of political independence. In some royalist garrisons, European and creole soldiers turned on each other, brawled in bars, and fought minor skirmishes. Apodaca's policy of granting automatic amnesties to former insurgents and incorporating them into the royalist ranks planted a highly untrustworthy element within the army. Throughout the country, cities and towns invoked articles of the Spanish Constitution to refuse tax support for district and regional militia forces. When this occurred, the counterinsurgency defenses created by Calleja crumbled. At that crucial juncture, Apodaca appointed Brigadier Agustín de Iturbide as commander of royalist forces in the region of Acâpulco—at the center of the strongest remaining insurgent strength. Instead of fighting, Iturbide made a deal with the insurgent leader Vicente Guerrero, and in the Plan de Iguala he declared the independence of Mexico. Much of the royalist army attached itself to this movement, and Spanish Mexico collapsed.

The insurgent and counterinsurgent terror evident early in the War of Mexican Independence accomplished little more than to harden attitudes and lengthen the conflict. The royalist armies won on the conventional battlefield, but they could not crush the isolated *focos* of insurgency. Equally, the guerrillas were able to maintain an existence, but they did not possess the military power to win a definitive victory. Although the use of spontaneous and planned terror on both sides declined toward the end of the war, guerrilla-banditry or common varieties of banditry entrenched violence in the society. The decade of conflict devastated Mexico's agriculture, mining industry, and commerce. In 1821 few Mexicans realized that insurgency, banditry, and other forms of violence would not disappear. As an independent nation, Mexico embarked upon a turbulent course.

NOTES

1. Christopher Dobson and Ronald Payne, *Counterattack: The West's Battle Against the Terrorists* (New York: Facts on File, 1982), xxi.

2. Ovid Demaris, *Brothers in Blood: The International Terrorist Network* (New York: Charles Scribner's Sons, 1977).

3. Dobson and Payne, *Counterattack*, 2.

4. Richard H. Shultz and Stephen Sloan, *Responding to the Terrorist Threat: Security and Crisis Management* (New York: Pergamon, 1980).

5. Benjamin Netanyahu, *Terrorism: How the West Can Win* (New York: Farrar Straus, 1986).

6. Dobson and Payne, *Counterattack*, 169.

7. *New York Times*, 24 May 1989, 4.

8. *New York Times*, 16 May 1989, 1.

9. Christopher Dobson and Ronald Payne, *War Without End: The Terrorists: An Intelligence Dossier* (London: Harrap, 1986), 192–93.

10. Christopher Dobson and Ronald Payne, *The Terrorists: Revised Edition: Their Weapons, Leaders and Tactics* (New York: Facts on File, 1982), 122–23.

11. Richard Clutterbuck, *Guerrillas and Terrorists* (London: Faber and Faber, 1977).

12. Walter Laqueur, *Terrorism* (Boston: Little, Brown and Company, 1977); and Laqueur and Yonah Alexander, *The Terrorism Reader: The Essential Source Book on Political Violence Both Past and Present* (New York: Penguin, 1987).

13. Alf Andrew Heggoy, *Insurgency and Counterinsurgency in Algeria* (Bloomington: Indiana University Press, 1972).

14. Alistair Horne, *A Savage War of Peace, Algeria, 1954–1962* (London: Macmillan, 1977).

15. David Galula, *Counterinsurgency Warfare, Theory and Practice* (New York: Praeger 1964).

16. Ranajit Guha, *Elementary Aspects of Peasant Insurgency in Colonial India* (Bombay: Oxford University Press, 1983).

17. William B. Taylor, *Drinking Homicide and Rebellion in Colonial Mexican Villages* (Stanford: Stanford University Press, 1979).

18. See Eric Van Young, "Millenium on the Northern Marches: The Mad Messiah of Durango and Popular Rebellion in Mexico, 1800–1815," *Comparative Studies in Society and History* 21 (1986), 385–413; and "Quetzalcóatl, King Ferdinand, and Ignacio Allende Go to the Seashore; or Messianism and Mystical Kingship in Mexico, 1800–1821," in Jaime E. Rodríguez O., *The Independence of Mexico and the Creation of the New Nation* (Los Angeles: UCLA Latin American Center Publications, 1989), 89–127. For interesting comparisons in nineteenth century India, see Ranajit Guha, *Elementary Aspects of Peasant Insurgency*, 256–68.

19. Christon I. Archer, *The Army in Bourbon Mexico, 1760–1810* (Albuquerque: University of New Mexico Press, 1977), 98.

20. Archer, *Army in Mexico*, 99.

21. See Enrique Florescano, *Precios del maíz y crisis agrícolas en México (1708–1810)* (México: Colegio de México, 1969); and John Tutino, *From Insurgency to Revolution in Mexico: Social Bases of Agrarian Violence, 1750–1940* (Princeton: Princeton University Press, 1986); and Eric Van Young, "Moving Towards Revolt: Agrarian Origins of the Hidalgo Rebellion in the Guadalajara Region," in Frederick Katz, ed., *Riot, Rebellion, Revolution: Rural Social Conflict in Mexico* (Princeton: Princeton University Press, 1988), 176–204.

22. Eric Van Young, "Islands in the Storm: Quiet Cities and Violent Countrysides in the Mexican Independence Era," *Past and Present* 118 (February 1988), 134.

23. Brigadier José de la Cruz to Viceroy Francisco Javier de Venegas, 30 November 1810, Archivo General de La Nación, Mexico, (cited hereinafter as AGN), Sección de Operaciones de Guerra (cited hereinafter as OG), vol. 140.

24. Francisco Amador to Juan Felipe de Mugarrieta, Otumba, 23 July 1811, AGN:OG, vol. 347.

25. Colonel Pedro Armijo to Viceroy Félix Calleja, Chilpancingo, 25 May 1814, AGN:OG, vol. 72.

26. *Ibid.*

27. Friar Miguel González to Calleja, Hacienda de los Cedros, 16 October 1810, AGN:OG, vol. 169.

28. Isidro Gómez de Vera, hacendado of Espiritu Santo to Calleja, 16 October 1810; and Julián de Cosío to Calleja, Real de Catorce, 17 October 1810, AGN:OG, vol. 180.

29. Venegas to Calleja, 8 December 1810, AGN:OG, vol. 170.

30. Callejo to Venegas, Guanajuato, 12 August 1811; and Venegas to Calleja, 18 August 1811, AGN:OG, vol. 190.

31. See Don W. Alexander, "French Military Problems in Counterinsurgency Warfare in Northeastern Spain, 1808–1813," *Military Affairs* 40, no. 3 (October 1976), 117–22; and *Rod of Iron: French Counterinsurgency Policy in Aragon during the Peninsular War* (Wilmington: Scholarly Resources Inc., 1985).

32. Cruz to Viceroy Venegas, Hacienda de la Goleta, 19 November 1810, AGN:OG, vol. 141.

33. Cruz to Calleja, Huichapan, 2 December 1810, AGN:OG, vol. 140.

34. Cruz to Venegas, Huichapan, 11 December 1810, AGN:OG, vol. 106.

35. Christon I. Archer, "Banditry and Revolution in New Spain, 1790–1821," *Bibliothecas Americana* 1, no. 2 (November 1982), 59–89.

36. This general approach was applied by the French in Algeria, and variations continue today in countries such as Guatemala. See for example the *Globe and Mail*, Toronto, 4 February 1984, 5; Richard Halloran, "U.S. Studies Rebels in Latin America: Military Research in Panama Seeks Ways to Defeat Left," *New York Times*, 8 February 1987, 4.

37. Alistair Horne, *A Savage War of Peace*, 331; and Robert B. Asprey, *War in the Shadows: The Guerrilla in History*, vol. 2 (Garden City, NY: Doubleday, 1975), 685, 921. For an interesting theoretical approach, see David Galula, *Counterinsurgency Warfare: Theory and Practice* (New York: Praeger 1964).

38. Venegas to Calleja, 13 November 1810, AGN:OG, vol. 170.

39. See for example Peter M. Dunn, "The American Army: The Vietnam War, 1965–1973," in Ian F. W. Beckett and John Pimlott, *Armed Forces and Modern Counter-Insurgency* (London: Croom Helm, 1985), 86–87.

40. Cruz to Calleja, Huichapan, 2 December 1810, AGN:OG, vol. 140; Cruz to Venegas, 1 December 1810, AGN:OG, vol. 142; and Christon I. Archer, "La Causa Buena: The Counterinsurgency Army of New Spain and the Ten Years' War," in Jaime E. Rodríguez O., *The Independence of Mexico and the Creation of the New Nation* (Los Angeles: UCLA Latin American Center Publications, 1989), 63–84.

41. Correspondence of José de Andrade, May and June 1811, AGN:OG, vol. 55.

42. Cruz to Calleja, 2 December 1810, AGN:OG, vol. 140; and Andrade to Venegas, Ixmiquilpan, 22 June 1811, AGN:OG, vol. 95.

43. Calleja to Cruz, Guanajuato, 5 December 1810, AGN:OG, vol. 140; and Venegas to Andrade, 24 June 1811, AGN:OG, vol. 95.

44. Calleja to Venegas, 15 October 1811, AGN:OG, vol. 192.

45. Calleja to Venegas, 7 November 1811, AGN:OG, vol. 195; and Calleja to Venegas, 28 February 1812, AGN:OG, vol. 198.

46. Reglamento ó instrucción general para la observancia de los comandantes de partidas partióticas que han de obrar en la circumferencia de sus respectivas lugares, 1 November 1814, AGN:OG, vol. 430.

47. Reglamento político militar que deberán observar bajo las penas que señala los pueblos, haciendas, y ranchos . . . , 8 June 1811, AGN:OG, vol. 186. Also see Brian R. Hamnett, "Royalist Counterinsurgency and the Continuity of Rebellion: Guanajuato and Michoacán, 1813–1820," *Hispanic American Historical Review* 62, no. 1 (February 1982), 24–26; and Brian R. Hamnett, *Roots of Insurgency: Mexican Regions, 1750–1824* (Cambridge: Cambridge University Press, 1986).

48. Calleja to Venegas, 11 August 1811, AGN:OG, vol. 190.

49. Calleja to Venegas, 11 February 1812, AGN:OG, vol. 165.

50. Calleja to the Minister of War, bo. 14 reservada, 5 September 1813, Archivo General Militar de Segovia, Spain, Sección de Ultramar (cited hereinafter as AGMS), leg. 232.

51. Fernando Miyares to Francisco Xavier Abadía, 27 February 1816, AGMS, Ultramar, leg. 226.

52. Conde de Venadito [Apodaca] to the Secretary of War, no. 108, 31 January 1820, AGMS, Ultramar, leg. 223.

53. Venadito to the Secretary of War, no. 111, 29 February 1820, AGMS, Ultramar, leg. 233.

54. Calleja to Brigadier Manuel de la Concha, 10 July 1816, AGN:OG, vol. 120; and Brigadier Domingo Luaces to Venadito, no. 61, 16 July 1820, AGN:OG, vol. 511.

55. Testimony of Cristóval Flórez, 26 March 1820, AGN:OG, vol. 325.

56. Concha to Venadito, Zihuatentla, no. 300, 20 January 1819, AGN:OG, vol. 124.

3

Middle Eastern Terrorism: Its Characteristics and Driving Forces

Khalid Duran

IS THERE A DISTINCT ISLAMIC QUALITY TO MIDDLE EASTERN TERRORISM?

The large number of terrorist acts committed in or emanating from the Middle East has given rise to speculations that there is an intimate connection between Islam and violence. These suspicions are not limited to time-honored Western prejudices against Islam. Many Muslims themselves have come to believe that there is some truth to this claim. The seemingly intractable conflicts between various Muslim states, the conflict of factions within Lebanon itself, and the conflict between the Palestinians and Israel—added to the gripping TV images of Middle Eastern terrorists seizing aircraft and Western hostages—seem to corroborate this judgment that Islam is a religion of violence.

The fact that the governments of Iraq, Iran, Libya, and Syria either maintain terrorist organizations as instruments of their foreign policy or provide support to, and avail themselves of, the services of terrorist groups serves to confirm this suspicion.[1]

However, to hold Islam responsible for the surge of Middle Eastern terrorism would be a mistake. While it is undeniable that with the demise of the Soviet Bloc Middle Eastern governments became the chief ones to sponsor acts of terrorism, the reason for this is neither cultural nor religious, but must be sought elsewhere. The way a number of Middle Eastern and North African regimes use terrorism as a means of achieving their political ends does not differ substantially from that of totalitarian regimes in other parts of the world.[2] Iraqi terrorist activities abroad bear no distinct Islamic or Arab stamp; rather they tend to follow the model of Eastern European terrorism.[3]

Saddam's opponent, Ayatollah Ruholla Khomeini, claimed to be autochthonous, but a glance at the nativism of Iraq's "Islamic Republic" reveals it to derive, except for a few Persian peculiarities, most of its police-state edifice from these same European totalitarian systems of this century and not from seventh-century Islam. On the practical side, the Mullahs' implementation of "Islamic policies" is even more indebted to the totalitarian molds of the much maligned West. (In Islamist literature, the term "West" usually includes all of Europe, often including Russia, because East and West are taken as synonyms of, respectively, Islam and Christianity.)[4]

Islam neither begets terrorism nor legitimizes it. Like Buddhism, Judaism, and Christianity, Islam enunciates essentially pacifist ethics. The very name *islam* is but a derivative of *salam*, which is the same as the Hebrew *shalom* and means "peace." During the Prophet's early career in Mecca, he was a pacifist altogether, and we find this reflected in the first revelations collected in *Al-Qu'ran* (Koran), the holy scripture of Islam. Later revelations in Medina lent a militant touch to Al-Qu'ran, but even then Muslims were allowed to take up arms only for defensive purposes.[5]

THE CONCEPT OF *JIHAD*—"HOLY WAR" OR "MORAL EFFORT?"

"Oppression is worse than fighting," says Al-Qu'ran, and this phrase was the basis for the declaration of a *jihad* against Saddam Hussein. Muslims are keen to point out that jihad has to be understood in its literal meaning as an "effort," more precisely as a moral effort. There is the "greater effort" and the "lesser effort." The greater jihad is to fight against one's evil inclinations, against immorality and sloth, and, most of all, against selfishness. It is a struggle to purify oneself, to be a better part of society, to become the "perfect man" upon whom others can rely for help, a pillar of the *civitas dei*, the "virtuous city" (*al-madina al-fadila*) of the Muslim philosophers and moralists.

To join the defense forces of the Muslin polity is but the "lesser jihad," even though the death of such a soldier turns him into a *shadid* ("martyr"). On return from one of the battles of the early community against the onslaught of the heathen tribes, the Prophet told his companions, "Now that the lesser jihad is over, it is time to dedicate yourself to the greater jihad."

The notion of a defensive war was sometimes interpreted fairly liberally to allow for preemptive attacks. On the other hand there has always been much discussion as to whether this or that war was a jihad or not. In order to declare a war a jihad, proof is needed that the opponent does harm to religion. It need not be Islamic religion. If Jewish religion is oppressed, Muslims are just as much called upon to rise in arms and defend their Jewish cousins-in-faith. In theory, Muslim states ought to have waged a jihad against Nazi Germany and Soviet Russia for the suppression of the Jewish and the Christian religion.

The ethical connotation of the term jihad is most clearly evident in a saying of Muhammad's to the effect that "the most virtuous jihad is to oppose a tyrant with a word of truth." On January 18, 1985, seventy-seven-year-old Mahmud Muhammad Taha was publicly hanged in Khartoum precisely for leading this type of jihad. The pacifist religious leader of Sudan had convened rallies of protest against the inhuman application of the *Shari'a*, the archaic punitive laws the dictator Numairi reintroduced to amputate the limbs of petty thieves in a time of famine.

Mahmud Taha also demanded a peaceful solution to the civil war between the arabized north and the animist south of Sudan. This courageous jihad of his—his standing up against brutality, his resistance to the insanity of the tyrant—ushered in a huge protest movement that eventuated in the fall of Numairi's regime.[6]

It is evident that the same *Hadith* (saying of Muhammad's) might be used to oppose a ruler who may not be a tyrant in the eyes of the vast majority but is regarded as such by a small band of fanatics seeking a religious legitimization. All the same, the Prophet did not recommend the murder of the unjust ruler—he wanted him to be exposed to brave criticism, to *kalimatu haqq* ("a word of truth").

No religion is safe against distorted interpretations. Buddhism, often hailed as a religion of peace, which it undoubtedly is, has not been able to turn its followers into angels. There have been terrible wars between Burmese and Thai Buddhists, with temple destructions in Ayuthaya, and brutal repression by the officially Buddhist government in Burma (now Myanmar).[7] The civil war in Sri Lanka is an ongoing massacre of the Buddhist Sinhalese and Hindu Tamils. For most Buddhists such deviations are shameful. The same pain is felt by many Muslims when they witness coreligionists resorting to a murderous interpretation of the jihad concept.

There are about a dozen terrorist movements that misuse the term jihad. Some of them bear a name that includes the words "jihad" or "*mujahidin*." A *mujahid* is someone who carries out jihad. Two groups that are clearly terrorist and bear the name jihad are *al-jihad* in Egypt and *al-jihad al-islami* in Lebanon. In both cases jihad stands for "holy war."

The al-jihad movement in Egypt says explicitly that Muslims have the obligation to make war against all infidels, that is, non-Muslims and lax Muslims alike. It is a movement led by a scholar of the religious law, Shaikh 'Umar' Abd-ar-Rahman. He is neither very intelligent nor profound, but an activist and a fanatic, a kind of Muslim counterpart to the assassinated rabbi Meir Kahane, an apostle of hatred who strikes the right chord with highly frustrated segments of society. 'Umar'Abd-ar-Rahman is a Muslim supremacist proud of his assassins who killed "the Pharaoh," Egypt's President Sadat. He is in and out of prison. Overall the government has been wise enough to permit him some agitation as this allows the security services a way to gauge the extent of his popular appeal.[8]

A book published by another ideologue of the movement bears the significant title *The Missing Obligation*.[9] Its theme is that Muslims are wrong in assuming that there are only five "Pillars of the Faith" (the confession of faith, ritual prayer, fasting, almsgiving, and pilgrimage). The sixth one—jihad— has wrongly been allowed to fall into disuse. It has to be reintroduced. Jihad means primarily *jihad bi-s-saif* ("to fight with the sword"), not *jihad bi-qalam* ("to fight with the pen"). According to this faulty history and dubious theology, Islam was always spread by war. Without war Islam would never have been a force in the world, and without war Islam will one day cease to exist. All other interpretations of jihad are decadent. The moralist interpretations of jihad by generations of Muslim scholars are declared shallow apologetics.

Out of a billion Muslims in the world, some 10–50 million know by heart the famous saying of Muhammad's according to which "Islam is built upon five" (*"buniya l-islam 'ala khamsa"*). It stands at the beginning of religious instruction for children.[10]

Therefore, little credence needs to be given to the untenable theological interpretation spread by the movement al-jihad. However, there is some basis to this historical interpretation of Islam, a view held by many in the Muslim world. Islam has had a history of the sword. The remarkable military exploits of the forebears of modern Islam were often responses to attacks on the nascent community of Islam. But posterity remembers them as military campaigns only, not as basically defensive ones. There is this divergence between the explicit tenets of Islam and the popular understanding of Islam among many of its largely illiterate followers.

We might be able to understand this better by drawing a parallel to the development of Spanish Catholicism and its popular imagery. The pacifism of Jesus was circumvented by inventing the cult of Santiago (Saint James), in whose name the Spaniards militarily overthrew the religiously-tolerant Moorish rule in Spain and in whose name the *conquistadores* conquered America, slaughtering and enslaving the indigenous people.[11] In time Santiago supplanted Jesus altogether, not in the theology of the Church, but in the psychology of the masses. How else could the capital city of Chile and a major city in Cuba be named Santiago if a popular following had not been built?

Similarly the "lesser jihad" has a stronger appeal than the "greater jihad," at least in some parts of the Muslim world and among some sections of the population. Leading ideologues of extremist Islamism, such as the Pakistani Maududi (d. 1979) and his Iranian counterpart, Ayatollah Ruhollah Khomeini (d. 1989), actually occupy a sort of middle-ground between the rabid war-mongering of al-jihad's 'Umar' Abd-ar-Rahman and the general view of jihad as a defensive war, held by the vast majority of the orthodox scholars.[12]

OLD-TIMERS OF THE MUSLIM BROTHERHOOD: A FAREWELL TO ARMS?

This, however, is not to say that fringe movements of religious fanatics are the major source of terrorism emanating from the Middle East. Islamism as a modern movement that combined religious fundamentalism with elements of Western political totalitarianism (in particular the fascism of Italy and Spain) emerged first in Egypt in 1928, and Cairo is still its major center despite much emigration and forced exile.[13] Its political party, the Muslim Brotherhood (*ikhwan*) gave its name to all Islamists (those taking Islam to be a political ideology)— be they called "fundamentalists," "extremists," "radicals," "Muslim fanatics," or whatever—from Indonesia to Mauritania.

The mainstream *ikhwan* in Egypt have, quite some time ago, dissociated themselves from terrorism. They used to be a major contributor to terrorist activity in Egypt although they were not necessarily the major contributor. They are probably correct in their assessment that terrorism did them more harm than good and that they might have been able to take over, at one stage or another, had they not alienated the people by resorting to terrorism.[14]

Consequently, the old-time Islamists have almost become a factor of stability in Egypt's political life, but they are being violently challenged by their illegitimate offspring, the fanatical *jama'at islamiya* ("Islamist Associations"), organized mostly in the underground, of which al-jihad is but one.[15]

Al-jihad and other Egyptian jama'at did take some assistance from Libya and from Iran in the past, but they are not part of the international terrorist network run by those states. Strongly xenophobic and idiosyncratic, al-jihad does not fall under the category of international or state-sponsored terrorism. This makes it, on one hand, easier to suppress the movement by depriving it of foreign support but, on the other hand, more difficult to do so because it is homespun, with a wide underground network.

Al-jihad al-islami in Lebanon is also partly indigenous and individualistic. In fact, it is a kind of a family affair, run chiefly by 'Imad Mughniya, a Lebanese Shi'ite seeking to release his relatives from prison in Kuwait. They had tried to assassinate the Emir but were not executed because of the pressure Mughniya was able to exert by dint of his hostage-taking enterprise called al-jihad al-islami.[16]

At the same time al-jihad al-islami worked in liaison with the Khomeinist establishment as an important component of its international terrorist network. It is, therefore, more appropriate to subsume al-jihad al-islami under the rubric of state terrorism. Mughniya's group is but one of several subgroups constituting the terrorist wing of the "Party of God" (*hezbollah*).[17]

THE DISPARATE SELF-CONCEPTS OF ISLAMIST TERRORISTS

Terrorists who feel inspired of Islam may have two views of their activity that are diametrically opposed to one another. First there are those who believe that terrorism is a form of warfare at which "the others" excel and which Muslims ought to learn and to master. The "others" are Americans, Europeans and Jews. Such Muslims sincerely believe that they must emulate other people who owe their strength to terrorism. Some of these Muslims know Islam does not teach terrorism; they may even know that it actually prohibits it. However, they also think that this is a weak point, and they are prepared to go against an express injunction of their religion for the sake of achieving worldly aims and competing with non-Muslims for power.

This self-concept runs totally counter to a common Western view of Middle Easterners as more given to terrorism than other people and of Muslims as being prone to terrorism because of their religion. Many people in the Middle East seriously think of Americans as terrorists *par excellence* and of Jews as terrorists *per se*. The carnage wrought in Iraq by American weapons will, unfortunately, reinforce this view. These people admire the West's advantage in "terrorism" as they admire her advantage in science and technology.

In this context it cannot be emphasized enough how the success of Israeli terrorism has influenced Arab and Iranian terrorism. Zionist militancy began early in the 1940s, preceding the flowering of Arab terrorism by three decades.[18] This point is not being made as an apology for terrorist acts committed by Arabs and Iranians, all of which deserve censure in their own right. But it would be patently wrong to underestimate the effect of Israeli terrorism on the region. From my own experience I would maintain that it had a stunning impact upon two or three generations in the Middle East.[19]

Israeli terrorism did not confine itself to eliminating opponents through assassination; it has often had the purpose of intimidating a whole class of foes, particularly the Arabs. Intimidation of a wider audience is, of course, a technical hallmark of terrorism. Such seems to be the purpose of the Israeli air force bombings of crowded refugee camps or Shi'ite villages in "retaliation" for a crime committed against Israel. This feckless effort simply provokes more counter-terrorism, in a wearying and futile cycle of violence. It creates a sense of inferiority and frustrated anger in Arabs and other Muslims identifying with them. It has become a major aspiration of many to overcome this complex by outdoing the Israelis, or at least by being as efficient and ruthless as they are.

Part of this syndrome is the conviction among many Arabs and other Middle Easterners that the Israelis are brave and determined, qualities lacking in the Muslims of today. The most convincing way of proving that this lamentable state of affairs has been overcome is to carry out terrorist acts compatible with the feats of the Mossad (Israeli Intelligence Service) if not more grandiose.

Second, there are the zealots, especially among Shi'ites, who disagree that terrorism runs counter to Islamic ethics. They may dispute the appropriateness of the term terrorism for what they regard as heroism; but they know what is meant, and they are proud of possessing in terrorism a weapon which they believe they use more effectively than others. Considering terrorism a specialty of Shi'ism, they actually confirm Western prejudices about Islam being a religion of violence.

This group seeks to overcome the sense of inferiority by propagating the idea that Jews really are cowards. Whatever they achieved was due to superior military and financial backing by the United States and European nations. Without such support, these Islamists claim, there would be no Israeli terrorism and, probably, no Israel.

By contrast, Shi'ites, lacking the technical means of great power patronage, are not frightened because the Almighty has blessed them with the spirit of martyrdom: the faithful who die while carrying out a terrorist act are to be considered "martyrs" (*shuhada*), just like any other combatant who dies in a just war.

I would like to stress that the difference between a guerrilla fighter and a terrorist is clear to most concerned people in the Middle East. The debate about who is a terrorist and who is a legitimate resistance fighter can be avoided if terrorism is regarded as a property of acts and not causes. Menachem Begin or Yitzhak Shamir may be considered freedom fighters in reference to some of the fighting they did, but in reference to some other acts of theirs it seems impossible to absolve them of the charge of terrorism. The same applies to Yasir Arafat.

It is a different matter, though, with young Iranians who underwent years of indoctrination alongside their training in terrorism. The brainwashing carried out by terrorism experts of the Khomeini regime has been proven to be extraordinarily deft and effective. Some of the *hezbollahis*, who have little other education, may actually not be any longer in a position to distinguish between terrorism and acts of self-sacrifice for a righteous cause. Such a victim of Islamist indoctrination will regard any Israeli soldier as a terrorist but an Iranian assassin as a *mojahed* and a potential martyr.

In the course of Iran's "Islamic Revolution," many observers, and quite a few protagonists, too, became convinced that Shi'ism has an innate capacity for martyrdom through suicide.[20] Countless Western writers presented the sacrificial spirit of Iran's young revolutionaries as a special quality only Shi'ism has been able to generate. The fact that so many opponents of the new regime were no less sacrificial was seen as a confirmation of the thesis about Shi'ism as the "revolutionary brand of Islam." The *mojahedin-e khalq* ("People's Mujahidin") who fought so bravely against Khomeini's theocracy were, after all, Shi'ites, too.

This notion of suicidal Shi'ites became widespread following the car-bomb attacks in 1983 by Lebanese Shi'ites on the embassies of the United States and Iraq, on the headquarters of the French paratroops, on an Israeli government office in Tyre, and on the American Marine barracks. This latter bombing shocked President Reagan into abruptly withdrawing the Marines from Lebanon and frantically erecting barricades around U.S. public buildings at home and abroad.

POLITICAL RIVALRY LEADS TO A COMPETITION IN BODY COUNT

However, shortly afterward, other political groups, including Communists and nationalists, surpassed the Islamists in suicide attacks. More than a dozen kamikaze type operations against the Israelis in Southern Lebanon were carried out by non-religious groups. A number were carried out by women, which raised interesting challenges to the "holy warrior" claims of the mullahs. Moreover, "because suicide missions have no necessary connection to Islam, they can be employed by brutal regimes of any ideological stripe."[21] In Lebanon, the Iranian-backed Shi'ites entered into some competition with groups aligned with Syria. Damascus allowed Teheran considerable latitude, but not a monopoly on terrorism.[22]

All this proved very vexing to the leadership of the hezbollah in Lebanon, especially after a film was made on the life of one of those heroines, Miheidalla. She was quite westernized in her manner and dress, and her motives were purely nationalistic and not Islamic. Shaikh Subhi At-Tufaili, a top cleric of the Khomeinist religious establishment, bitterly denounced those suicide missions as fruitless and counterproductive.[23]

This denunciation smacked of envy. It is true that most of those later kamikaze actions did not inflict much damage on the enemy, what with the increased security precautions being taken. This, however, did not mean that Khomeinist Shi'ites were more effective terrorists. They had established the pattern, and once the pattern was known, defenses such as vehicle barriers made success come harder.

Envy became apparent in many other ways. Many terrorist acts in Lebanon, or emanating from Lebanon, were claimed by several groups simultaneously. A mad race for terrorist exploits began, all contributing to the prestige of terrorism as such. The terrorist became the hero of the day and terrorist prowess the highest virtue.

As a result, terrorist acts began to be traded as they acquired fetish-like attributes, being performed to acquire a strange sort of legitimacy. The hezbollah would actually kidnap Lebanese Communists and threaten them with execution, but set them free in exchange for assistance rendered to hezbollah terrorists in places where they lacked logistics or the necessary infrastructure.

GRUESOME PRECEDENTS IN MUSLIM HISTORY

It is undeniable that Muslims as a community have been beset by political violence throughout history, perhaps no more than some other cultural traditions, but certainly not less than others. Three of the four "Right Guided Caliphs," the first rulers of the early community, were assassinated: 'Umar (Omar), 'Uthman (Osman), and 'Ali. Bands of zealots and sectarians made the assassination of the "impious" their credo. "Impious" was anyone who did not share their particular interpretation of the Holy Book.

Periods of rampant terrorism were followed by centuries of remarkable tranquility, only to be disrupted by renewed turmoil and terrorist activity. In the eleventh century we have the notorious *assassins*. The word, which entered most European languages with the connotation of political murderer, derives from the Arabic *hashashin*. A hashash is someone who uses hashish. The Shi'ite leader in Persia, Hasan Bin Sabah, called the "Old Man of the Mountain," allegedly would dispatch his men to murder political opponents after intoxicating them with hashish.[24] We commemorate this by using the words "assassinate" and "assassination," loanwords from a Persian tradition that is Islamic only in name. On one hand such excesses resulted in a stigma on political murder. Countless theologians condemned such aberrations as antithetical to Islamic moral teachings. However, political assassination became a definite strand in Muslim tradition, and from time to time some extremists emerge who make the resuscitation of this particular strand their life's mission.

The late Ayatollah Ruhollah Khomeini resembled the "Old Man of the Mountain" not only in appearance and in spreading a gigantic terrorist network of his own out to all corners of the globe but also by publicly calling for the assassination of Salman Rushdie, the Indian-born novelist who wrote *The Satanic Verses*.[25] Egyptian Nobel Prize-winner for Literature, Naguib Mahfouz, did not hesitate to call the Ayatollah an assassin and a terrorist.[26]

The present-day equivalent of the hashashin are called hezbollahis. *Hizb-Allah* or, in Persianized spelling, hezbollah, means "Party of God" or "God's own party."

Hezbollah became prominent in Lebanon, where it fought mainly against a rival Shi'i organization called *Amal* (it means "hope" in Arabic). Amal, a larger and more progressive group, was founded in 1975 by Nabih Berri. It is a decidedly more nationalist group than hezbollah (which identifies itself totally with Iranian pan-Islamism) although it is often an ally if not an agent of Syria.[27] Significantly, hezbollah fought more against Amal than against anyone else among the warring factions, including the Maronite Christians and the Israelis.[28]

Similarly, hezbollah in Afghanistan fought more against the independent and nationalistic Shi'ite organization *shura* than against the Russians. In fact, some hezbollah did not fight the Russians at all.[29]

As a result of the reporting about Lebanon in the world press, a common misconception in the minds of many Westerners is that hezbollah is a party just of Lebanese Shi'ites. In reality, hezbollah is present wherever you have any sizable number of Shi'ites following the "line of the Imam (Khomeini)," be it among the predominantly Shi'ite population of Bahrain, among the numerous Lebanese in African states such as Sierra Leone, Ivory Coast, Senegal, Zaire and Gabon,[30] or among the large community of *siriolibaneses* in Buenos Aires, Tucuman, and other Latin American cities. The regime even dispatched a high ranking cleric, Ayatollah Rabbani, to Buenos Aires along with politically well-trained young functionaries. The Shi'ite mosque in Argentina's capital was also active in mustering support for Iran from local political parties.[31]

Most of all such activities served the purpose of creating a solid infra-structure for Teheran's terrorist network. The Khomeini regime's resolute-ness in procuring for itself such a vantage position in terrorism has generally been underestimated.[32] Specialists on Iran do not tire to point out that the regime is beset by deep divisions and that the "moderates" or "pragmatists" centered on Rafsanjani have gotten the upper hand over the "radicals" united around Khomeini's son Ahmad and the former Interior Minister Mohtashami.[33]

It is difficult to predict the future developments of Iranian policy under the clerics. The fanatical defenders of the "Imam's line" still possess many trump cards. However, even if they were decisively defeated, which is highly unlikely, this would be no guarantee that the "pragmatists" would totally renounce their fifth columns abroad.

In 1990 terrorism was temporarily shelved by Teheran, but the efficient network was not disbanded. The impressive structures, set up in Europe especially, in the early 1980s, remain intact. Thousands of Iranians abroad were recruited by hezbollah, and tens of thousands more were sent abroad as students, businessmen, refugees, and in other capacities.[34]

One Iranian specialty is to use male nurses accompanying invalids sent to Europe for the treatment of their war injuries as agents. Several European countries wishing to reestablish commercial relations with the "Islamic Re-public" were very generous in filling their hospitals with the wounded of the Iran–Iraq war. Spain, which had accepted more refugees from the Iranian revolution than any other European country, tried to improve its relations with Teheran by accepting a large number of wounded Iranian soldiers for medical treatment. Similarly, both Germanies prior to reunification treated victims of Iraqi poison gas attacks. Each invalid was accompanied by a male nurse, almost all of whom were not only hezbollahis but *pasdaran* ("Revo-lutionary Guards").[35]

In England, Teheran was able to recruit several hundred Shi'ites from the Arab Gulf countries for the hezbollah. Their mosque at Dorset Square became a major center for Khomeinist indoctrination in Europe. In France Khomeini's emissaries found a sympathetic hearing with many frustrated North Africans, quite a few of whom were only too eager to go to Iran for "further training."[36]

The most rewarding of all was the recruitment of Western converts to Shi'ite Islam. Some of them converted first to Islam and were won over for terrorism afterwards; others came first to terrorism and converted to Islam afterwards. They are British, French, German, Spanish and Latin American young people; some are militant American blacks. Their ranks swelled in the wake of the Soviet Empire's collapse. Young radicals in search of a militant cause got attracted to Khomeinism because of its blatant defiance of the superpowers, with particular vitriol for the West. Thus the chairman of Ger-many's Anti-Apartheid League became an ardent spokesman of Khomeinism, with the argument that Iran was the only oil producing country refusing to sell to South Africa. Where such grotesque make-belief was possible, it should not surprise us that frustrated blacks from the bleak slums of Philadelphia or New York should hurry to Iran for training in terrorist tactics targeting the United States.[37] It should, however, worry us.

THE NEGLECTED TERRORISM: PAKISTAN'S AFGHAN WAR

Attention has usually focused on Libya, Syria, Iraq, Iran and Yemen as countries sponsoring terrorism.[38] Another Middle Eastern country deeply involved in terrorism, Pakistan, has been exempt from the stigma despite the fact that the Islamabad government instigates more terrorism than do all of the above-mentioned Arab governments and the PLO combined.

Pakistan, it must be said, has never indulged in the kind of terrorism these other governments and groups are accused of. The ISI (Directorate of Inter-services Intelligence), Islamabad's military security service, has not (to my knowledge) assassinated any political opponents abroad nor has it kidnapped dissidents from London or contracted to place explosives in airplanes or public places.[39] Pakistani involvement in terrorism has gone largely unnoticed because it hides behind the veil of Afghan liberation.[40] When criticism of killings within the Afghan resistance mounted in Europe and the United States, Islamabad was, at best, accused of negligence or passivity. Very few analysts took the Pakistanis to task, and hardly anyone pinpointed the ISI as the chief agent responsible for the murders of Afghans in Pakistan and in Afghanistan itself.

Actually, Pakistan has itself been a victim of terrorism. Separatist groups from among the smaller nationalities of Pakistan's multi-national population have many times resorted to terrorist acts, mostly at the behest of India or the Soviet Union. WAD (formerly KHAD), the secret service of Kabul's Soviet-installed regime, has killed several hundred people—Afghans and Pakis-tanis—in Pakistan, and cross-border violations by the Afghan and Soviet military were responsible for still more.[41]

By 1989 there were 3.4 million registered Afghani refugees in Pakistan and another 400,000 unregistered.[42] General Zia ul-Haq saw this influx of refugees as both a threat and an opportunity. In 1970, on assignment in Jordan, he saw firsthand the near toppling of King Hussein by the PLO during "Black September." He realized that armed refugees can threaten a regime; the Pakistani military determined to place the *mujahidin* under firm control.[43] The opportunity presented by the Soviet invasion was the possibility of es-tablishing a "malleable regime" in Afghanistan. With the prospect of billions of new dollars flowing into Pakistan, the Pakistani military found itself well-placed to effect both of these outcomes.

The CIA determined that the ISI would be the appropriate agent to funnel funds to be used against the Soviet occupation of Afghanistan, and to all appearances things worked well: the Russians were made to leave Afghanistan, which was all that counted in the eyes of the CIA operatives. Their local partners from the ISI were more professional and efficient than comparable services in other Third World countries. Therefore, the CIA did not insist on more direct dealings with the resistance commanders, leaving the distribution of weapons, money and supplies to the ISI.[44]

The distribution of the American supplied arms became a decisive weapon in the hands of the Pakistani authorities. They supplied the bulk of the arms shipments to the faction of their choice and left little to the six other partners in the alliance of seven Afghan *mujahidin* parties forcibly married to one another by the ISI, the so-called Afghan Interim Government (AIG). These seven themselves were but a fraction of the whole resistance movement.[45] Being utterly dependent on arms supplies, the commanders in the field had no choice but to affiliate themselves with Islamabad's favorite among the resistance leaders, Gulbuddin Hekmatyar, a Pashtun and leader of the Islamic Party (*hezb-e islami*), the most radical of the fundamentalist parties in the AIG. As a result, Hekmatyar soon emerged as the strongest among the party bosses, despite the fact that few Afghans found him to their taste.

Hekmatyar has had a bad reputation as a wanton killer ever since he murdered the leftist student leader Saidal at Kabul University back in 1972. This happened at a time when Hekmatyar was switching his affiliation from the pro-Soviet *parcham* faction of the Democratic People's Party (the Communist Party still in control in Kabul) to the fundamentalist *ikhwan* ("Muslim Brothers"), whom he was to infiltrate on behalf of parcham. Saidal was an independent leftist with Chinese sympathies whom the Soviets wanted eliminated. At the same time Hekmatyar used this murder as a means of ingratiating himself with the "Muslim Brothers" and gaining their confidence.

He was given refuge in Pakistan in 1975, where the party of Zulfikir Ali Bhutto, the PPP (Pakistan People's Party) found common interest with the Pakistan military in supporting an Islamist of Pashtun descent who may help resist Pashtun irredentist claims to northern Pakistan. When Pakistan's Islamist party (*jama'at-e islami*) ran afoul of the government and was suppressed, and the Islamists were about to be banned, Hekmatyar managed to hang on. He is widely considered to be a stooge of the ISI.[46]

Justifying Islamabad's choice of the budding terrorist, an ISI officer confidentially assured me that Hekmatyar was neither a Communist nor an Islamist, but an opportunist:

In the whole of Afghanistan you cannot find a dirtier guy than him, and that is exactly what we need. He suits our purposes ideally because we have the means of controlling him and he cannot escape our grip [This was a veiled reference to Hekmatyar's homosexuality.] We can put him to any use. We have had so many problems with Afghanistan and we are sure to need someone like that in the future in order to ward off trouble from Kabul.[47]

Some twenty years later a *Task Force on Terrorism and Unconventional Warfare* of the U.S. House of Representatives concluded that Gulbuddin Hekmatyar's

...personal involvement with the highest echelons of the Khomeini regime and the ensuing cooperation of his men in anti-US international terrorism should have made him ineligible for any US assistance, let alone the bulk of it. Yet, ISI and the CIA steadfastly shielded, promoted and propped up their man.[48]

STATE TERRORISM SERVING GEOPOLITICS

What does Islamabad have in mind by choosing Hekmatyar and insisting on installing him in Kabul against all odds? Afghanistan and Pakistan are closely related to one another in geography, religion, and ethnicity. Their international border in the Hindu Kush, the Durand Line, is not recognized by Afghanistan and has never served as a cultural, political, or territorial boundary.[49] Through most of history they were joined together as part of the various Persian empires and, at other times, part of various Indian empires. When Pakistan separated from India and gained independence in 1947, Afghanistan was the only country to oppose it; India recognizes the Najibullah government in Afghanistan. Having been landlocked since the days of the British colonial advance toward Kabul, Afghanistan wished to get back the western half of Pakistan, which is inhabited by the Pashtun people who are the dominant nationality in northern Pakistan and in Afghanistan. On two occasions the neighboring states almost went to war because of Pashtun irredentism propagated by Kabul.[50]

Under the Shah the Pakistanis were able to station their air force in Iran and prevent its destruction during the 1970 war with India, just as the Iraqi aircraft took shelter in western Iran during the Gulf War. Since Pakistan never ceased to prepare for another go-around with India, incorporating Afghanistan, or at least parts of it, into Pakistan, could provide the "strategic depth" that had been lost in Iran.[51]

The country is eternally overshadowed by its huge and hostile neighbor, India. Thus, the fact that Pakistan has nearly as large a population (121 million) as all the Arab states combined gets overlooked. It has also a stronger scientific, industrial and military base than the combined Arab states. Pakistan is the only Islamic nation sure to possess nuclear weapons.[52] While other Islamic states do in fact rely heavily on Pakistan for scientific and technical expertise, her expertise is considered venal and, therefore, treated contemptuously.

From the viewpoint of the Pakistanis, their country ought to be considered more important. Lacking oil, they feel the snub of being regarded less important than neighboring Iran, their technical and demographic inferior. Their frustration finally gave birth to a particularly determined chauvinism, shared by the entire political spectrum, from Islamists like Nawaz Sharif to Islamic Social Democrats like Ms. Bhutto alike. All parties are equally resolved to employ any means in order to obtain their country's "rightful place in the sun." Absorbing Afghanistan is the critical first step.

EMULATING THE KHMER ROUGE: AN ELITE IS LIQUIDATED

A major difficulty is the new educated class of Afghanistan. Grown up in confrontation with Pakistan, Afghanistan's elite tended to look with alarm at Islamabad's ruling class. General Zia ul-Haq, for eleven years Pakistan's military dictator, was born into Britain's colonial army (his father was an army Mullah) and personified every inch the type of Punjabi mercenary loathed by the Afghans. Furthermore, these intellectuals, educated in Moscow or in Europe, found the traditional practices such as the veiling of women and selling children as brides unacceptable for a modern state.

The ISI harbored no illusions as to the possibility of winning over the fiercely independent Afghans by ordinary means. They knew that many of the promising guerrilla commanders were intractable nationalists. From early to mid–1980, many forces in the Afghan resistance were not Islamist at all. The National United Front of Afghanistan (NUFA) was a movement of the independent left that united many intellectuals seeking independence from both Moscow and the fundamentalists. Under the leadership of young professionals such as Majid Kalakani and Gol Mohammad Rahimi, it was formed to resist the Soviet-backed dictatorship of Hafizollah Amin in 1978. When the Islamists were about to be organized by several different foreign intelligence services (U.S., British, French, Iranian, Saudi), NUFA remained wholly indigenous.[53]

The ISI gave these foreign intelligence services freedom to organize resistance groups in Peshawar, the provincial capital of northwest Pakistan, while proceeding with its own plan of replacing the Afghan elite with one thoroughly indoctrinated by the Pakistani brand of Islamism and subservient to Pakistan.

Both the Soviets and the Pakistanis sought the elimination of Afghanistan's political and intellectual elite through "education" and individual murder.[54] The Soviets took 20,000 Afghan students to the Soviet Union with the aim of creating a reliable popular base for the regime installed in Kabul. Similarly, the fundamentalists established schools in the camps to indoctrinate their new elite in ways that most Afghans opposed.

In the course of the war years, hundreds of educated Afghans were murdered in Peshawar and in the interior of Pakistan; many others disappeared and have not been heard from.[55] As a result, few members of the Afghan elite stayed in Pakistan. More than 200 Afghan medical doctors found employment in Germany alone while virtually the same number of medical relief personnel were recruited in France to serve with the resistance in Afghanistan. Foreigners were permitted to enter and leave Pakistan and to pass over into rebel held territory inside Afghanistan; Afghan professionals risked their lives if they did not join Hekmatyar's "Islamic Party," (*hezb-i islami*), so many fled for the sake of their lives.

The killing and kidnapping was done almost exclusively by the *hezb-i islami*, a development many Alfghans and some specialists have been warning against since 1980.[56] But Washington and most European governments were slow in recognizing this. Afghans were often hesitant to uncover Islamabad's doings for fear of reprisals against relatives among the refugees. A true state of terror has been created.

The most prominent victim of this terror campaign was Professor 'Abd-ol-Qayyum Rahbar-Kalakani, the chairman of NUFA. On January 27s, 1990, he was on his way to Islamabad, where he was to board a plane for Frankfurt the following day as the invited guest of the German Social Democratic Party. He had not yet left the outskirts of Peshawar when four gunmen jumped out of a Toyota jeep and riddled the 48 year old politician with bullets from their Kalashnikovs, killing him instantly and wounding his driver.

Having spent many years in the political underground, the slain NUFA leader was extremely circumspect and moved with utmost caution. However, as an Afghan wishing to travel abroad from Pakistan he needed an exit visa—which is issued by the ISI. In other words, no one but the ISI knew about his exact travel plans. Ironically, only a few years earlier, the Afghan politician was assured by the then ISI chief of Peshawar, General Hayat, that nothing would happen to him. Hayat boasted that none of the many political assassinations—ostensibly committed by religious extremists—ever took place without the consent of the ISI. More often than not the assassins were actually commissioned by the ISI.[57]

A clear indication of the government's culpability was that Islamabad reacted as if nothing at all had happened after the professor's murder. Over the last decade, several governments on friendly terms with Pakistan repeatedly urged the authorities in Islamabad to grant protection to Afghan personalities known to figure on the hit lists of Islamist gunmen. For the embattled Prime Minister, Benazir Bhutto, the murder of the prominent resistance leader should have been a golden opportunity to assert herself against the headstrong officers of the military intelligence with their Islamist storm troopers among the Afghans.[58] However, there was never any word from Ms. Bhutto on the tragic murder, and no comment whatsoever from anyone in her government. Afghan policy remained a preserve of the military throughout, and the Bhutto interlude (she was ousted in August 1990) made no difference.

The assassination of the NUFA chairman at the eve of his departure for Europe was a message by the ISI to the governments of the European Community, warning them that Pakistan would neither allow those countries to have a say in Afghan affairs nor tolerate any mediation aiming at a solution of the conflict other than what is decided in Islamabad.

The SPD (Social Democratic Party) of Germany regarded the NUFA as a viable alternative to the extremists presently dominating the Afghan scene. A "hearing" at the party's political foundation (Friedrich-Ebert-Stiftung) in the summer of 1989 had convinced SPD parliamentarians and experts that among the non-Communist and non-Islamist forces in Afghanistan, 'Abd-ol-Qayyum was the ablest leader with the largest following as well as a serious and realistic reform program.[59] With veteran party leader Willi Brandt demanding renewed efforts at finding a solution to the conflict in Afghanistan, the Social Democrats chose NUFA as their Afghan counterpart. Professor 'Abd-ol-Qayyum had the additional qualification of speaking fluent German, having previously taught Arabic and Persian at the University of Kiel in Northern Germany.

Such a move on the part of an important political party in Western Europe (at that time it looked as if the Social Democrats were about to win the parliamentary elections) ran counter to the designs of the Islamist generals in Islamabad. The future government of Afghanistan was not to be one of Afghan nationalists but of Islamists loyal, above all, to Pakistan. Independent Nationalists such as 'Abd-ol-Qayyum and his NUFA following were not even allowed to open an office in Peshawar.

Pakistani intelligence officers would often pretend to be helpless in the face of what they termed "Afghan factionalism." They would shed crocodile tears over the "Lebanonization" of Pakistan that was, in reality, more their own doing than that of anybody else. The ulterior motive was to deprive Afghans of their elite; an elite that would have been neither subservient to a superpower such as the Soviet Union, nor to regional powers such as Iran and Pakistan. Professor 'Abd-ol-Qayyum has neither been the first nor, unfortunately, the last member of Afghanistan's elite to be murdered by Islamists.[60]

"ISLAMIC KILLING" OR "KILLING ISLAM"?

These facts are spelled out here in such detail because they have rarely been publicized, let alone analyzed. Pakistan does not rank among the states stigmatized as terrorist, and yet, more murder has been committed on Pakistani orders than on that of any other Middle Eastern state, with the possible exception of Iran.[61]

Pakistani terrorism goes by the name of Islam, but a closer look reveals that this is nationalism, or rather chauvinism, of a type not different from Iraqi or Iranian nationalism. In the Pakistani mode of thinking, whether consciously or unconsciously, Islam stands for self-interest, or what elsewhere would be called "national interest." The Pakistani military would like to see the creation of an Afghan Islamic Republic giving it "strategic depth" when the next war with India occurs. In the future there are bound to be political reorientations, but this generation of generals is still possessed by revenge. Above all, they are irredentist with regard to Kashmir. In a plebiscite, the overwhelming majority of Kashmiris would vote for Pakistan. Knowing that India would never cede Kashmir peacefully, Pakistan's generals prepare for war. The "strategic depth" required for such a war with India can only be obtained if Afghanistan is confederated with Pakistan.

While there are natural bonds of culture and religion between these countries, Islamism has not brought them any closer; rather it has estranged them from one another. Pakistan sponsored Islamist terrorism against Afghan nationalists and the elimination of Afghanistan's elite has caused havoc and turned two brother nations into bitter enemies.

Islamabad's attempt to gain control of Afghanistan by supporting extremists among the *mujahidin* eventuated in what the Afghan population has come to call "Islamic killing," viz. the liquidation of Afghanistan's nationalist and independent elite by terrorists under the banner of Islam, unleashed by Islamabad's military intelligence.

Judging by the present mood of things in the region, Western prejudices regarding Islam as a "religion of the sword" seem obliquely justified. The mood in Afghanistan is reminiscent of the anti-Catholicism among Republicans during the Spanish civil war. To look here for a confirmation of the view that terrorism is related to the Islamic religion would be not only superficial but also misleading. It certainly does not tell us much about the root causes of terrorism in the Middle East or why the volume of terrorist acts is at present comparatively high in that part of the world.

CONCLUSION

Terrorism is frequently associated with the Islamic faith, especially with Shi'ism. There is a long-standing tradition to explain this pseudo-religious connection. A closer look reveals this to be little more than the exploitation of religion for political ends with which we are familiar in Western and other cultures. In Lebanon, the particular terrorism that takes recourse to a religious legitimization has had difficulties in competing with such terrorism as is avowedly secular. The frequency of terrorist acts in the Middle East during the 1970s and 1980s was due in part to a race among competing ideologies and a state of latent civil war in artificially created nation states lacking identity, forged by colonial powers forcing artificial boundaries across different groups.

Looked at from within, Middle Eastern terrorism is the only resort of peoples still seething under the yoke of colonialism. This, at least, is the self-view of the Palestinians, and with them many Arabs and other Muslims, too. The Palestine issue is not the single most important stimulant of terrorism emanating from the Middle East, even though it appears as such to many westerners. Palestinian terrorism may be the most conspicuous, but in several countries power politics operate with terrorism more frequently than do the PLO and its numerous offshoots.

The lack of democracy and an extremely unequal distribution of wealth between individuals and between states ("Oil-Arabs" and the others) engender a host of protest movements that entail terrorism. Enormous disparities exist in population (rich but underpopulated Libya versus poor and overpopulated Egypt; industrialized and overpopulated Pakistan versus undeveloped and underpopulated Afghanistan), in size and resources (big Iraq, rich in agriculture and oil, next to small Jordan, arid and bereft of oil), as well as in education (educated Sudan contrasting with uneducated Yemen). All of these factors contribute to hegemonical aspirations of an intensity unknown to Latin America or East Asia, at least during the second half of the 20th century. These hegemonies and their ideologies (Arabism, Islamism, etc.) have produced more terrorism than the Palestinian struggle for self-determination. This is little noticed.

A major source of Middle Eastern terrorism is the expansionism of several states seeking to play a role out of proportion to their size and population. Iran's "Islamic Revolution" is an ideological legitimization for Persian designs on neighboring countries with Shi'ite minorities.

Pakistan exemplifies the opposite case. Its population and general potential are more than twice that of Egypt's; yet it has never been accorded even half the importance given to Egypt, be it in terms of political wooing, financial support, military aid, or simply media coverage.

In contrast, the religion of Islam, as enshrined in the revelation of Al-Qur'an, is unequivocal in its rejection of terrorism (and suicide). The pacifist strand in the Islamic tradition has rarely been recognized outside the realm of Islam, despite the fact that it has had an impressive record even in the 1980s. Daniel Pipes has aptly summarized that "IRA starvations reflected the politics of Ireland in 1981, not the nature of Celtic culture. Similarly, suicide bombings in the Middle East result from specific historical developments, not the permanent verities of Islam."[62]

NOTES

1. Although ETA, the IRA, and other terrorist organizations have accepted funding or training from rulers with grandiose ambitions, such as Libya's Qaddafi or Syria's Assad, these organizations were neither created by these governments nor do they follow their directives. The relations are much more symbiotic.

2. See Samir al-Khalil, *Republic of Fear: The Inside Story of Saddam's Iraq* (Berkeley: University of California Press, 1989) for a discussion of the roots of Ba'thism and the police apparat in Iraq in the totalitarian tradition in Europe.

3. See "How the Iraqis Tried to Kill a Dissident in the U.S.," *The Wall Street Journal*, 27 February 1991. The article reports on the activities of Abu Nidal's orga-

nization, the most radical of all Fatah splinter groups. However, detailed reports were published already back in 1987. See "Abou Nidal: affaires a l'Est," *L'Express*, 31 July 1987. Also Walter S. Mossberg and Gerald F. Seib: "Ominous Pattern—Before Its Invasion, Iraq Strengthened Ties To Terrorist Network," *The Wall Street Journal*, 20 August 1990.

4. See the small "classic" written by an Egyptian historian to refute this view of the world: Ahmad Amin, *Ash-Sharq wa l-Gharb* (*East and West*) (Cairo: Dar-al-ma'arif, 1955).

5. See Mahmoud Mohamed Taha, *The Second Message of Islam*, trans. by 'Abdullahi A. An-Na'im (Syracuse NY: Syracuse University Press, 1987).

6. Khalid Duran, "The Centrifugal Forces of Religion in Sudanese Politics," *Orient* 26, no.4 (December 1985).

7. William H. Overholt, "Burma: The Wrong Enemy," *Foreign Policy* 77 (Winter 1989–90):172–91.

8. See the portrait of Shaikh 'Umar 'Abd-ar-Rahman in Khalid Duran, *Islam und politischer Extremismus* (Hamburg: Deutsches Orient-Institut, 1986).

9. See *Al-Farida Al-Gha'iba*, translated by Johannes G. Jansen as *The Neglected Duty: The Creed of Sadat's Assassins and Islamic Resurgence in the Middle East* (New York: Macmillan, 1986). Professor David C. Rapoport does an excellent exegesis of this piece in his "Sacred Terror: A Contemporary Example from Islam" in *Origins of Terrorism: Psychologies, Ideologies, Theologies, States of Mind*, ed. Walter Reich (New York: Cambridge University Press, 1990), 103–30. His exposition agrees with my view by showing how this terrorist manual and movement disagrees with it.

10. At age thirteen I won an essay-writing contest in Sunday school for Muslim children. The title of the competition was *The Five Pillars of Islam*. The essay was subsequently translated and published in a Pakistani children's magazine. This would hardly have happened had there actually been *Six Pillars*, as insisted upon by the al-jihad movement.

11. See Americo Castro, *The Spaniards: An Introduction to Their History*, trans. by Williard F. King and Selma Margaretten (Berkeley: University of California Press, 1971).

12. *Jihad* was the title of the first book written, in 1927–30, by Abu l-A'la Maududi, then a budding Urdu journalist in Haidarabad, India. It did not declare jihad to be a "missing obligation" or a Sixth Pillar of Islam, but it presented a very militant interpretation and a rejection of the intellectual approach common among reformist thinkers such as Sayyid Ahmad Khan (d. 1887) in India and Muhammad 'Abduh (d. 1905) in Egypt.

13. Founded by Hasan al-Banna (1906–1949). See Richard P. Mitchell, *The Society of the Muslim Brothers* (London: Oxford University Press, 1969).

14. See Fathi Osman, *"Shura and Democracy,"* *Arabia* (London: May 1984) and by the same author, "Terrorism: A Search for Justice in the International Jungle," *Arabia* (London: August 1985). See also Muhammad Salahuddin, "Democracy in Egypt hinges on Islamists," and Fahmi Howaidi, Egypt's Democratic Experiment," *Arabia* (London: July 1984).

15. See Robert Bianchi, "Islam and Democracy in Egypt," *Current History* 88, no. 535 (February 1989).

16. See Caryle Murphy, "Bombs, Hostages: A Family Link," *The Washington Post*, 24 July 1990. See also Daniel Pipes, "Kuwait's Terrorism Policy Sets an Example," *The Wall Street Journal*, 18 November 1986.

17. I have dealt with these issues at some length in my book *Islam und politischer Extremismus* (Hamburg: Deutsches Orient-Institut, 1986).

18. Two prominent Israeli terrorist groups were *Irun Zva'l Leumi* (National Military Organization) and *Lohamei Herut Israel* (Fighters for Israel's Freedom), members of the former being credited with the bombing of the King David Hotel, the billet of British officers during the Mandate period. The parallel to the bombing of the Marine barracks in Beruit is disturbing and should be taken seriously.

19. The distinguished author Jochanan Bloch, whose book *Judentum in der Krise* and person I came to admire while a student in Berlin in 1967, sent shivers down my spine when he boasted of assassinations he had helped plan and carry out during the Israeli struggle for independence. Both Englishmen and Arabs were targeted.

20. See Ariel Merari, "The Readiness to Kill and Die: Suicidal Terrorism in the Middle East," in Reich, *Terrorism: Psychologies, Ideologies, States of Mind*, 192–207.

21. Daniel Pipes, "The Scourge of Suicide Terrorism," *The National Interest* 4 (Summer 1986): 99.

22.

The Syrian regime has best demonstrated its versatility. Of the 15 suicide attacks it sponsored against Israel in 1985, 6 belonged to the Ba'th Party, a secularist pan-Arab organization; 5 belonged to the Syrian Social Nationalist Party, espousing secularist pan-Syrianism; 2 belonged to Amal, the Shi'ite organization aligned with Syria; and one each belonged to the Communist Party and to an Egyptian opposition group. One of the suicides was a Druze, 4 were Shi'ite Muslims, and 10 Sunnis. (Pipes, "The Scourge of Suicide Terrorism," 100)

23. See Rene Backmann's interview with the former French intelligence chief Pierre Marion. "Ces Etats qui manipulent les terroristes." *Le Nouvel Observateur*, September 26–October 2, 1986.

24. The *Nizari* sect founded in 1094 by Hasan Bin Sabah waged guerrilla warfare from his mountain fortress in Persia, Alamut. The heirs of this sect became successful businessmen with well-organized welfare practices and peaceful ways. The sect is centered now in India. See Edward Mortimer, *Faith and Power: The Politics of Islam* (New York: Random, 1982), 48.

25. Published by Viking Penguin (London) in 1988. For a perceptive discussion of the case with all of its implications and ramifications see Daniel Pipes, *The Rushdie Affair: The Novel, the Ayatollah, and the West* (New York: Carol Publishing, 1990).

26. See his interview with *Der Spiegel*, 8 January 1989.

27. See Augustus Richard Norton, *Amal and the Shia: Struggle for the Soul of Lebanon* (Austin: University of Texas Press, 1987): 144–87 for a full discussion of the differences between these rival Shi'ite groups.

28. See Hussein Sirriyeh, "Lebanon: Dimensions of Conflict, *Adelphi Papers* 242 (London: International Institute of Strategic Studies, Autumn 1989): 17–20.

29. See Khalid Duran, "Afghanistan—Islamischer Widerstand gegen den Sozialimperialismus der russischen Kolonialmacht," in *Weltmacht Islam*, ed. Rudolf Hilf (Munich: Bayerische Landeszentrale fuer politische Bildungsarbeit, 1988). For the full background see Michael Pohly, "Der afghanische Widerstand (Afghan Resistance)" (Ph.D. diss., Institut fuer Iranistik der Freien Universitaet Berlin, 1991).

30. See Robin Wright, "Hezbollah Seen Setting Up Terror Network in Africa," *Los Angeles Times*, 27 February 1989.

31. I accompanied several delegations of Afghan resistance parties on lecture tours

of Latin America in 1985 and 1986. On each occasion we were invited to the Shi'i mosque in Buenos Aires. What impressed us most was the knowledge of the young functionaries sent there by Teheran as *politkommissars*.

32. Against the background of a "hearing" on the violations of human rights in Iran, sponsored by the Swiss League of Human Rights in Geneva in 1982, in which I participated, I dare say that all other reports on the theocratic regime's involvement with terrorism are, at best, piecemeal work. See Judith Miller, "World Terrorism: A Report to NATO Paints a Dark Portrait," *The New York Times*, 14 November 1986; George Lardner Jr., "Lawmakers Rebuke Iran For Policy of Terrorism," *The Washington Post*, 19 July 1990; and Robert Oakley, "International Terrorism, *Foreign Affairs* 65, no. 3 (1987): 611–29.

33. Shireen T. Hunter, "Post-Khomeini Iran," *Foreign Affairs* 68, no. 5 (Winter 1989/ 90): 133–49 gives a good review of this debate.

34. On November 25, 1989, Spanish authorities arrested ten hezbollah members for trying to smuggle eighteen pounds of plastic explosives into Spain in jars of jam for attacks on U.S. and other Western targets. Wright, "Terror Network."

35. The Islamic Revolutionary Guards Corps (*Pasdaran-e Ingilab-e Islami*) was formed in June 1979 as armed politico-ideological keepers of the faith who monitored left-wing organizations and guarded key personalities and facilities. They formed company- and larger-sized units that fought on the Iran–Iraq front and suppressed insurgencies like the *Waffen-SS*. See Edgar O'Ballance, *The Gulf War* (London: Brassey's, 1988), 21–22. Many of these "nurses" managed to hang on in Europe by dint of European passports and identity cards stolen by hezbollah.

36. See Laurent Greilsamer, "Anatomy of a Middle Eastern Terrorist Network," and "Fouad Saleh—The Militant Who Declared War on France," *Le Monde*, 30 January 1990. English reprint in *Guardian Weekly*, 11 February 1990.

37. See Todd Robberson, "The Unfinished Journey of Isa Abdullah Ali," *The Washington Post Magazine*, 16 December 1990.

38. See United States Department of State, *Patterns of Global Terrorism; 1989* (Washington DC: U.S. Government Printing Office, 1990).

39. One is led to speculate about the cause of the crash of the plane that carried Zia ul-Haq, his leading associates, and the U.S. ambassador to their deaths on August 17, 1988. After "a leading Shi'ite, Allama Arif Hussain al-Hussaini was assassinated in Peshwar...the Shias responded by crying 'Blood for Blood!' This led to suspicion of the possible role of Shia militants in Zia's death." Mahnaz Ispahani, *Pakistan: Dimensions of Insecurity, Adelphi Paper 246* (London: Brassey's for the International Institute for Strategic Studies, 1990): 20.

40. See Barnett R. Rubin, "The Fragmentation of Afghanistan," *Foreign Affairs* 68, no. 5l (Winter 1989/90), 150–68, for mention of this involvement in an account that raises more questions than it answers.

41. Ispahani, *Pakistan*: 45. "...by August 1988, 1,456 acts of sabotage in Pakistan's cities had resulted in 801 dead and 2,940 wounded."

42. Ispahani, *Pakistan*: 44. A refugee family must be registered to one of the parties recognized by the Pakistani government as "official" to receive any aid. This gives the parties control over the camps and the ISI control over the parties. Rubin, "Fragmentation," 162.

43. James Rupert, "Afghanistan's Slide Toward Civil War: U.S. Policy and the *Mujaheddin*," *World Policy Journal* 6, no. 4 (Fall 1989): 764.

44. Rubin, "The Fragmentation of Afghanistan," 154.

45. The seven Pakistan-based parties who were pressured into forming a *shura* (traditional council) to be called the Afghan Interim Government (AIG) were those groups deemed acceptable to the Pakistan military. Among the groups excluded were leftists or those with ties to Kabul, Shi'ite groups close to Iran, and those groups allied to the former king, Zaher Shah. The fact that these excluded groups represented sizable constituencies (and ethnic factions) in Afghanistan and carried out the bulk of the resistance made the AIG a farce. See Oliver Roy, *Islam and Resistance in Afghanistan* (Cambridge: Cambridge University Press, 1986) for a detailed account of these parties.

46. Rubin, "The Fragmentation," 154, and Rupert, "Afghanistan's Slide," 765.

47. This is from my personal notes. While teaching at the Sociology Department of Islamabad University, I also worked in the ghost writer team headed by Mr. Yusuf Buchh, then special advisor to Prime Minister Z. A. Bhutto. In any event, I was a little surprised to find this statement more or less reproduced in an official document. See Vaughn Forrest and Yossef Bodansky, "A Question of Trust" in *Task Force on Terrorism & Unconventional Warfare*, House Republican Research Committee (Washington, D.C.: U.S. House of Representatives, 1990).

48. Forrest and Bodansky, "Question of Trust," 48.

49. Ispahani, *Pakistan*, 43.

50. Over Baluchistan and over insurrection in the Sind, Ispahani, *Pakistan*.

51. Rubin, "Fragmentation of Afghanistan," 164.

52. Leonard Spector, *Nuclear Ambitions: The Spread of Nuclear Weapons 1989– 1990* (Boulder Co.: Westview Press 1990).

53. See Pohly, *Afghanische Widerstand*.

54. See Arnold Hottinger, "Mord als politisches Instrument in Afghanistan—Eli- minierung der politischen und intellektuellen Eliten," *Neue Zuercher Zeitung*, 4 Au- gust 1990. The fact of the factional killing is mentioned by Rubin, "Fragmentation of Afghanistan," 159, by Rupert, "Afghanistan's Slide," 764 *passim*, and Ispahani, *Pakistan*: 45.

55. An Asia Watch report "Human Rights Abuses by Elements of the Afghan Resis- tance," 3 November 1989 reports that thirty fighters of *jamiat-e-islami* (the Tajik party) were ambushed and killed by hezb-i-islami members on July 9. Rubin reports this incident, too, "Fragmentation," 159. Asia Watch suggests that many politically motivated threats, kidnapping, and killings of Afghan aid workers and intellectuals are attributable to Hekmatyar's group. These are the tip of the iceberg.

56. See the coverage of Afghanistan by Pierre Metge in the French daily *Liberation* in 1980–81.

57. See Michael Pohly and Khalid Duran, "Pakistan: Setback for Peace in Afghani- stan," *International Report* 8, no. 1 (February 1990).

58. In her autobiography, *Daughter of Destiny* (New York: Simon and Schuster, 1989), 332–3, 389, she worries about the danger the mujahidin pose to her own safety. Cited in Ispahani, *Pakistan* no. 24, p. 72.

59. See "Afghanistan—Testing Ground for Global and Regional Powers," *Inter- national Report* 7, no. 2 (July 1989).

60. I append here the briefest sketch of the fate of three colleagues and friends whose stories typify the intent of Islamabad toward an independent Afghan elite. In 1988 the distinguished sociologist Professor Baha'uddin Majruh was murdered

after releasing an opinion poll showing that fewer than 2 percent of the refugees were supportive of any union of Afghanistan and Pakistan. Richard M. Weintraub, "Exiles Killing jars Afghans in Pakistan," *The Washington Post*, 17 February 1988.

In 1989 Dr. Nasim Luddin, the only child specialist in Peshawar, established overnight nineteen emergency clinics to deal with the casualties from the botched assault on the Soviet-occupied city of Jalabad. The *mujahidin*, furious with the Islamist leadership, elevated this physician to the status of a hero. He was immediately assassinated.

Dr. A'zam Dadfar, a psychiatrist and NUFA leader, had to abandon the only psychiatric clinic in Peshwar and flee to Germany in 1990 to escape a death squad. His work was reported in Henry Kamm, "Afghan Doctor Tells of Nation's Mental Scars," *The New York Times*, 2 May 1988.

61. Forrest and Bodansky, "Question of Trust."

62. Daniel Pipes, "The Scourage of Suicidal Terrorism," *The National Interest 4* (Summer 1986), 95.

4

How Terrorists Think: What Psychology Can Contribute to Understanding Terrorism

Martha Crenshaw

Terrorism is a particular style of political violence, involving attacks on a small number of victims in order to influence a wider audience. This specific type of violence used to oppose governments is the subject of this chapter. No pejorative connotation is implied by this selective focus. The behavior of such groups often appears rational, in the sense of being a logical means to an end, but some of their actions are puzzling. If no rational explanation can be found, then we must look beyond what might be called a *strategic choice theory* to *psychological* factors. What important questions about oppositional terrorism can psychology help answer?

First, why do some radical opposition groups resort to terrorism when it appears to outside observers that other choices are available, especially when alternative methods of action are less costly? Certainly the resort to terrorism is a high-cost method of opposition. The personal risks are high. Furthermore, in many cases other methods of political action might be more effective. In his chapter, Brian Jenkins poses the question: how do the ends justify the means? A related question is: how do terrorists justify their actions? The choice of ends does not automatically imply the choice of means. Many people who share the same objectives disagree over appropriate ways of achieving them.

Thus terrorism is always a choice among alternatives. The decision to use terrorism is not determined by circumstances, and even the weakest group operating in the most oppressive society has other options. People with the same ideological convictions can either accept or reject terrorism as a method. Within opposition movements, both in democracies and in authoritarian regimes, there is typically an internal debate over the use of terrorism. It is an extreme method, recognized as such by the people who use it. Indeed, they would not use it if it were not extreme; outrageousness is precisely its attraction. Why is it, then, that within a single political movement some activists choose terrorism, while some prefer other methods?

A second related question to which a psychological answer may be appropriate is: Why do some radical opposition groups continue to use terrorism long after it ceases to be effective or necessitated by circumstances? Why use terrorism when it cannot be justified in terms of expediency or as a "last resort"? Consider, for example, the Basques in Spain. Basque terrorism against Franco was understandable as the only means of opposing a repressive regime that suppressed Basque culture as well as political expression. In 1975 Spain became a democracy with a freely elected socialist government. Despite the fact that the new socialist government made significant concessions to Basque autonomy, violence increased. In fact, terrorism escalated after the transition to democracy when the most compelling justification for it had disappeared. How do we explain this occurrence? Was it rational for Basque separatists to continue violence, or is a psychological explanation more plausible?

A third question concerns the diversity of terrorism, which despite the implied homogeneity of the phenomenon actually takes many different forms. These forms include both hostage seizures—a form of coercive bargaining—and simple assassinations and bombings. Why did hijackers demand ransoms for the release of hostages in the Middle East, but not in Latin America? Why did diplomatic and business kidnappings begin in Latin America? Why has the IRA rarely kidnapped people and never hijacked airliners? In sum, how do we explain the choice of a particular method? Most people who study terrorism explain the choice in terms of the technical possibilities and availability of resources and opportunities. But psychology may also contribute to explaining a particular method. Some methods of terrorism are psychologically easier or more attractive than others.

The last question to be addressed is, How should governments respond to terrorism? From a psychological point of view, the question should be rephrased: What can psychology tell us about how radical opposition movements respond to what governments do? What are the psychological effects of different government policies on underground conspiracies?

Now let me suggest some answers, starting with the first question. What is particularly satisfying about using terrorism? What are the psychological incentives for terrorism as opposed to other forms of resistance? This question has another dimension. What is it that enables people who presumably possess the same moral inhibitions as the rest of society to perform acts of violence that many of their peers regard as excessive? As I have noted, terrorism has strategic value to its users precisely because it violates moral, political, and legal rules. Terrorism is deliberately meant to demonstrate the illegitimacy of generally accepted standards. It would not be effective if it did not shock an audience. Undoubtedly, many people who use it are adept at psychological manipulation. But what enables such people to go beyond the bounds of what society regards as conventional and acceptable behavior? Part of what distinguishes terrorism from other forms of political violence is the willingness of its users to violate the expectations of the majority in society.

Turning to the issue of incentives, what drives or motivates people to perform actions such as the bombing of Pan Am 103 or the hijacking of the *Achille Lauro*? One of the strongest motivations behind terrorism is vengeance, particularly the desire to avenge not oneself but others. Vengeance can be specific or diffuse, but it is an obsessive drive that is a powerful motive for violence toward others, especially people thought to be responsible for injustices. But it also leads to aggression against victims most societies would consider innocent because such targets are readily accessible and because conceptions of responsibility are distorted.

Furthermore, the perpetrators of terrorism tend to be impatient. They are frustrated with talk, debate, and endless argument. Most are not intellectuals or philosophers, but people who seek action.[1] The advantage of terrorism to radical underground movements, particularly very small ones that are weak in resources, is that it can be quick and easy. Terrorism is economical since little is required in the way of manpower or weapons. Of course, many acts of terrorism involve extensive planning, and hence delayed gratification, but much terrorism is quickly implemented. It need not require mobilization of masses of people through slow, painstaking organizational work. It is also exciting to belong to a radical underground that uses violence. There is a certain grim satisfaction in living in the underground, knowing secrets that other people do not, and belonging to a closed conspiracy.

Terrorism can also be a way of building self-esteem and of exercising power over other people. Certain types of people enjoy stress. Being in danger and at the center of events is thrilling. Moreover, the publicity that terrorism generates is gratifying. Attention is a reward, especially for people who have felt ignored and neglected by society. The image constructed by the media builds an identity that is otherwise lacking. Even superficial or negative publicity is better than obscurity.

In addition many people who belong to these kinds of undergrounds feel a certain sense of superiority. They consider themselves members of an elite, an exclusive group composed of the only people who are willing not only to act for the masses of people but to break all the rules. Those who oppose terrorism are seen as cowardly or risk averse. Interestingly, terrorists regard themselves simultaneously as both heroes and victims. They often think of themselves as the victims of persecution and the representatives of the oppressed. In fact, an organization in Lebanon was named the "Group of the Oppressed on Earth." Nevertheless, many of the people who belong to radical undergrounds are not themselves the oppressed. They are more likely to be of middle-class background and often are university students. This paradox may create psychological discomfort that can only be relieved through dramatic action.

Such emotional contradictions can also be reconciled through the belief system that members of the group share. Justifying violence is important to those who use it, although the public tends to think of "terrorists" as callous people who are unconcerned with justification. In many cases they develop elaborate conceptions of causation. Brian Jenkins mentions how obscure and arcane the language of the terrorist is. Much of their ideological jargon is indeed confused, but it is also devoted to justification.[2]

The second part of the question of motivation concerns overcoming inhibitions. Belief systems are one way. For example, violence is interpreted not as a choice but as an obligation. Patterns of socialization must also be considered. In certain groups, particularly in Palestine, Northern Ireland, or in some areas of Latin America, individuals are socialized into violence from early childhood. Generally people who have experienced violence are more likely to use it. At the same time the members of groups in other situations, such as Germany or Italy, have not been socialized into violence. Perhaps to compensate for this deficit in the upbringing of their recruits, some groups devote extensive effort to indoctrinating their members. Once recruits enter such groups, leaders try to teach them a certain set of values and to develop organizational routines that make violence easier to perform. Once someone enters a group, the first thing he or she is asked to do is to break the law and, second, to commit an act of violence. This initiation prevents them from returning to normality and rejoining society. Individuals become accustomed to performing acts of violence and yet, paradoxically, may also develop feelings of guilt. One way to overcome guilt and avoid remorse is to continue violence, in order to prove that the decision was right in the first place. The more someone performs acts of violence, the easier it becomes. The performance of acts of violence is context-dependent. Conditioning through repetition and belonging to a group that sanctions violence enable people to do things that they would not ordinarily do.

In underground groups one also finds a tendency to dehumanize the enemy.[3] This labeling is of course not exceptional in conflict situations. It is easier to perform acts of violence against an enemy who is not considered a person but the system or the "establishment." In Italy the enemy was the "multinational imperialist state," an abstraction rather than real people who might suffer. In the literature of these groups most references are to the enemy and to themselves. They say little about the people who are the actual victims. If they do, they argue that they are all members of a general enemy category, which is imperialism, capitalism, or an equally vague and diffuse concept. By focusing on the evilness of the enemy, they may avoid thinking about the people they are killing.

Members of such groups may also experience survivor guilt. Joining a radical underground group that has turned to violence, particularly to terrorism, means that one will face a high rate of attrition in the organization. Many comrades will be killed. The survivors would be letting them down if they did not continue the struggle, however self-defeating that struggle might be. All of the individual's values are bound up in comrades who are now being killed or, even more important, imprisoned by a government that all regard as evil and cruel. This creates a feeling of desperation among the survivors and may account for many attempts to secure the release of prisoners.

Personality clearly matters in certain instances, such as that of Abu Nidal, the leader of the Fatah Revolutionary Council, but in general it is not the individual who matters but the group. One of the strongest factors that permits people to overcome moral inhibitions is group or peer pressure. The individual does not want to let the group down or incur its disapproval. The need to fulfill the group's expectations creates an enormous pressure to do whatever the group wants. Group pressure is almost irresistibly strong in a very small group that lives in concealment, pursued by the government, and isolated from society. Members associate only with other members of the group. Their sources of information are restricted. They are forbidden even to maintain friendships with outsiders.

This discussion leads to the second question: Why would groups continue using terrorism when it has become counterproductive? Why does terrorism persist when it does not accomplish the goals originally claimed for it, such as overthrowing the state or changing a particular government policy? Similarly, as in the case of the Basques, why does terrorism continue when the group appears to have attained significant concessions? The answer may lie in the fact that terrorism serves the important social psychological function of *maintaining the group*. The members of the group have lost their individual identities (or may not have had a stable sense of identity) and assumed the collective identity of the group. These are usually small groups, in many cases face-to-face or primary groups, composed of people who make decisions through personal discussions. To let the group down or challenge a collective decision is very risky in psychological terms. If all the individual has to rely on in the realm of personal relationships is the group, he or she is unlikely to dissent or exit from the group. Cohesiveness and solidarity are strengthened by the danger that all mutually confront. Simply keeping the group together may be the reason for continuing. It may not even be desirable for some groups to get what they say they want. If collective purposes were achieved, the group would no longer have a reason for being. There would be no cause for action.

For example, consider the Palestinian question, particularly the role of extremist factions such as the Abu Nidal group. This faction opposes the mainstream PLO. If some form of Palestinian self-government were established, Abu Nidal would be unlikely to have any role in it. Why should he support a resolution to the conflict? Occasionally the leaders of such groups become respected political leaders, but such outcomes are rare.

Thus what keeps the group going may be terrorism itself, more than the promise of a homeland or of revolution. The opportunity for action motivates participation. If the group becomes inactive, frustration will build among the militants for whom the attraction was the opportunity for action. Leaders must keep the action going or lose control of their followers. All are bound up together, so all must continue until militants become so weary or so disillusioned that they abandon the struggle. This suggests another important question for psychology: When do people take the risk of being rejected by the group and challenge what the group says? How do groups disintegrate? Why do members "exit" from the group? These questions may be even more pertinent, especially to governments, than those related to causation.

Discussions of the importance of group solidarity to terrorism often stress the similarities between terrorists and soldiers under combat conditions. The military also indoctrinates, demands obedience, enforces discipline, and relies on peer pressure. Many of the theories used to explain terrorist behavior are borrowed from studies of military personnel. Terrorist groups style themselves as the Red Brigades or the Japanese Red Army. They frequently compare themselves to soldiers and use military titles. Yet several differences should also be noted. One involves levels of social support. Within the world of terrorism, large diversified organizations that either represent or claim to represent specific ethnic, religious, or racial constituencies usually enjoy more social support than small, isolated undergrounds. Yet the armed forces of nation-states enjoy much more secure support, in both domestic and international spheres. Furthermore, the organization of a national military is much more bureaucratized and complex. And in democracies the military establishment is ultimately accountable to civilian leaders who possess political legitimacy. This is not to say that the armed forces of nations may never engage in terrorism, but that the psychological dynamics of participation in violence are not the same.

The third question concerns why terrorism takes specific forms. Terrorism varies widely in terms of degree of discrimination, ranging from the single assassination to the destruction of an entire airliner, killing hundreds of people. At the same time terrorism also differs in terms of whether or not it is used as a bargaining tool. One of the most significant innovations in terrorism in the twentieth century has been the use of terrorist tactics in order to bargain with governments. Until the late 1960s terrorism was not usually employed in order to make specific demands on governments. Instead it was a one-shot deal—a simple and direct form of political communication. A political statement was made with the bombing or the assassination. A few kidnappings occurred, but they were rarely linked to explicit political demands. Hijackings, kidnappings, and other hostage seizures are modern attempts to put pressure on governments to get them to yield in specific circumstances.

Within this range there are a variety of methods of violence. Terrorism can involve mass casualty bombings, in most cases time bombs, an impersonal form of violence. Terrorism also involves armed assaults, for example at airport ticket counters. A rash of shootings occurred at synagogues in Western Europe and in Turkey in the mid 1980s. These attacks involved face-to-face personal violence of an extremely indiscriminate nature. Furthermore, hostage takings include kidnappings as well as barricade incidents—taking over a building and holding a large group of hostages in a "fishbowl" situation. Neither the hostages nor the hostage-takers can escape, as opposed to a kidnapping where the hostage-taker is usually free to let the victim go and vanish into obscurity. As a consequence, the personal risk is less.

Considering all these varieties of terrorism, what psychological considerations are involved in choosing a method? It is harder for most people to kill someone face-to-face than at a distance. It is probably not surprising that most terrorist acts are bombings. Not only is a bombing often easier in a technological sense, but it is easier psychologically to place a bomb that will explode later. Not only is the individual risk reduced, but also the bomber can avoid a personal encounter with victims.[4]

On the other hand, some terrorists may enjoy such contact with their victims, which confers a sense of power and control. Furthermore, a psychological advantage to hostage-taking is that terrorists can blame the outcome on the government. Their argument is: "We have no intention of killing anyone and we are convinced that the government will give in to our demands." When the government refuses to concede, hostage-takers consider themselves forced by the government to kill. Consequently they are able to evade personal responsibility for their actions.

Other psychological considerations may also be significant. The person who actually takes hostages may not be the real decision-maker, who gives orders from behind the scenes. Role differentiation and specialization exist within such groups. The agents who are actually on the ship or the airliner are usually taking orders from above. They can act as the impersonal agents of higher authority. They are also subject to peer pressure. Consider the alternatives confronting terrorists who have seized an airliner. If they refuse to carry out the group's orders, what will happen to them? They might be captured by the government, which is not an attractive prospect. At the same time, if they manage to get themselves out of the dilemma without being captured, they must return to the group and admit failure. The admission of failure would be extremely painful, in many ways, but if they do not return to the group, they must stay on the run indefinitely.

Discussions of hostage taking often refer to the "Stockholm syndrome," a belief held by policy-makers that hostage-takers will develop friendly relationships with hostages that will prevent or at least impede violence against the hostages if the government mounts a rescue attempt. Presumably assault forces coming in to rescue passengers on an airliner or cruise ship or diplomats held in an embassy will have a brief moment before the hostage-takers bring themselves to start shooting. Actually, such emotional bonding is unlikely. It is more likely that the hostage-takers will panic, especially if the situation involves acute time-pressure and constraints on alternatives.

Note the incident in Karachi, when a Palestinian group, probably the Abu Nidal faction, seized a Pan Am airliner en route from India. The electricity went out on the airliner, probably a result of mismanagement on the part of the Pakistani troops who were surrounding the plane. They had no immediate plan to intervene. The hijackers, who had been extremely nervous throughout the hijacking, immediately panicked and began firing indiscriminately on the passengers and crew.

Proceeding to the fourth question, what advice can be offered to policy-makers other than "Don't trust in the Stockholm syndrome"? One of the issues Brian Jenkins raises in his chapter concerns the use of force against terrorists. The use of force includes police or military actions at home as well as military operations abroad. In foreign policy the use of force is complex. It includes hostage rescue attempts, which constitute a limited and precise resort to force; the apprehension of terrorist suspects, such as the interception of the Egyptian airliner carrying the hijackers of the *Achille Lauro*; and military retaliation against terrorist groups or against states suspected of sponsoring, aiding, or assisting nonstate terrorist groups. The raid on Libya is an excellent example of the last option.

Interestingly enough, only three states have pursued a policy of military retaliation: South Africa, Israel, and the United States. There is no evidence that such a policy works to deter or prevent terrorism. Judging success is, of course, difficult, but using force against small groups for whom terrorism is a primary if not exclusive method may not only reinforce their self-image of themselves as persecuted victims but also confirm their image of the government as a hostile and unrelenting adversary. Terrorists need to think of the government as implacably hostile. It is necessary for them to believe that the world is sharply divided between good and evil, with themselves on the good side. Military retaliation, especially if ineffective, can thus strengthen their self-esteem and uphold their world view.

In addition, retaliation may provide extremists with the publicity they seek. Many radical groups are inconsequential on the world scene except for their ability to use terrorism. Many have no popular following and are often manipulated by governments for their own purposes. But these small factions want to be recognized. They want attention. If the American Navy and Air Force can be provoked into bombing them, then they have become somebody.

Thus large scale and indiscriminate military retaliation may be counter-productive with certain groups. But what about covert methods of dealing with terrorism? Israeli intelligence led a clandestine campaign against the former members of Black September in Europe in the 1970s. The American government recently debated the issue of whether or not to remove restraints on the assassination of leaders of terrorist groups. The psychological effect of the removal of a key leader might be extremely detrimental to group morale, but the risk of making a mistake is high. If the group were dependent on a charismatic and dominant leader, a government might provoke the disintegration of the group, but it is unlikely that governments will be sufficiently precise and well-informed. The Israeli Mossad is considered one of the best intelligence agencies in the world, but in tracking down Black September operatives they mistakenly assassinated a Moroccan waiter in Norway.

If the use of force can backfire, what are the psychological problems associated with negotiating with terrorists? Do negotiations only reward bad behavior? Psychological factors are probably most important in negotiations in barricade situations, which involve direct and sustained contact between government representatives and hostage-takers, but they are also significant in kidnappings. In barricade situations, both sides rely on an implicit threat of the use of force if negotiations do not succeed, while in kidnappings the kidnappers possess the advantage if their location is concealed from the government. Governments recognize the psychological basis of negotiations and frequently rely on trained hostage negotiators and behavioral scientists. In general, negotiations seem to be struggles for psychological control and dominance. At the same time, they involve establishing relationships of mutual trust despite the existence of animosity and threat. It is extremely important to terrorists that they be recognized as valid negotiating partners because they regard recognition as a step toward political legitimacy. Governments tend to resist recognition for the same reason, but without it negotiations cannot succeed. It is also helpful to introduce elements of predictability and routine into negotiating relationships, to reduce the level of emotionalism and prevent panic. Consistency and reliability on the part of the government are critical.

Clearly, any policy toward terrorism, whether coercive or conciliatory, must be context-oriented and thus be developed on a case-by-case basis. Policymakers must have detailed knowledge of the group in question, including the type of psychological interactions within the group, relationships between leaders and followers, beliefs prevalent in the group, degree of commitment of militants, and psychological incentives for remaining in the group. It is important to know who occupies positions of authority and what the sources of their authority are. There are no general prescriptions.

For example, the Italian government supposedly ended terrorism with the so-called repentance laws, which offered rewards for cooperation rather than punishment for resistance. The government rewarded activists for abandoning terrorism and aiding the authorities. Yet it is important to remember that in Italy the terrorist underground had already fallen on hard times. The Red Brigades began to break up after the abduction and murder of Aldo Moro in 1978. The efficiency of the Italian security forces had increased dramatically while public support for extremism had declined. Another catalyst for internal dissent and subsequent defection was the murder of the brother of one of the first *pentiti*, who had gone over to the government and turned state's evidence.[5] However, group disintegration does not always lead to a decline in terrorism. Sometimes factions start fighting both each other and the government. Perhaps the psychological discomfort that members experience because they are losing their collective identity goads them to lash out indiscriminately. The remaining members of a disintegrating organization become desperate and frustrated. They may resort to violence in order to restore group solidarity and prevent further "exit." Extremists may attack moderates within the movement.

In sum, we cannot understand terrorism without the contributions of psychology, although this knowledge does not provide a magic answer to dealing with terrorism. Three points should be remembered. One is that the group performing the act of terrorism is more significant than the individual. Although Marxists condemned terrorism as "individual" and not mass action, it is actually small group behavior. Second, it is important to the people who use terrorism to be able to justify what they do. Perhaps terrorism declines when its practitioners can no longer justify it to themselves. The last point is that the stated goal of terrorism may not be what the perpetrators really want. We should reject the easy inference that the outcome of an act of terrorism reveals the purpose behind it. We cannot assume that there is always a rational calculated strategy, which if traced back far enough would reveal a master plan. In many cases there is no master plan but only small plans. Terrorism may be more petty, more incremental, and more erratic than we think. Understanding the psychology of terrorism, which is not unlike the psychology of other forms of violence or extreme behavior, demystifies the phenomenon.

NOTES

1. See Walter Laquer, *The Age of Terrorism.* (Boston: Little Brown, 1987) and the review of Jerrold M. Post, "Terrorist Psychologic," in *Origins of Terrorism; Psychologies, Ideologies, Theologies, States of Mind* ed. Walter Reich (New York: Cambridge Univesity Press, 1990).

2. See Bonnie Cordes, "When Terrorists Do the Talking: Reflections on Terrorist Literature," *Journal of Strategic Studies* 10, no. 4 (December 1987): 150–71.

3. Sam Keen's powerful *Faces of the Enemy: Reflections of the Hostile Imagination* (San Francisco: Harper and Row, 1986) details this process with illustrations from war propaganda of many nations.

4. "Stanley Milgram Explores Closeness to the Victim as a Variable Mediating the Amount of Electric Shock People Are Willing to Administer to Another Person," in *Obedience to Authority* (New York: Harper & Row, 1974).

5. Alison Jamieson, "Entry, Discipline and Exit in the Italian Red Brigades," *Terrorism and Political Violence* 2, no. 1 (Spring 1990): 16.

5

Becoming a Terrorist: Social and Individual Antecedents

Nehemia Friedland

The use of political violence for political ends is obviously not new, and there exists a historical continuity between present and past forms of terrorism. However, the incidences of politically motivated terrorist acts and their impact on public awareness have reached unprecedented dimensions in the last two decades. This change in trend has created a need for a thorough understanding of the causes and antecedents of political terrorism.

The study of political terrorism is beset by a number of difficulties. A most obvious one is the difficulty of defining the phenomenon. The worn-out aphorism "one's terrorist is another person's freedom fighter" points to the very core of the problem: Political leanings and value judgments bias attempts to demarcate the phenomenon, and criteria used to distinguish between terrorism and other forms of politically motivated violence are often ambiguous.

Additional difficulty results from the uncertain quality of data that are available to the student of terrorism for analysis and from its scarcity. Much of the intelligence gathered by branches of government is classified. Opportunities to conduct direct interviews with members of terrorist groups are limited. And even data that are more readily available, such as counts of terrorist incidents and of the number of casualties, have to be treated with caution.[1] Wide discrepancies between estimates may be expected, due in large measure to the definitional ambiguity alluded to above. For example, the RAND corporation estimated that 1022 international terrorist incidents occurred in the ten-year period, 1968–1977.[2] The Central Intelligence Agency's estimate, concerning the same period, was 2690.[3]

The difficulty is compounded by the heterogeneity of the phenomenon. Terrorist groups show large variability in size, in national and religious composition, and in stated motivation. Ideological credos range from the extreme right to the extreme left. Many groups adhere to a composite social-political ideology, and some are known to have replaced an ideology held initially with a radically different one.

Ambiguity and diversity notwithstanding, a convenient framework for the analysis of the antecedents of political terrorism can be designed on the basis of three generalizations. First, terrorism is a group phenomenon. Although individuals may employ terror in the pursuit of criminal or personal ends, political terrorism is usually perpetrated by organized groups whose members have a clear group identity—national, religious or ideological. Furthermore, group processes are evident in terrorists' selection of targets. Those attacked are usually singled out according to group or class characteristics rather than on the basis of individual attributes. Second, political terrorism has its roots in intergroup conflict. Third, "insurgent terrorism," unlike "state terrorism," which will not be discussed in the present chapter, is a "strategy of the weak." It is employed, characteristically, by groups with little numerical, physical or direct political power in order to effect political or social change.

The second generalization verges on the tautological, and it is presented only as an antithesis to the view that terrorist behavior is driven by personality disorders or psychopathologies.

A brief digression is needed in order to comment on explanations of terrorist behavior that draw from models of individual psychology. Such explanations hold, for example, that the turning to terrorism may be attributed to abusive child-rearing.[4] Gustav Morf, on the other hand, maintained that the rejection of the father and his values plays a dominant role in the making of terrorists.[5] David Hubbard found a clue in terrorists' faulty vestibular functioning of the middle ear and in its attendant effects: an arrested process of learning to walk, dizzy spells, visual problems, and general clumsiness.[6] Robert Frank noted that terrorism is prevalent in societies where fantasies of cleanliness are prevalent.[7] Peter Berger attributed terrorist behavior to the sense of fulfillment and power that individuals presumably derive from absolute dedication, commitment and self-sacrifice, and from the infliction of pain and death.[8]

These theories promote the notion that political terrorists are psychologically deviant or abnormal. By implication, important insights on the nature of terrorism and its antecedents are to be found in the fields of psychopathology and psychiatry.

The validity of such theories may be questioned on both a-priori and empirical grounds. Some of the theories, for example Berger's, are logically circular. In addition, most of them are predicated on a single, core proposition and their predictive power is thereby curtailed. For instance, many reject their fathers' values at a certain age, yet only a negligible few turn to terrorism. As for empirical support, to date there is no compelling evidence that terrorists are abnormal, insane, or match a unique personality type. In fact, there are some indications to the contrary.[9]

The critique of the attribution of terrorist behavior to individual idiosyncrasy or pathology is not meant to imply that individual predispositions play no role whatsoever in the emergence of terrorist groups and in eruptions of terrorist action. However, as will be argued later, the influence of individuals has to be examined as an element of group and intergroup processes.

By setting political terrorism in the context of intergroup conflict, as a strategy employed by relatively weak groups to bring about social or political change, the generalizations presented above raise three questions that must be answered in order to gain insight into the causes of terrorism.

1. What are the conditions that produce a movement toward social and political change?
2. What are the dynamics that turn such a movement to violence?
3. Why has terrorism acquired unprecedented dimensions in the last two decades?

THE MOVEMENT TOWARD SOCIAL AND POLITICAL CHANGE

Recent work on intergroup conflict and, particularly, on the social psychology of minority groups yields important insights on the instigation of movement toward social and political change.[10] Most revealing is the proposition that underprivileged groups are likely to reject their disadvantaged status, and will move to improve their lot when (a) the social system is viewed as unstable and (b) inequitable distributions of power, rights, and resources are deemed illegitimate.

This proposition appears to be entirely consistent with the recent, accelerated emergence of movement toward worldwide social and political change. The evolution and growing acceptance of democratic philosophies has fostered the view that discriminatory social structures and political systems are neither immutable nor legitimate. The view of authority as a prescribed right is no longer accepted. It was replaced with the attitude that authority has to be earned, constantly justified and, by the same token, challenged. Moreover, mass communication has helped disseminate the belief that social change is possible, by turning the success of some social change movements into models that other groups can hope to emulate. Thus, if terrorism is viewed as a strategy of social and political change, its heightened incidence may be explained in the context of disadvantaged groups' growing drive to reassert their rights.

The preceding speculation is quite compelling, and it appears to offer an adequate explanation of why some groups turn to terrorism. For example, Palestinian terrorism and the growing international acceptance of the PLO as the legitimate representative of the Palestinian people is consistent with this speculation. However, as a general explanation of political terrorism it cannot be accepted without some qualifications. The recent history of political terrorism suggests, for one, that all else being equal, groups' adoption of the terrorist solution is more probable under the least oppressive regimes than under the most oppressive ones. In the Basque provinces of Spain, for example, terrorism did not abate, and even intensified, after much of the autonomy demanded by the Basques was granted. In addition, data yielded by terrorist biographies are often incongruent with the attribution of terrorism to the growing assertiveness of minority groups. For example, a profile compiled from the biographies of about 350 members of terrorist groups indicated that the great majority consisted of males between ages twenty-two and twenty-four. Most came from affluent, urban, middle- or upper-class families and had some university education or a college degree. Among the older members, many were professionals and may have practiced their professions prior to joining the terrorist groups.[11]

This profile is common among members of ideologically motivated groups that emerged in countries such as France, West Germany, Italy or Japan, exposing their own countries to what became known as "domestic terrorism." In other words, members of such groups do not typically belong to an identifiable disadvantaged minority but rather to the privileged majority, and they cannot convincingly justify their attacks as a response to wrongs committed against them. In fact, most of them do not even pretend to be victims of injustice or discrimination. Instead, it is their identification with suffering others that is quite often presented as the cause of their turning to terrorism. For example, Baumann, a member of the "June 2nd Movement" in Germany, attributed his embrace of terrorism to the killing of a student demonstrator on June 2, 1967, by a policeman, during a visit of the Shah of Iran to Berlin and to the fact that the policeman was not punished.[12] Renato Curcio, founder of the Italian Red Brigades, was presumably turned to violence by the police killing of two demonstrating farmers in Aola on December 2, 1968.[13] Horst Mahler, co-founder of the German Red Army Faction, noted that the massacres in Vietnam and the indifference of the German government drove him and his colleagues, Ulrike Meinhof and Gudrun Ensslin, to terrorism.[14]

The difficulty of applying social psychological or sociological explanations to the emergence of groups such as the Baader-Meinhof or the Italian Red Brigades has led some students of terrorism to the conclusion that the attribution of terrorism to social conflict should be rejected altogether.[15] Franco Ferracuti suggested that "available facts, at least in Europe, contradict [explanations based on adverse social conditions], unless they are seen as internal obstacles, not related to social realities. . . . Terrorism . . . is fantasy war, real only in the mind of the terrorist."[16]

The rejection of the social antecedents of some terrorist movements stems from an excessively narrow conception of the nature of social conflict. This conception ascribes "reality" to conflicts of interest, concerning tangible resources, power, or rights only. On the other hand, ideological conflicts, or disputes over values, are deemed "unreal," a mere figment of imbalanced or irrational individuals' imaginations.

Psychologically, the distinction between "real" conflicts and "imaginary" ones is indefensible. For members of the German Red Army Faction or the Italian Red Brigades, their ideological conflict with the majority or the establishment is as real as any conflict of interest. Logically, the distinction is untenable as it derives from a classification of conflicts into those that have a "sufficiently good cause" and those that do not, which is totally arbitrary and subjective. It appears that an expansion of conflict theories, to include cases of *intra*group conflict whose core is ideological, is needed sorely. A widened perspective will make the theory more useful for understanding radical movements of social change.

THE TURN TO VIOLENCE

The turn to violence is not a necessary consequence of the drive to effect social or political change. Violence does not assure the successful realization of such change, and, conversely, history contains striking examples of dramatic changes that were brought about peacefully. Therefore, the understanding of the emergence of political terrorism requires that the analysis of social change movements be supplemented with an analysis of group violence.

Social psychological and sociological explanations of group violence, civil strife, and rioting, as well as explanations advanced by political scientists, draw heavily on the frustration–aggression (FA) hypothesis.[17] The hypothesis is essentially a proposition about the cause of individual violence. Nevertheless, the adaptation of the hypothesis to the explanation of group violence was done by various authors with little apparent regard for modifications that the transition from the individual to the group context might necessitate. For example, Dollard and his associates linked the rise of German anti-Semitism to the humiliation suffered by the German people in the wake of the treaty of Versailles and to subsequent economic hardship. Leonard Berkowitz relied on the hypothesis quite heavily in attempting to account for black rioting that occurred in the United States in the 1960s.[18]

Sociologists and political scientists substituted the FA formulation with the conceptually close notion of "relative deprivation" (RD).[19] Ted Gurr's proposition has been the most influential or, at least, the most widely quoted:

"Relative deprivations" (RD) is the term used . . . to denote the tension that develops from the discrepancy between the "ought" and the "is" of collective value satisfaction, that disposes men to violence. . . . The frustration–aggression relationship provides the psychological dynamic for the proposed relationship between intensity of deprivation and the potential for collective violence.[20]

The straightforward adaptation of the FA hypothesis, from the individual to the group level, was criticized by a number of authors. Joseph Van der Dennen criticized those who applied the hypothesis to the explanation of group processes for being oblivious or indifferent to the fact that the validity of the hypothesis is questionable, even for the explanation of individual behavior.[21] He proposed that the simplicity of the hypothesis, more than its validity, explains its popularity among social scientists. Michael Billig considered explanations of group violence that derive from the FA hypothesis "altogether too neat."[22] He was particularly disturbed by the fact that theories of individual aggression cannot explain the uniformity of group and mass behavior. The possibility that pent-up emotions in a group of individuals erupt simultaneously implies an inconceivable coincidence or a degree of coordination that the FA hypothesis does not and cannot explain.

This criticism does not necessitate, however, the complete rejection of the FA hypothesis as an explanation of group violence, but rather a more comprehensive perspective that bridges the gap between the individual and group contexts. First, the group must articulate its discontent and develop a unifying ideology that gives meaning to its grievances. In the absence of a clearly articulated core ideology, individual frustrations will result in disorganized individual action. Leadership, of course, plays a critical role in the crystallization and channelling of group discontent. Second, violent group action must be seen as an intergroup process. Any attempt by one group to alter a political or social status quo necessarily elicits an attempt by another group to preserve it. It might not always be clear which group instigated the violence, but, doubtlessly, it is perpetuated by a cycle of violent action and counteraction. Moreover, the ever-present threatening outgroup enhances the unity and uniformity of each group's action that, as already maintained, the FA hypothesis cannot explain.

Certain cases of intense terrorist action can be linked to frustrations and grievances suffered by their perpetrators. Such is clearly the case in Ulster or in the Middle East. However, an explanation of terrorist violence that draws from the assumed FA link is considerably less convincing when applied, for example, to the emergence of terrorist groups in Western Europe. As already suggested, it is difficult to identify the frustrations and deprivations that caused the members of these groups to turn to terrorism. But even if frustrating, adverse social conditions were identified, it would still be necessary to reconcile theoretical predictions, stemming from the FA and RD notions, with actual data: Adverse social conditions normally affect large groups. Yet, to date, ideologically motivated groups, acting within their own democratic societies, attracted a very limited membership. For example, the French Action Directe had a hard core of about twenty members. In Belgium, the Combatant Communist Cells numbered less than twenty active members. The German Red Army Faction commands a group of about two hundred "part-time" activists, but its core consists only of a score of members. The active cells, or "columns," of the Italian Red Brigades contained a membership of about fifty. The Japanese Red Army is known to have about forty-five members.[23] Thus, two queries have to be answered convincingly if the FA or RD hypothesis is to be retained as an element in a general explanation of political terrorism: What are the characteristics of the modern democratic state that frustrate privileged members of society? Why is it that so very few undertake terrorism?

A tentative answer to the first query is offered by the sociology literature. Hannah Arendt attributed violent political action to the anonymity of the modern bureaucratic state and the resultant sense of political helplessness and frustration.[24]

The sense of political helplessness, along with the notion of "blocked societies," figures prominently in the writings of Italian sociologists. Ferracuti maintained that

Terrorism is a response to the lack of political education in Italy. It is a tragic response to an overabundance of political stability.... The country is a democracy, but its institutions are not run according to democratic criteria. Youth and the new urban classes are cut off from power. Political parties and trade unions carry a heavy responsibility for the birth and outgrowth of terrorism since they have neglected the energy and demands of the young ones.[25]

Luigi Bonanate held that "A society that knows terrorism is a *blocked society*, incapable of answering the citizens' requests for change, but nevertheless capable of preserving and reproducing itself.... A situation seems blocked when there seems no innovation capable of bringing about a new situation."[26]

The concept of "blocked societies" is similar to the "lack of alternatives" justification that terrorists use and that is found also in the writings of some students of terrorism:

I can find no single case in which recourse to terrorism was not forced on the organization in question by denial of all other means of fighting against social injustice. Whenever I have seemed to come upon such a case, it has turned out that although other means existed in theory, they have been found useless in practice.[27]

In different terms, frustration, that might turn individuals and groups to violent action, is assumed to result from a discrepancy between a desire to stand out and to leave a mark on the course of political events and the actual ability to do so.

This proposition has two corollaries: One, the more stable the political system, the wider the aforementioned frustrating discrepancy. Echoes of this corollary can be heard in justifications of violence that ideological radicals present often: Violence is justified insofar as it shakes a complacent society out of its apathy and lethargy. Second, the more individuals believe that they deserve or have the right to influence, the wider the discrepancy and the stronger the frustration brought about by failure to do so.[28] This corollary might explain the relatively high incidence of terrorism in democracies as well as the involvement of affluent, well-educated, middle- or upper-class individuals.

Having identified frustrating conditions that might drive well-to-do citizens of democratic states to terrorism, we are still faced with the need to account for the inability of terrorist groups to attract a large membership and constituency. As already argued, social immobility and blockades affect many, but only a negligible few become terrorists.

The resolution of this apparent inconsistency requires the consideration of individual predispositions. Failure or perceived inability to bring about social change affect different individuals in different ways. Some might simply give up in disillusionment. Others might persist in their attempts to elicit change through nonviolent, legitimate and legal means. Only those that are predisposed to violence will embrace the terrorist solution.

Analyses of the emergence of terrorist groups in Western Europe elucidate, somewhat, the role of individual dispositions. Herbert Hess' analysis, for example, describes a process that progresses through a number of steps.[29] The origin is a widespread social protest movement. Confrontations with authorities lead to the experience of repressive violence. Such violence and the failure to enlist the support of segments of the population that were expected to become the movement's constituency lead to the fragmentation and deterioration of the movement. The remnants organize in small, clandestine cells. Their members maintain little external contact and fierce group loyalty. Under these circumstances, violent individuals become prominent, shape the violent character of the group and establish terrorism as the group's preferred *modus operandi*. The turn to violence is facilitated and hastened by the presence of external models. German groups, for example, were strongly influenced by foreign groups such as the Tupamaros and Palestinian groups.

The attribution of the emergence of terrorist groups to an interaction of social processes and individual dispositions appears reasonable, indeed obvious. Yet, the utility of this interactive approach is bound to remain limited unless conditions that affect the relative weight of social and individual factors are specified. I propose that individuals' dispositions have a relatively minor effect on a group's turning to terrorism, under the following three conditions: (1) deprivation is intense, the group is denied satisfaction of basic needs and the exercise of elementary rights; (2) the group has articulated and ideologized its discontent; and (3) group members have a strong group identity and the group is cohesive and clearly differentiated from outgroups. Under these conditions, individuals' adoption of the terrorist response is not necessarily indicative of violent predispositions. Thus, for example, the predicament of the Palestinians in the wake of Israel's war of independence, the fact that many of them have since been refugees, and the emergence of a strong national identity and ideology provide a sufficient explanation for the rise and actions of the PLO. Given these conditions it appears hardly necessary to attribute to members of the PLO a greater propensity to violence than one would attribute to, say, soldiers in any nation's regular army.

Individual dispositions, particularly the disposition to violence, become paramount when (1) the radical movement does not aim to satisfy specific basic needs or to reclaim elementary rights but rather to implement a general social ideology; (2) the ideology is incoherent and unrealistic; and (3) the group lacks a unique, separate identity. Terrorist groups in Western Europe are a case in point. The protest movements from which these groups sprouted did not consist of underprivileged, discriminated against segments of society. Their ideology was typically incoherent, and their group identity was diffuse, as they possessed, in effect, many of the class characteristics of the "establishment" against which they waged war.[30]

In principle, the empirical confirmation of these propositions rests on measurements of variance. If the propositions are valid, then members of organizations such as the PLO should be shown to be more heterogeneous in their dispositions to violence than members of, say, the Italian Red Brigades or of the French Action Directe. Such evidence is extremely difficult to obtain, however, and, at present, the propositions can be supported only indirectly. It may be reasoned that groups that emerged as a result of political circumstances or necessity would attract a larger membership than those that came into being as an association of violent individuals. The data support this reasoning: while ideological terrorist groups, such as those operating in Europe, consist of scores of active members only, groups such as the PLO have rosters of thousands.

THE RECENT INCREASE IN TERRORIST ACTIVITY

The recent increase in the incidence and intensity of terrorist activity can be attributed, at least in part, to changing assumptions about the stability and legitimacy of established social orders and to new attitudes toward authority. These, as argued in previous sections of this chapter, stimulated a worldwide movement toward social and political change, which, under certain circumstances, seeks expression in terrorist action. However, the explanation of the proliferation of terrorism in the last two decades is certain to remain incomplete if the analysis remains confined to the search for root causes and ignores facilitating conditions. I propose, in other words, that a major contribution to said proliferation is due to the relative ease with which terrorist strategy can be implemented nowadays.

Salient among the facilitating conditions are advances in transportation, communication, and weapons technology.[31] The ready accessibility of fast and efficient air transportation has increased the reach of terrorist groups and the range within which they can select targets. Planning and organization have been considerably simplified by efficient modes of communication. Recent developments in the miniaturization of weapons provide terrorists with small, portable, cheap, accurate, and easy-to-operate weapons, such as hand-held, heat-seeking surface-to-air missiles. Plastic explosives that are difficult to detect, along with cheap and highly accurate day-date watches and long-life miniature batteries, have increased the quality of amateur-made bombs and the safety with which such devices can be used.

Recent developments have made terrorism not only easier to execute but also more effective. Increasing dependence on advanced technologies and the growing centralization of the technological infrastructure heighten the potential threat posed by terrorists. This growing threat was described by Robert Kupperman:

Commercial aircraft, natural gas pipelines, the electric power grid, offshore oil rigs, and computers storing government and corporate records are examples of sabotage-prone targets whose destruction would have derivative effects of far higher intensity than their primary losses would suggest.... Thirty years ago terrorists could not have obtained extraordinary leverage. Today, however, the foci of communications, production and distribution are relatively small in number and highly vulnerable.[32]

Yet the greatest contribution to the heightened potential effectiveness of terrorism is due to the current technical capabilities and orientation of the news media. Their ability to broadcast events in real-time to every corner of the globe, and news editors' adherence to the principle that events must be reported immediately, as they transpire, magnify the effect of terrorist acts manifold. Taking advantage of the capabilities and operating philosophy of the news media, practitioners of terrorism have become highly "cost effective."

SUMMARY

This chapter explored psychological and social psychological antecedents of political terrorism. Three specific questions were addressed:

1. What are the conditions that produce a movement toward social and political change?
2. What are the dynamics that turn such a movement to violence?
3. Why has terrorism acquired unprecedented dimensions in the last two decades?

Theories of intergroup conflict and recent propositions about the social psychology of minority groups provide a framework within which the first question can be answered. However, the generality of the answer is qualified by examples of terrorist groups that emerged out of privileged majority groups rather than out of disadvantaged minorities. The conditions that lead to the rise of such groups, driven by ideology rather than by adversity, have yet to be specified by social psychological and sociological theory.

The FA and RD hypotheses give grounds for answers to the second question. However, in applying these hypotheses to the explanation of terrorism it is imperative to consider differences in the nature and potency of frustrations and deprivations experienced by different groups. The frustrations of young radicals in North America are incomparable to the plight of a national group that has lost a homeland. In the former case, frustration appears to be insufficiently intense to produce a mass terrorist movement. Hence, to explain the behavior of the few that do turn to terrorism, it is necessary to take into consideration personal attributes and dispositions.

The possible role that individual attributes play in the dynamics of terrorism constrains the generality of group and conflict theories of terrorism. No analysis of the predicament of minority groups or of intergroup conflict in the United States can convincingly explain the doings of the twelve who comprised the Symbionese Liberation Army. This is not to suggest that social psychological and sociological explanations are invalid, but rather that they might be more valid with respect to some cases or varieties of terrorism than to others.

The various theoretical approaches explored do not account fully for the increase in the incidence of terrorism in the last two or three decades. This increase does not necessarily imply that there are, nowadays, more or more compelling causes for terrorist action. The answer to the third question might reside in facilitating conditions that make the practice of terrorism easier and more effective.

NOTES

1. See Grant Wardlaw, *Political Terrorism: Theory, Tactics, and Counter-measures*, 2nd ed. (New York: Cambridge University Press, 1989).

2. Brian M. Jenkins, "International Terrorism: Trends and Potentialities," *Journal of International Affairs* 32 (1978): 114–23.

3. Central Intelligence Agency, *International Terrorism in 1979* (Washington, D.C.: The Central Intelligence Agency, 1980).

4. Alice Miller, *For Your Own Good: Hidden Cruelty in Childrearing and the Roots of Violence* (New York: Farrar, Straus, Giroux, 1984), 241.

5. Gustav Morph, *Le Terrorisme Quebecois* (Montreal: Editions de l'Homme, 1970).

6. David Hubbard, "Bringing Skyjackers Down to Earth: Views of a Psychiatrist," *Time*, 4 October 1971, 64–65.

7. Robert S. Frank, "The Prediction of Political Violence from Objective and Subjective Social Indicators." Paper presented at International Political Science Association Conference, Edinburgh, 1976.

8. Peter L. Berger, cited in the Introduction to *Political Terrorism*, vol. 2, 1974–1978, ed. Lester A. Sobel (New York: Facts on File, 1978), 8.

9. See Lauran Paine, *The Terrorists* (London: Robert Hale, 1975) as well as Martha Crenshaw, "The Causes of Terrorism," *Comparative Politics* 13 (1981): 379–99.

10. For example, Henri Tajfel, *Human Groups and Social Categories: Studies in Social Psychology* (Cambridge: Cambridge.University Press, 1981); John C. Turner and Roger J. Brown, "Social Status, Cognitive Alternatives, and Intergroup Relations," in *Differentiation Between Social Groups: Studies in Social Psychology of Intergroup Relations*, ed. Henri Tafel (London: Academic Press, 1978); Roger J. Brown and Glenn F. Ross, "The Battle for Acceptance: on Investigation into the Dynamics of Intergroup Behavior," in *Social Identity and Intergroup Relations*, ed. Henri Tajfel (Cambridge: Cambridge University Press, 1982).

11. Charles A. Russell and Bowman H. Miller, "Profile of a Terrorist," *Military Review* 58 (August 1977): 21–34.

12. See Zdenek Zofka, *Denkbare Motive und Mogliche Aktiosformen eines Nuklear-terrorismus* (Essen: Auge, 1981).

13. See Alessandro Silj, *Never Again Without a Rifle* (New York: Karz, 1979).

14. See William H. Nagel, "A Socio-legal View on the Suppression of Terrorism," *International Journal of the Sociology of Law* 8 (1980): 213–26.

15. Peter G. Kielmansegg, "Politikwiessenschaft und Gewaltproblematik," in *Der Weg in die Gewalt*, ed. Heiner Geissler (Munich: Olzog, 1978).

16. Franco Ferracuti, "A Sociopsychiatric Interpretation of Terrorism," *The Annals of the American Academy of Political and Social Science* 463 (1982): 120–49.

17. John Dollard, Leonard W. Doob, Neal E. Miller, O. H. Mowrer, and Robert R. Sears, *Frustration and Aggression* (New Haven: Yale University Press, 1939).

18. Leonard Berkowitz, "Frustrations, Comparisons and Other Sources of Emotional Arousal as Contributors to Social Unrest," *Journal of Social Issues* 28 (1972): 77–91.

19. James C. Davies, "Toward a Theory of Revolution," *American Sociological Review* 27 (1962): 5–19; Ivo K. Feierabend and Rosalind L. Feierabend, "Aggressive Behavior Within Politics, 1948–1962: A Cross-National Survey," *Journal of Conflict Resolution* 10 (1966): 247–71; Ted R. Gurr, *Why Men Rebel* (Princeton: Princeton University Press, 1970); Peter A. Lupsha, "Explanation of Political Violence: Some Psychological Theories versus Indignation," *Politics and Society* 2 (1971): 89–104.

20. Gurr, *Why Men Rebel*, 23.

21. Joseph M. G. Van der Dennen, *Problems in the Concept and Definition of Aggression, Violence, and Some Related Terms* (Groningen: Polemological Institute, 1980).

22. Michael Billig, *Social Psychology and Intergroup Relations* (London: Academic Press, 1976), 150.

23. See Richard L. Clutterbuck, *Terrorism and Guerrilla Warfare: Forecasts and Remedies* (New York: Routledge, 1990).

24. Hanna Arendt, *Crisis of the Republic* (Harmondsworth: Penguin, 1973).

25. Cited in Alex P. Schmid and Albert J. Jongman, *Political Terrorism* (Amsterdam: North Holland Publishing Company, 1988), 122–23.

26. Luigi Bonanate, "Some Unanticipated Consequences of Terrorism," *Journal of Peace Research* 16 (1979): 205.

27. Edward Hymas, *Terrorists and Terrorism* (New York: St. Martin's Press, 1974), 170.

28. See John W. Thibaut, Nehemia Friedland, and Neil Walker, "Compliance with

Rules: Some Social Determinants," *Journal of Personality and Social Psychology* 30 (1974).

29. Herbert Hess, "Terrorismus und Terrorismus-diskurs," *Tijdschrift voor Criminologie* 4 (1981): 171–88.

30. See Philip E. Devine and Robert J. Rafalko, "On Terror," *The Annals of the American Academy of Political and Social Science* 43 (1982): 129–49.

31. Wardlaw, *Political Terrorism*.

32. Robert Kupperman, *Facing Tomorrow's Terrorist Incident Today* (Washington, DC: U.S. Department of Justice, Law Enforcement Assistance Administration, 1977), 1.

6

Terrorism and the Media: Freedom of Information vs. Freedom from Intimidation

Alex P. Schmid

INTRODUCTION

More than one hundred years ago, in 1881, a San Francisco paper called *Truth* wrote "*Truth* is two cents a copy, dynamite is forty cents a pound. Buy them both, read one, use the other."[1] That was the time when media and terrorism began to interact, in the United States as well as in Russia. Nearly fifty years ago Franklin Delano Roosevelt announced on January 6, 1941, to Congress the "Four Freedoms" that the United States would uphold in its fight against tyranny:

1. Freedom of speech and expression;
2. Freedom of worship;
3. Freedom from want; and
4. Freedom from fear.

A question I would like to pose is whether the first freedom—the freedom of information—is compatible with the fourth—the freedom from fear or intimidation. Do the Western media, by informing us on acts of terrorism, not also intimidate all those who own a radio or TV set or read a paper and identify with the victim of a particular act of terrorism?

Thirteen years ago, during the so-called Hanafi incident in Washington, D.C., Andrew Young, then President Carter's ambassador to the United Nations, suggested that the First Amendment of the U.S. Constitution, which guarantees the freedom of the press, should "be clarified by the Supreme Court in the light of the power of the mass media." Although President Carter felt nothing for this suggestion, the fact that the issue was raised demonstrated

that the terrorist–media relationship had begun to intrude on the fundamentals of American society.[2]

What is the relationship between terrorism and the media? There are three
schools of thought:

1. There are those who argue that the media reduce uncertainty about acts of violence.
   By informing about terrorism they prevent rumour and panic. In this perspective
   media coverage reduces the impact of terrorism.

2. Then there are those who argue that terrorism existed long before today's media
   and that the mass media, like jetliners, are just one more modern commodity used
   by terrorists as well as by other people.

3. Finally, there are those who argue that the media inspire and encourage terrorism—
   that they are the oxygen terrorists need to stay alive.[3]

While there is some truth in all three propositions, I tend to subscribe to
the last one. It is, however, a qualified subscription that depends on what
one labels "terrorism" and, to a lesser extent, even what counts as media.

Acts of terrorism have three basic purposes. They can serve (1) to intimidate
a target audience; (2) to blackmail a target, for example, a government; or
(3) to make propaganda.

For the first purpose, intimidation of a population, media can be helpful—
as in show trials—but not absolutely necessary for the execution of state
terror. The intimidation can also be achieved by rumours or public executions. That's the way state terrorism works and it is perfectly compatible with
censorship of the media. In fact, the media are more often than not a hin-
drance rather than a support mechanism for state terrorists. For the second
purpose, the blackmail business, you don't need the public media. Criminal
kidnappers, for instance, loath the media. For the third purpose, to call the
attention of a wider audience to presence or cause of armed men, the media
are very important.

I will herein focus on insurgent terrorism, by which I mean non-state
ethnic and social revolutionary terrorism. For this sort of terrorist activity to
intimidate a target audience media coverage is essential, certainly in the early
stages of a terrorist campaign. By terrorism I mean unprovoked violent attacks
against non-combatants who might be chosen randomly from a general target
population. Attacks can also be symbolic or representative (for example,
killing off-duty servicemen). These latter acts are distinct from assassinations
of a particular figure, say President Kennedy. Both symbolic and random
attacks are meant to convey a message of terror, of demands, or of propaganda
to a target population. By media I mean the news media, television, radio
and newspapers that now are able to report events almost in real time. Fiction
in the movies also plays a role in the contagious effects of terrorism, but I
will not dwell on that in this chapter.

When we look at the relationship between insurgent terrorists and the

Western news media, it is important not to consider it in isolation. It is part of a relationship between at least five parties:

1. The terrorists;
2. The victims/hostages;
3. The public/audience;
4. The government; and
5. The media (editors and journalists).

The relationship between these five parties cannot simply be reduced to users and used, such as that the terrorists abuse the media for purposes of propaganda. There are various types of relationships. These differ from country to country, period to period, medium to medium, and from terrorist movement to terrorist movement, leaving little room for bold generalizations and clear-cut guilt attributions. Each of these parties—terrorists, victims, public, government, and media—has a perspective based on its role in the theatre of terror. Each party has its own agenda and when something happens each one (except the audience) tries to control the event by steering the effects of it in a direction which fits the open or hidden agendas of the protagonists of the social drama. Sometimes there are parallel interests and unholy alliances between two or more parties, sometimes their interests clash.

Next, I will discuss briefly the aspects of each of these perspectives, beginning with the terrorists themselves.

THE TERRORISTS

How do terrorists and other violent activists think about the media? While our knowledge in this area is still inadequate, we nevertheless have some cues about how they view the power of the media. A Dutch radical group called Revolutionary Anti-Racist Action, or RARA ("Guess Who?"), which through a series of arsonist attacks managed to coerce a Dutch multinational corporation to sell its business in South Africa, wrote, "According to the rules of TV democracy, those with most access to the media win."[4]

This thought is widely shared outside terrorist circles as well; think, for instance, of the advertising industry. How much truth there is to this insight is of secondary importance. As long as terrorists believe this, they will act on the basis of this assumption.

However, it is important to point out that there is a distinction between obtaining coverage of terrorist acts in the media and having regular access to the media. Indeed, it can be argued that one of the reasons terrorists engage in shocking acts of violence is because they do not have habitual access to the media the way the government does.

Hans-Joachim Klein, a former German terrorist, expressed it in these words: "If they do not listen to us, then we throw a couple of bombs."[5]

Consider another example from the Provisional IRA, the underground group that kills people, giving above-ground members of Sinn Fein a chance to explain to the public what the meaning behind the violence is. When the British government sent a new army commander to Northern Ireland and he, in turn, wanted to give his first news conference, announcing that the battle against terrorism was going well, the Provisionals decided to deny him the front page of the local paper. Maria McGuire, then member of the Provisionals, wrote, "We drove him [commander Sir Harry Tuzo] off the front pages of the Belfast Evening Telegraph with a dozen bomb explosions in Belfast, demonstrating very clearly who was winning in the Six Counties."[6]

Such examples can be multiplied. In the late 1950s, for instance, an Algerian leader of the Front de la Liberation National instructed his gunmen and bombers, "We must have blood in the headlines of all the newspapers."[7]

The nature of this "propaganda by the deed" is illustrated with two more quotes from Bommi Baumann, a member of the West German "June 2nd Movement":

Without journalistic reporting we would find ourselves facing a certain vacuum. It is through the press that our cause is maintained in the just manner . . .

The RAF [Red Army Faction] has said, this revolution will not be built up by political work, but through headlines, through its appearance in the press, which reports again and again that *guerrilleros* are fighting here in Germany.[8]

They were, of course, not genuine *guerrilleros*. Guerrillas attempt to conquer physical territory and create an alternative state in these liberated areas. These urban terrorists try to conquer space in the papers, on the airwaves, and ultimately in our hearts and minds. They are waging a media war, exploiting the media for political ends by staging newsworthy acts of violence.

This media war was already foretold in the 1960s by Marshall McLuhan who predicted that "the next war will be fought with images."[9]

The recipe of the terrorists' political communication strategy has already been formulated in 1936 by Joseph Goebbels, the Minister of Propaganda of the Third Reich: "Violence arrests the attention of all who are within sight and hearing of the action . . . it focuses the attention of everybody in the audience on the terrorists' propaganda message."[10]

One hundred years ago it was the rotary press that spread the terrorist message to hundreds of thousands of readers. Fifty years ago it was state-controlled radio that brought the message of totalitarian invincibility to millions of listeners. Today it is television that reaches hundreds of millions of viewers.

It has been said, with some exaggeration, that television is so ideally suited to terrorism that the medium would have invented the phenomenon if it had not already existed.[11]

What do the media do for the terrorist? In my study, *Insurgent Terrorism and the Western News Media*, first published ten years ago, I identified more than thirty active and passive uses. They range from using the public media as an external communications network between terrorists to magnifying the impact of fearful events. There is no space to discuss all of these uses here, but let me stress one point that forms the historical basis for media-oriented terrorism. This is "Herostratism." Herostratus was the Greek who set the Artemis temple in Ephesus on fire in the year 356 B.C. with the explicit aim of being remembered by us. The destruction of this temple—one of the seven wonders of the ancient world—was meant to confer status on Herostratus, to give him identity. The fire was the power generator to immortalize his name. The Greek word "pseudo" means "false" or "meant to deceive." Not the temple but we were the ultimate target of this arson. One could call this fire the first "pseudo-event."

Daniel Boorstin wrote a book, *The Image*, in the 1960s, wherein he introduced the concept of a pseudo-event, "the new kind of synthetic novelty which has flooded our experience." He situated its origin in the interwar period. To my mind, Herostratus was the inventor of the pseudo-event. Boorstin defined it in these terms:

1. It is not spontaneous, but comes about because someone has planned, planted, or incited it.

2. It is planted primarily (not always exclusively) for the immediate purpose of being reported or reproduced. Therefore its occurrence is arranged for the convenience of the reporting or reproducing media. Its success is measured by how widely it is reported.[12]

Herostratus has found many imitators. One of them was John Hinckley, Jr., the young man who almost killed President Reagan. When he was apprehended his first question was, "Is it on TV?" He had deliberately planned to shoot the President with the cameras rolling, declaring, "No crime carries as much publicity as the assassination of the President of the United States." In a couple of seconds he had gone, as he himself declared, from "obscurity to notoriety," emphasizing that "the entire civilized world knows who I am."[13]

Hinckley was an insane young man, but he was clever enough to grasp the working principle of many terrorists. Attack the president of the United States and you have some 240 million concerned Americans. Attack the Roman Pope and you have the attention of 900 million Catholics. Satellite-linked television is a tremendous magnifier. While the Chinese saying which explains the essence of terrorism was "Kill one, frighten ten thousand," today you can reach mega-audiences of two billion people within twenty-four hours. The victim matters more for his news value than for the motive behind the deed as is illustrated by a quote from Hans-Joachim Klein, the German terrorist who at one time was a member of the Red Cells (Rote Zellen): "I then proposed to kidnap the princess of Monaco, because she was much written about in German magazines at that time..."[14]

We find the same logic in the selection of the Munich Olympic Games as a theatre for a Palestinian terrorist operation back in 1972.

In other words, a new kind of violence has come about in the last few decades, a kind of violence performed in order to be reported. If it is not reported, it cannot be successful. This principle applies to other certain non-terrorist events as well. In the Netherlands, where there is a colorful extra-parliamentarian action tradition, there are many political demonstrations planned for Saturdays. The organizers call up a television station and try to cajole the editor to send a camera team to record the event. There are sometimes thirty such requests and only one or two are selected by the editor for coverage. An interesting phenomenon is that some demonstrations are cancelled when the organizers learn they will not be covered in the Saturday evening news.

Terrorists can, by producing newsworthy violent events, be more sure of coverage. A mere handful of terrorists can, in such a way, bomb or shoot a nonviolent demonstration of ten thousand people from the TV screen. Such is the news value system that guides editors. The rise of the newsworthy violent pseudo-event has, in my opinion, begun to poison journalism. It has started a feedback process in which the media, and television in particular, reflect reality less than reality has begun to reflect television's news values. The implications of this shift from neutral news gathering to calculated news-making by actors in and recorders of events are profound for the global electronic village.

Ben Bagdikian wrote already in the early seventies: "For most of the people of the world, for most of the events in the world, what the news system does not transmit did not happen. To that extent, the world and its inhabitants are what the news media say they are."[15]

The commercial and public media, following the principle that "good news is bad news and bad news is good news," have made a lion out of a mouse. Most terrorists are weak. Mario Moretti, referring to the kidnapping of Aldo Moro, the Italian Premier in the 1970s, said "for a few necessary minutes [the Red Brigades] can be the strongest."[16]

Yet these short moments of terrorist strength can be endlessly prolonged by media coverage: fifty-five days in the case of the kidnapping of Aldo Moro and 444 days in the case of the seizure of U.S. embassy personnel in Tehran.

Ample media coverage of terrorist episodes and their aftermath occupies space in our minds, and we attribute a significance to the phenomenon of terrorism that is not warranted. In the last two decades probably fewer than 500 American civilians were killed by what is called "international terrorism," yet many Americans perceive terrorism as one of the major problems of our times.

What do terrorists use the media for besides magnification of their deed

and amplification of their message? The attention they get through perpe-
trating atrocities gives them status—a negative status in the eyes of many, but
status nevertheless. Violence, however trivial or despicable its cause, always
demands respect, due to the irreversible results it can have.

A negative status can, in a world where former terrorists become statesmen
and winners of the Nobel prize for peace (Menachem Begin), be turned into
a positive one. Without attention to begin with, there can be no hope for
recognition of the right to exist and ultimately, acknowledgment of the legitimacy of the political position taken by terrorists. It is here that the media
can play a decisive role, as Ronald Crelinsten has pointed out:

The central element in the relationship between terrorists and the media is therefore
the struggle for legitimation between those seeking power and those holding power.
By choosing to cover or not to cover terrorism and, when covering it, by choosing
to present it in certain ways, the media become vehicles for these legitimation
struggles.[17]

The media, then, do more than inform us when reporting on terrorism.
They give tiny numbers of violent men access to millions of homes and allow
the terrorist newsmakers to horrify us by sudden unprovoked killings of
innocents. In fact, we become secondary victims, some of us more than others,
depending on the degree of identification with the primary victims. When
the public's freedom of information becomes a freedom of terrorists to intimidate the public through predesigned shocking acts of violence, something
has clearly gone wrong. But can it be changed? Is the system of the free flow
of information in our media affected by terrorism because of what the media
are or because of what the media do? Are they helpless accomplices or
partners in crimes? Before addressing the question of media (self-) regulation,
let me turn to the other perspectives, beginning with the one of the victims.

THE VICTIMS' PERSPECTIVE

In a certain sense, we are all victims of terrorism as it is constructed for
us by the mass media, our primary and usually only source of information.
We change our travel habits or our vacation destinations out of fear of becoming victims. The rationale for this fear is small—it is more likely that we
will be killed by lightning than by terrorists—but the fear of victimization is
real, especially among heavy media consumers. Whenever we think, reading
or hearing about a new terrorist bombing, shooting or kidnapping, "It could
have been me!", we are identifying to some degree with current victims and
the pain they suffer directly becomes a psychological pain for us. This is
especially true of former hostages. Hearing of a new hijacking through the
media, former victims of hijackings can regress into their own former victimization and experience frightening images in intrusive recollections.[18] A pro-

cess of identification takes place not only with former victims and likely future victims but with all those in the audience who share some "victim characteristics."

Audience identification means enhanced attention, which is a valuable commodity in the media business. Acts of hostage-taking, and to a lesser extent, kidnappings are the stuff that fits the standard programming formats of television. Such events are open-ended and potentially deadly social dramas that make for "good TV." Victims can be personalized, especially when family members are brought into the story. This process of enhancing the value of the victim is sometimes strengthened by the terrorist themselves, who send videotapes of kidnapped victims or their execution. The hostages and the terrorists have an identical interest that the government gives in to blackmail. In this way the hostages can be made spokesmen for the interests of the terrorists. When wives of hostages and kidnapping victims fight for the release of their husbands, or mothers for their children, and the desire to get the loved one back clashes with reasons of state, all the ingredients are present to turn a personal tragedy into a national affair with yellow ribbons being tied around old oak trees and candles being lit from the hostage's home to the White House.

Powerful pressure groups are created, demanding the safe return of the victims of kidnappings at almost any price. I have heard an intelligence officer from Israel express concern that President Reagan was willing to hand over the entire nation of Lebanon to Syria for the safe return of seven kidnapped Americans. The release of these hostages was a major reason why the U.S. president sent arms to Iran. In the case of the hijacked TWA Flight 847 (June 14–30, 1985) the media exposure of the hostages generated enough pressure for the American president to make concessions. A White House staffer later reported:

Like everyone else, the President watched television for his information, occasionally making major policy decisions, against the best advice of his most senior cabinet officers, on the basis of what he saw . . . Reagan had to be restrained by Secretary of State, George Shultz, from making concession to the hijackers of TWA Flight 847. Reagan reacted just like millions of other viewers did—he identified with the plight of the hostages. But unlike the other viewers of the latest humiliation, he had the power to do something about it. He was ready to cave in. It took more than an hour of strenuous argument, mainly by . . . Shultz, to persuade the President to suppress his feelings about the hostages and hang tough publicly against any concessions to the terrorists.[19]

Ultimately the president gave in, agreeing to exchange 766 Shiites in Israeli camps for the thirty-nine Americans. "The public will demand satisfaction," Reagan said in explaining the deal.[20]

Similar pressure was generated by hostage support groups such as the Families Liaison and Action Group (FLAG) at the time of the U.S. embassy occupation in Tehran. In France, for instance, Joelle Brunerie, a gynecologist nationally known for her campaign to legalize abortion, organized another campaign when her husband, the journalist Jean-Paul Kaufmann, was kidnapped by Hezbollah in Beirut. To get her husband back, she not only visited French ministers in the Elysee but also went to Beirut to negotiate with Amal leader Nabih Berri. Perhaps most important of all, she sent daily, for many months, a letter to her husband. This letter was broadcast day after day by the powerful radio station France Inter.[21] She, too, managed to get her husband back, when election time came in France.

While it can be argued that some hostages have been saved by the media attention given to them, there also have been cases where hostages were endangered by the media. In the Hanafi incident in Washington, D.C. in 1977, journalists broadcasted pictures on television that could have informed the terrorists that there were more people in an occupied building than were in the hands of the terrorists. Reporters calling up by phone have given terrorists ideas such as when they were asking for ultimata deadlines when no ultimatum had been set by the terrorists themselves.

In a hostage incident in the Netherlands in 1978, a radio news report identified by name two prominent hostages among fifty-six public officials taken hostage in the Provincial building in Assen. The terrorists promptly decided that "the highest go first." The two country aldermen were handcuffed and placed against the window as the ultimatum was about to expire. When the Marines stormed the place to prevent the executions, the terrorists managed to fatally wound one of the persons singled out in the news bulletin. Being mentioned and assigned news value in the 12.30 ANP radio broadcast brought thus death to county alderman Trip.[22]

Not all deaths related to hostage incidents wherein the media play a role can be rightfully blamed on the media. In the case of the TWA Flight 847 hijacking in June 1985, for instance, the father of a hostage, flight engineer Christian Zimmermann, died of a heart attack when he learned from the media that his son had been hijacked.[23] However, the remote shock he experienced could perhaps have been cushioned if he could have been prepared for the bad news by a face-to-face personal communication rather than hearing from media that probably did not even think of delaying the broadcasting of the story until all relatives had been notified.

Real-time newscasts can be fatal, as in the case of a German captain of a Lufthansa jet hijacked to Mogadishu in October 1977 who passed information about the hijackers to the authorities. This fact was reported by a radio station. The hijackers, who were listening to the broadcasting journalist, decided to kill the captain.[24]

Even more blame can be placed on the media in the case of a hijacking of a Kuwaiti airliner by Hezbollah in Algiers. The hijackers had heard on the radio that the British authorities had sent the Special Air Service commandos after them. In order to deter their arrival on the scene they killed one hostage and told the control tower to tell the British Prime Minister to keep the SAS at home. It turned out that the report that the SAS was under way had not been accurate to begin with and that they had acted on information that turned out to be wrong.[25]

Media coverage, then, can bring life or death to hostages, and it is difficult to tell which before the fact. When Americans were asked in an opinion poll whether they would wish to maximize press coverage if held by terrorists, 47 percent answered in the affirmative, but almost as many, 43 percent, said the opposite.[26]

During and after captivity, hostages and their families are torn between wanting to use the media and resenting the intrusion of the media in their private lives. On one occasion, a hostage recalled, his teenage son received a phone call from a journalist at two o'clock in the morning, wherein the boy was asked to comment on the fact that "the latest reports indicate that your father will be executed in 2 hours."[27]

After an incident hostages are sometimes very angry at the media, comparing reporters to vultures who would rather have them dead than alive because it made for better TV. The release situation where family members, security forces, politicians, and reporters fight for access to the hostages is, of course, a situation where frustration has to be released and in search of a convenient object for aggression the media serve as scapegoat.

In summary, the victims of terrorism have an ambiguous relationship with the media. They often are used—sometimes with deadly consequences—but at the same time, their own use of the media can, at times, enhance their chances of survival.

THE PUBLIC AUDIENCE

The media love big audiences because these potential consumers can be sold to advertisers. To get and hold the audiences they turn to producers able to appeal to large numbers of people. Some of the productions bought are fictional programs, involving, among other things, sex and violence as bait for audiences. I see a certain parallel between commercial advertisers sponsoring violent action series and terrorists performing acts of violence. In both cases the violence serves to attract audiences, which then can be exposed to a message: "buy me" or "obey me." One difference is that the advertisers have to pay for reaching audiences while the terrorists do not. Another is that the advertiser's violence is largely fictional whereas that of the terrorists is real. Yet in both cases violence serves to send messages to mass audiences. Apparently, the masses like violent action programs and feel a need to watch news programs containing violence.

In a market society the audience gets from the media what it wants—education, information, and entertainment, with an emphasis on entertainment. In fact, news programs also have to be entertaining if they want to keep their audience. And that is what regularly happens with terrorist stories. George Ball, the former Under Secretary of State, labelled the U.S. network coverage of the ordeal of the embassy personnel in Teheran "the greatest soap opera of the year."[28]

In this section I will raise two questions:

1. What do the terrorists expect from the audiences provided by the media?
2. What does the public think of the media's coverage of terrorism?

In order to discuss the first question, some distinctions have to be made. First we have to keep in mind that the two types of terrorist groups considered here differ in significant aspects. The social–revolutionary terrorists lack mass allegiance, while ethnic terrorists have a natural constituency that usually is a minority (or a majority in a minority position) within a state from which they want to be liberated. These people are supposedly sympathizers of the terrorists, sharing their goals if not their methods.

When performing violent deeds, terrorists play for one or more audiences. Generally, we can distinguish between terrorist violence that sends, through the choice of victims and the manner of victimization, signals to at least half a dozen particular audiences:

1. World public opinion;
2. The national majority which is generally opposed to the goals of the terrorists;
3. The national minority or social class for which the terrorists claim to fight;
4. The national government which is the direct opponent of the insurgent terrorists;
5. Rival political movements, both terrorist and non-terrorist;
6. The terrorists and their direct supporters.

Depending on which audience is foremost in their mind, terrorist violence comes in different forms. Basically, the terrorists want to affect (change or reinforce) the opinion of relevant audiences and thereby influence the political situation in their favour. However, one of the problems they encounter is that different audiences assign different meanings to their violence. An act of violence might be successful in mobilizing new recruits to the movement. That, for instance, was one effect of the Palestinian attack on the 1972 Olympic Games. However, the same act might not lead to the ideological conversion of other audiences; rather than opening their eyes to the grievances of the terrorists it might alienate them. With their communiques and claims of responsibility, terrorists try to explain to various relevant audiences how a particular act should be understood and how it relates to the common goal. In practice, it is very difficult to structure violence in such a way that both the terrorists' natural or desired constituency and a wider public react favorably. The fact that they are able to reach the mass media might give them the illusion that they can reach, through them, the masses themselves and open their eyes. The belief that a majority of people share our personal opinions is a fallacy to which not only the terrorists are prone. Living in the underground and acting in small cells of three to five people, the terrorists are, through their choice of tactics, unable to interact freely with their reference group and observe what the state of public opinion actually is. The risk that they confuse their own rhetoric with reality is therefore substantial.

How their violence is understood by the target audience depends, among other things, on the way the target group—whose allegiance or compliance they desire—relates to the government.

Sometimes terrorists want to demoralize the public at large so that it ceases its support for the government on a particular issue. The Provisional IRA, for instance, hopes that the British public will get sick and tired of seeing British boys being killed in Northern Ireland and withdraw its support to the government's policy on Northern Ireland. In other cases, for instance in West Germany in the 1970s, the Red Army Faction (RAF) hoped to provoke widespread government repression that would radicalize the proletariat and drive it into the arms of the revolutionaries. By killing bankers, they hoped to win the sympathy of the workers; by attacking U.S. generals, they hoped to find a positive echo with the peace movement. In Germany, therefore, left-wing terrorism was focussing on rather narrowly defined representatives of business, the military, and the state. Right-wing terrorists, on the other hand, generally direct their attacks against common people, exploding bombs in railway stations, trains, or beer halls, in the hope that there will be public outrage and a massive demand for law and order and a strong authoritarian leader.

Whether these reactions actually can be provoked in such a way with any degree of certainty is another question. In fact, I suspect that in many cases the terrorists and their immediate supporters are the only ones who appreciate the results of their violence. Auto-propaganda, whereby the terrorists are both perpetrators and chief audience, is a very important element. A bomb set off, an opponent killed, and the media coverage that goes with it boost their morale much more than it lowers that of their opponents. The terrorist message to the "true believers"—the community of insiders—might be more important than the message to the outsiders.[29]

How does the audience actually react to media-reported terrorist incidents like kidnappings, hostage-taking, and political murder? Members of the audience are—if they are not predominantly identifying with their own government as the target of terrorism demands—likely to identify with one or another perspective:

1. They can identify with the victim of aggression. This is likely when the victim shows group characteristics such as same nationality, same class, or same social position as members of the (sub-)audience.

2. They can identify with the perpetrators of aggression. This is likely to happen if the victim is hated by members of the audience, if the goals of the terrorists are identical to the ones of the (sub-)audience, and if the manner of victimization can be justified or rationalized in one way or another.

The way the actual identification goes is likely to be co-dependent on the way the mass media portray a particular terrorist incident.

Whenever violence occurs and we are made witnesses, either face-to-face or in front of a television screen, we tend to determine whether or not the victim deserves what he gets and whether or not the perpetrator of violence is on our side or not. In short, we want to know who are the "good guys" and the "bad guys," "our" guys and "their" guys. With terrorism often victimizing innocent non-combatants, we react strongly to the fact that bad things happen to good people. We identify with the victim of violence and are imbued with feelings of compassion and sympathy in the face of the victim's distress. Yet we can do very little to aid the victim on the television screen; therefore, we, too, are likely to be frustrated, humiliated, and intimidated— a victory of sorts for the terrorist. On the other hand, if we identify with the man with the bomb who is prepared to die for his ideals and executes his deed with cool precision, the terrorist has won a new ally. Either way he is strengthened. The terrorist's invitation to identification is brought home to us by the public and private media: they are identification machines, printing the sporadic atrocious deeds of numerically insignificant underground groups into the brains of millions of people who are induced to take sides, to identify with the victim or the victimizer. Through the magnifying and amplifying instruments of the news media, mass audiences are faced in their homes with moral dilemmas created by distant terrorists with no moral scruples.

Yet these are speculative thoughts. What empirical evidence do we have about the relationship between public opinion and terrorism? There is disappointingly little evidence available that would allow comparisons in time and cross-nationally. The near-absence of systematic longitudinal data makes statements on public attitude changes problematical.[30]

Christopher Hewitt has brought together some data that allow statements on the level of public concern with regard to terrorism; the image the public has of the terrorists; the degree of support for the goals of the terrorists; and public attitudes toward government anti-terrorist policies.

Public concern about terrorism tends to rise as the number of acts of terrorism increases. Yet, paradoxically, Hewitt's findings indicate that in regions habituated to terrorism, such as the Basque country and Northern Ireland, terrorism in itself is seen as less of a problem. In the United States, on the other hand, terrorism has been a matter of great public concern despite low casualty rates for most years. This disproportionate concern can be interpreted in several ways:

1. Large media coverage could induce large public concern.

2. Large government preoccupation with terrorism (which might be either the result or the cause of media interest) could induce public concern. (Hewitt does not speculate on this particular aspect.)

An important finding of Hewitt is that the view that terrorists will damage their image by killing people is less true for groups like ETA and the Provisional IRA than for social–revolutionary groups like the Italian Red Brigades and the Baader-Meinhof group in Germany. This might be linked to the different targeting practices. The two ethnic groups tend to target more military men than civilians. In this regard they are closer to rural guerrillas than to urban terrorists. Nationalist groups tend to enjoy more legitimacy than social revolutionary groups with their constituencies. People who agree with the political goals of a group tend to have a positive image of a terrorist group. Terrorist atrocities directed against an ethnic enemy do not decrease public support for nationalist goals. In ethnically divided societies, the polarized groups disagree about who is to blame for the violence as well as what should be done about the violence.

Hewitt found that in Germany, Italy, and Uruguay social–revolutionary terrorism generated a strong backlash, with public opinion demanding tougher law-and-order measures. Germans, in particular, were even willing to give up some of their personal freedom in order to fight terrorism. The Germans were also willing to submit to a news blackout, while the Uruguayans did not believe that censorship was justified. Hewitt concluded that the most obvious political consequence of revolutionary terrorism was a law-and-order-backlash benefitting the conservative parties. Perhaps it is for this reason that in some countries (for example, Italy) some left-wing terrorist campaigns appear to have been provoked by if not conducted by right-wing elements linked to the government's secret services.

Social–revolutionary terrorists, it would seem, might not get from the public audience what they hope for: support. At best, they can gain attention. Gabriel Weimann, an Israeli researcher, studied the effects of press coverage of terrorist acts in distant countries. He and his students found that "Press attention appears to be sufficient to enhance the status of people, problem, or cause behind a terrorist event. Terrorists' successes in attracting media attention may then guarantee worldwide awareness and recognition of the political, racial, or religious problem that caused the event."[31]

Weimann's finding on the written press would seem to parallel the suggestion made by George Gerbner that "representation in the world of television gives an idea, a cause, a group its sense of public identity, importance, and relevance."[32]

This result might very well be a causal factor. Another researcher, Connie de Boer, noted in 1979 that 78 percent of the American public (and 60 percent of the British) held that it was a major cause of terrorism that "acts of terrorism receive so much coverage in the news that it encourages terrorists to further acts of terror."[33] Twelve percent in the United States listed this as a minor cause (20 percent in the United Kingdom).

Another survey, conducted by the Times Mirror group in Los Angeles, polled the attitudes of the American public with regard to terrorism and found that the impact of media coverage of terrorism was considerable, both in a negative and a positive sense. Six out of ten persons questioned also held that chances of future terrorist attacks increased by coverage, although only three out of ten persons expected that the amount of sympathy for the terrorist causes would increase through coverage. Some of the public responses were contradictory in this survey. With regard to hostage safety, 33 percent felt that media coverage made it safer for the hostages, 25 percent said less safe, while 28 percent saw no effect. At the same time only 21 percent held that through media coverage the chance that the government will give in to terrorist demands increases (63 percent saw no such effect while 4 percent held that it decreases). Almost two-thirds of the public felt that coverage of terrorism helps "the public interest" (23 percent held that it harms the public interest while 12 percent said they did not know). The public perception contains a paradox: on the one hand 60 percent of the respondents felt that media coverage increased the chance of future attacks, while 65 percent held that it helps the public interest. Apparently two-thirds of the public would not want to miss coverage of terrorist incidents even when it has harmful effects.[34] If we look at the results of opinion surveys focusing on particular incidents, we receive some confirmation for this suggestion.[35] One public opinion survey conducted during the TWA Flight 847 crisis found a slightly higher public support of the news media than a subsequent poll two months later, despite criticism of sensationalism and extensive coverage.

This was not exceptional. Other terrorist incidents scored almost equally high.[36] Apparently, the gripping social drama co-produced by the terrorist and the networks has a high appeal for an overwhelming majority of the public. Live television of such events apparently offers the audience gratifying identification opportunities, almost like fairy tales. One researcher, Sharon L. Sperry, has tried to interpret television news in such terms, and she comes, in my mind, close to the secret of the appeal of terrorist real-life dramas. In her article "Television News as Narrative" she writes,

As the keystone of each network's evening programming, television news attempts to build and hold its audience by lifting elements of that mythic formula which is the basis of its entertainment programs. [According to] Av Westin, former president of ABC News [the audience is] asking "Is the world safe and am I secure?" There is clearly a link between that question and the answer provided by a news structure that plots events along the lines of a hero story:

The world at peace is disrupted by some event (say an act of terrorism). That event, which becomes the evil, is named and, if possible, analyzed and understood. It is then attacked by some leader, the hero figure, often a representative of the people.[37]

However, the audience is not the only one that sees the theater of terror in these terms. There is a mirror image operative on the side of the terrorists.

Stepniak, a Russian terrorist of the 19th century, once said, "The terrorist is beautiful, terrible and irresistibly fascinating because he reunites two types of human grandeur: the martyr and the hero."[38]

Apparently, both sides—the terrorist and the audience—enjoy the theater of terror, although they might differ about who is the villain and who is the hero.

It is here that the government comes in. The government cannot allow the terrorist to be a hero.

THE GOVERNMENT'S PERSPECTIVE

In the United States the freedom of the press is firmly established in the Constitution, and censorship of news on terrorism is not considered. In other countries, however, the government has a tighter grip on the media. Within NATO countries, the situation is worst in Turkey. In the first five years since the end of military rule no less than 2,127 journalists have been tried in Turkey. Some of them have been given prison sentences of more than 600 years—seven years for each offensive article.[39]

In Great Britain, the government banned the broadcasting or televising of statements made by members of Irish terrorist organizations, their allies, and sympathizers. This ban does not apply to the printed media. In order to make the public aware of the restrictions imposed, the BBC (TV as well as the world service) has used the same method used in reporting on South Africa, namely indicating each time clearly that they consider themselves limited by the government in their way of reporting.[40]

In Great Britain the government can invoke Section D of the Official Secrets Act, which provides for the prosecution of anyone who reports information that the police consider should not be reported for security reasons. Abroad, it has to rely more on persuasion than on coercion to prevail in the media war with the terrorists.

In its attempt to influence relevant publics to counter the influence of the terrorists, the British government, working through the British Information Services, which has its American headquarters in New York, keeps in touch with the editorial writers and foreign editors of all the leading American media, briefing them on British policy.

The government of the United States tries to influence coverage of terrorism by keeping good working relationships with the networks, suggesting to them stories as well as warning that certain stories might be harmful to the national interest. In writings of the security forces of the United States on low-intensity conflict, it is recognized that "the media has [sic] the potential either to hamper or to enhance chances for success." Indeed, it is recognized that "The role of the media in counterterrorism and . counterinsurgency is especially critical."[41]

How far the government's role goes in shaping the news on political violence has been brought to light by the revelations of one Contra leader, Edgar Chamorro.[42] The selling of the Contras to the American and the European publics probably outdid everything in terms of media manipulation compared to what insurgent terrorists ever achieved.

The government is generally the main source of news on insurgent terrorism and has all the advantages that fall to the "primary definer of topics." It has been calculated by Michael Parenti in a more general context that no less than 78 percent of news stories in *The New York Times* and the *Washington Post* were based on government officials as sources.[43]

In the psychological war between insurgent terrorists and the sitting government, the public media are the main battleground. The actions of the terrorists can win them a degree of public support or can, at least, discredit the government. The terrorists have the advantage of the initiative. Their communiques often reach the media before the government can present an official version of an incident. The official version, however, might be as biased as the terrorists' version. In 1989, an officer in charge of the investigation into the Lockerbie disaster complained that the false information deliberately given by government sources to the news media could disrupt the investigation.[44] Generally, the balance between the government and the terrorists as definers of reality for media audiences is in the favor of governments. While we like to see the media as a critical watchdog of government actions, most of the media most of the time faithfully follow the government line in Western democracies. This is even more true in countries where Article 19 of the United Nations' Universal Declaration of Human Rights is less respected than in Western democracies.[45]

What does the American public think of government control of media coverage of terrorism? In a survey conducted in the mid–1980s by the Times-Mirror group, only 29 percent of the respondents held that "the government should have more control," while 64 percent said that most decisions on how to report a terrorist story should be made by news organizations themselves. The same survey found, however, that the public wants the news media to adopt a fairly restrictive code of professional responsibility.[46]

THE MEDIA PERSPECTIVE

The gut reaction of a reporter when writing a story is to tell the truth and damn the consequences. However, in many cases he reports not the truth but one or another party's view of a newsworthy event. He might faithfully record what his source says, but his source might be biased or misinformed.

If he is a careful reporter he will check statements with other sources. This will, however, delay his story, and he might miss a scoop. The deadline of a paper or electronic medium, combined with the pressure of competition, can impair the quality of reporting.

Above the journalist stands the editor, who acts as a gatekeeper. Yet he, too, is keeping in mind what the competition does. In addition, with the time interval between the breaking of a news story and the time it goes on the air or in print becoming smaller and smaller, there is less time for careful deliberation and editing. Live coverage of incidents brings special problems due to the possibility that terrorists sometimes react on the basis of the pictures and words broadcasted in real-time or near-real time.

The authorities especially loath interviews with terrorists because this allows them to make unedited propaganda statements. Another worry is statements on military or police moves around the scene of an act of terror. However, sometimes leaks from officials form the basis of such stories and it is not clear whether they were planted deliberately or were truly careless slips of the tongue.

Sometimes telling the truth can be lethal to somebody else. Hostages try to improve their survival chances by downplaying their own importance. If media, in such situations, contradict hostage statements and reveal the governmental links of certain hostages, this can reduce their chance of survival. The assessment of the likely or possible impact of media statements during on-going terrorist episodes is therefore something that should be kept in mind.

In the past fifteen years, many media have developed internal guidelines to deal with some of these tactical questions. These guidelines refer to matters such as not providing terrorists a platform for unedited statements and not endangering victims of terrorism by live reporting and resulting feedback processes.

In addition, however, it is also worth considering whether the media should not make a point that existing terrorist know-how (for example, how to get a weapon into a plane) is not transmitted to other potential terrorists. In the same vein, current anti-terrorist know-how (for example, how aircrafts are stormed by commandos) also should not be needlessly revealed so future rescue attempts are not thwarted.

However, these are minor problems for which solutions can be found with some good will. The major problems caused by media coverage, however, are not addressed by most current guidelines. I see three major problems:

1. Agenda-setting,

2. Contagion, and

3. Intimidation.

By agenda-setting, media experts refer to the phenomenon that viewers of television assign importance to what they see in proportion to the amount of time they see it.[47] It has been said that television might not be able to tell people what to think but that it is successful in telling people what to think about.

Some examples will illustrate this. When the American news media began to see what mileage they could get out of the Teheran embassy occupation story in 1979, they not only got higher ratings from an interested public, they also set the agenda of the Carter presidency. By focusing on this story even when there were no new developments, the media managed to maintain a crisis atmosphere and thereby paralysed the Carter presidency for months.

During the TWA Flight 847 incident in 1985, the three major networks spent two-thirds of their evening news time on this one hostage story, thereby blocking out other important news. President Reagan's agenda was for two weeks determined by the TV diplomacy where anchormen and reporters talked to hostages, terrorists, and ministers in Lebanon, Israel, and the United States and prepared the ground for the swap of hostages for Shi'ite prisoners in Israel. The media, in this case, too, did much more than merely record and report what was going on. They became the showmasters, switching public attention from one protagonist to the other and thereby forcing these to act under the eye of the camera in ways that did not reflect the long-term interests of the nation.

The second problem not addressed by most guidelines refers to the phenomenon of contagion. By having a marked preference for terrorist stories because of the human interest these manage to generate, the media invite crazies and political desperados to take up terrorism themselves. It is impossible to prove this without interviewing scores of terrorist imitators. Yet I am not alone in seeing such an impact. Charles Fenyvesi, a journalist who himself became a hostage during the Hanafi incident, wrote in 1977, "It is a gnawing suspicion that the news media awaken, legitimize and ... stroke fantasies of violence which might otherwise lie dormant, and on a level deeper than any court can probe, newsmen are responsible for a climate congenial to terrorism."[48]

This climate of violence is not only nourished by real violence and terrorist pseudo violence, but also by the numerous crime and action series sponsored on television by advertisers. These also prepare the ground for a disinhibition to hurt and kill in susceptible members of the audience. In time, this might also contribute to terrorism. An example of how fictional terrorism turns to real terrorism is provided by the impact of the movie *Doomsday Flight* by Rod Serling. When this extortion attempt by means of an altitude bomb placed aboard an airliner was televised, the first terrorist threat based on the scenario came in while the movie was still on the air. Within twenty-four hours, there were four more such threats to airline companies. When the movie was shown in Australia, it led to a copycat crime that cost Qantas Airways half a million dollars.[49]

Agenda-setting by the media and contagion of violence through the media can result in intimidation from the media. In a TV commercial, ABC anchorman Ted Koppel once described the task of the media as "to tell people about what's going on in the world."

This is clearly impossible in the little time and space that papers, let alone television, have. The best one can hope to do is to mirror reality in a balanced way. Yet when we look at the actual coverage of events we find—especially with foreign news—an overemphasis of extremely violent events. Yet even this violence is covered in ways that do not mirror the occurrence of political violence in different regions of the world or reflect its rise and fall. The selection depends on criteria such as visual appeals, which have more to do with media formats likely to appeal to mass audiences than with the weight of the story itself.[50] The predilection for the dramatic, the conflictual and violent events that U.S. news media have, makes for gripping images and large audiences. Yet these audiences are not just informed, they are also intimidated. Following the saturation coverage of the TWA Flight 847 incident, Europe and the Mediterranean countries noticed a new phenomenon: the scared American. It was estimated that 1.8 million Americans changed their travel reservations to foreign countries as a result of a media-induced terrorist scare.[51]

CONCLUSION

In the beginning of this chapter I quoted Franklin D. Roosevelt. During the depression he declared that the American public had nothing to fear but fear itself. Perhaps this call ought to be repeated with an eye to the media's preoccupation with violent pseudo-events staged to instill fear into our hearts. It is time that we realize we should not have our minds captivated by messages of intimidation that are administered to us under the guise of information. I do not deny that there is a place for reporting violence in our societies. Yet I think that an attempt should be made by the media to distinguish between genuine violence that would have taken place anyway and histrionic violence for audience manipulation. Whenever the latter is suspected, coverage should be minimal.

Let me finish by referring once again to Herostratus, the Greek who put the Artemis temple on fire the night Alexander the Great was born. The reason we know why Herostratus did what he did in 356 B.C. was his personal confession that he wanted to immortalize his name. The people of Ephesus thereupon decided to counteract his intent by prohibiting the mentioning of his name. Yet one man called Theopompus leaked the story, and so we know of him. The first news blackout in recorded history failed. You might argue that there will always be a Theopompus somewhere. It is true that in open societies where media compete with each other, news blackouts are difficult to bring about. Yet I am not advocating a total blackout of violent pseudo-events. Between a blackout and saturation coverage there is room for a reasonable compromise. I believe that some forms of restraint, agreed upon between the editors of all major media, would not be in conflict with the First Amendment of the U.S. Constitution.[52]

While terrorism has communicative objectives, such acts constitute—as the legal scholar Cherif Bassiouni has pointed out—"conduct" and not "speech" and thereby fall outside the constitutionally protected expression.[53]

If the terrorists cannot claim the privilege of the First Amendment, why should the media give it to them?

NOTES

1. Bernard Johnpoll, "Terrorism and the Mass Media in the United States" in *Terrorism: Interdisciplinary Perspectives*, eds. Yonah Alexander and Seymour Maxwell Finger (New York: John Jay Press, 1977), 160.

2. Alex P. Schmid and Janney De Graaf, *Insurgent Terrorism and the Western News Media* (Leiden: Center for the Study of Social Conflicts, 1980), 40.

3. Zoe C. W. Tan, "Media Publicity and Insurgent Terrorism: A Twenty-Year Balance Sheet," *Gazette* 42 (1988): 4.

4. See *Bluf!* [Periodical of Squatters in Amsterdam], no. 275, 25 June 1987: 5.

5. Schmid and de Graaf, *Terrorism and the Media*, 44.

6. Robin Gerrits, "Huivier en Luister! Een verkennend qualitatief onderzoek naar het gebruik van publiciteit door terroristen in Europa, 1875–1975" (Masters thesis, Erasmus University, Amsterdam, 1989), 144.

7. Alex P. Schmid, *Political Terrorism* (Amsterdam: North Holland Publishing Company, 1984), 221.

8. Schmid and de Graaf, *Terrorism and the Media*, 48.

9. The Ted Koppel Report "Television," Rebroadcast by NCRV on Dutch TV, 7 November 1989, 22.45 hours.

10. Eugene H. Methvin (senior editor of *Reader's Digest*) panel presentation to a conference held on 14 April 1983 published in *Terrorism and the Media in the 1980s*, eds., Sarah Midgely and Virginia Rice (Washington, D.C.: The Media Institute, 1984), 17.

11. Neil Livingston quoted in Gabriel Weimann, "Media Events: The Case of International Terrorism," *Journal of Broadcasting and Electronic Media* 31, no. 1 (Winter 1987): 23.

12. Daniel J. Boorstin, "From News Gathering to News Making: A Flood of Pseudo-events," in *Drama in Life: The Uses of Communication in Society*, eds. James E. Combs and Michael W. Mansfield (New York: Hastings House, 1976), 182–83.

13. Daniel Schorr, "The Encouragement of Violence," in *Terrorism: How the West Can Win*, ed. Benjamin Netanyahu (New York: Farrar, Straus and Giroux, 1986), 115.

14. Gerrits, "Huiver en Luister!" 132.

15. Ben Bagdikian, *The Information Machines: Their Impact on Men and the Media* (New York: Harper and Row, 1971), xii–xiii.

16. Robin Erica Wagner-Pacifici, *The Moro Morality Play: Terrorism as Social Drama* (Chicago: The University of Chicago Press, 1986), 272.

17. Ronald D. Crelinsten, "Terrorism and the Media: Problems, Solutions and Counterproblems" forthcoming in *Political Communication and Persuasion* here quoted from MS, 15.

18. This has been reported by Dutch hostages of South Moluccan train-jackings.

19. See Robert Kupperman and Jeff Kamen, *Final Warning: Averting Disaster in the New Age of Terrorism* (New York: Doubleday, 1989), 163.

20. David C. Martin and John Walcott, *Best Laid Plans: The Inside Story of America's War Against Terrorism* (New York: Harper & Row, 1989), 185.

21. *De Journalist* 36, no. 21, 2 December 1985.

22. Schmid and de Graaf, *Terrorism and the Media*, 328.

23. Martin and Walcott, *Best Laid Plans*, 189.

24. Rudolf Levy, "Terrorism and the Mass Media," *Military Intelligence* (October–December 1985): 37.

25. Robert Kupperman and Jeff Kamen, *Final Warning: Averting Disaster in the New Age of Terrorism* (New York: Doubleday, 1989), 167.

26. *The People and the Press*, Part 2 (Los Angeles: Times Mirror, September 1986), 12.

27. L. Paul Bremer, *Terrorism and the Media* (Washington, D.C.: Department of State, Bureau of Public Affairs, Current Policy No. 986, 1987), 3.

28. Combs and Mansfield, *Drama in Life*, 142.

29. The distinction "message to insiders/message to outsiders" is made by several authors. The terms used here are from Ralph E. Dowling's article "Terrorism and the Media: A Rhetorical Genre" *Journal of Communication* 36 (1986):16–17.

30. This is the conclusion of Christopher Hewitt, "Terrorism and Public Opinion: A Five Country Survey," *Terrorism and Political Violence* 2, no. 1 (Summer 1990): 145–70. The following discussion draws on data from Hewitt's survey of the public attitudes in Uruguay, Spain, Italy, Germany, and Northern Ireland.

31. Gabriel Weimann, "The Theater of Terror: Effects of Press Coverage," *Journal of Communication* 33, no. 1 (Winter 1983): 44.

32. Cited in Ralph E. Dowling, "Terrorism and the Media: 14.

33. Connie de Boer, "The Polls: Terrorism and Hijacking," *Public Opinion Quarterly* 43 (Fall 1979): 413–18.

34. *The People and the Press*, Part 2 (Los Angeles: Times Mirror, 1986), 12–13.

35. Lawrence K. Grossman (President of NBC News), "Television and Terrorism, A Common Sense Approach," *TVI Report* 6, no. 4 (1986): 1.

36. *The People and the Press*, Part 1 (Los Angeles: Times Mirror, January 1986): 34.

37. Sharon L. Sperry, "Television News as Narrative," in *Television as a Cultural Force*, eds. Richard E. Adler and Douglass Cater (New York: Praeger, 1976), 135.

38. *Time* (European edition), 19 November 1979, 23.

39. *International Herald Tribune*, 25 February 1989.

40. *NRC-Handelsblad*, 7 November 1988 and *International Herald Tribune*, 20 October 1988.

41. Headquarters United States Army Training and Doctrine Command, Office of the Commanding General, *Joint Low Intensity Conflict Project Directive* (Washington, D.C.: Department of the Army, 1 July 1985): 5–10 cited in Robert T. Terrell and Kristina Ross, "Terrorism, Censorship and the U.S. Press Corps," *Gazette* 42 (1988): 37–38.

42. Edgar Chamorro, *Packaging the Contras: A Case of CIA Disinformation* (New York: Institute for Media Analysis, 1987).

43. Michael Parenti, *Inventing Reality: The Politics of the Mass Media* (New York: St. Martin's Press, 1986), 51.

44. *International Herald Tribune*, 4 February 1989.

45. Article 19 of the U.N. Declaration of Human Rights reads: "Everyone has the right to freedom of opinion and expression; this right includes freedom to hold opinions without interference and to seek, receive and impart information and ideas through any media regardless of frontiers."

46. *The People and the Press*, Part 2, 13.

47. Shanto Iyengar and Donald R. Kinder, *News That Matters: Television and American Opinion* (Chicago: University of Chicago Press, 1987), 10.

48. Charles Fenyvesi, "Looking into the Muzzle of Terrorists," *The Quill* (July–August 1977), 18.

49. Thomas G. Krattenmaker et al., "The Political Context of Televised Violence" *Virginia Law Review* 64, no. 8 (December 1978), 1,134.

50. Michael X. Delli Carpini and Bruce A. Williams, "Terrorism and the Media: Patterns of Occurrence and Presentation," in *Terrorism, Political Violence and World Order*, ed. Henry H. Han (Lanham: University of America Press, 1984), 105.

51. See Harvey J. Iglarsh, "Fear of Flying: Its Economic Costs," *Terrorism: An International Journal*, 10, no. 1 (1987): 46–47.

52. "Congress shall make no law respecting an establishment of religion, or prohibiting the free exercise thereof; or abridging the freedom of speech, or of the press, or the right of the people peaceable to assemble, and to petition the Government for a redress of grievances"—1st Amendment of the U.S. Constitution (1789).

53. M. Cherif Bassiouni, "Media Coverage of Terrorism: The Law and the Public," *Journal of Communication* 32, no. 2 (Spring 1982).

7

Preserving Liberty in a Society under Siege: The Media and the "Guildford Four"

Abraham H. Miller

INTRODUCTION

Can a democratic society under terrorist siege properly balance its desires for liberty with its needs for order? Or will violence invariably push liberty aside as the quest for freedom from fear of terrorism becomes more important than liberty? And how does a free media strike its own balance between openly reporting the news while restraining itself from being unwittingly manipulated by terrorists?

In the aftermath of the TWA 847 episode, the professional community of journalists as well as the U.S. Congress expressed deep concern, if not outrage, at television's exploitation of the hostage crisis for ratings.[1] Not since the 1979 Tehran hostage situation had media ethics hit such a low ebb, and that episode had prompted the editors of *T.V. Guide* to take out an ad in the *Wall Street Journal* saying, "We have seen enough unwashed Iranians chanting their slogans and waving their fists on cue to last a lifetime. . . . Let the ratings be damned."[2]

T.V. Guide was pointing to the dramatic increase—a full 18 percent—in the size of the networks' news audience. With audience size determining advertising revenue, the portrayal of angry Shi'ite militants, an octogenarian holy man, and captive Americans could dramatically enhance revenue.

When the 1979 crisis subsided, the media took stock of itself and spoke of its own excesses, lessons learned, and mistakes not to be repeated.[3] All these were ignored in the midst of the drama of TWA 847, prompting the U.S. House Subcommittee on Europe and the Middle East to hold hearings on the media's involvement in the TWA hostage taking.[4]

At one point in the hearings, ABC vice president Robert Sigenthaler attempted to justify ABC's conduct in its transmission of live interviews with

Americans being held at gunpoint by Shi'ite terrorists by noting that ABC would have ended the interview if requested to do so by the hostages.

If the ethical issues raised concern, this attempt at rationalizing the media's behavior raised outrage, as Thomas Luken (D. Ohio) pointedly said to Sigenthaler:

This is so palpably offensive to me. He [the reporter] is still talking to people who are under complete control [of the terrorists]... You wouldn't even [have] had them on if the captors didn't deliver them to you. And you don't have the sophistication to recognize that the captors would have told them what to say? Privately or publicly?[5]

In all such controversies, there is talk of capping the lens and looking to the British experience, where prior restraint exists and the First Amendment does not. In Britain the Prevention of Terrorism Act coupled with internal broadcast procedures inhibits giving access to members of prohibited groups—meaning groups given to violence on both sides of the Ulster issue.[6] But the British denial of access to the camera for terrorists is not without its own set of problems.

For Irish nationalists, the policy raises questions of media bias and trust-worthiness. Within the journalistic profession, it raises questions of implicit censorship and restrictions on one's pursuit of the news—if not the "truth." (British journalists, unlike their American counterparts, who take a more pragmatic view of what journalists are capable of pursuing, espouse a professional ethos of pursuing truth.[7]) And it creates for journalists—always disproportionately dependent on government sources for information—an increased dependency because those sources are made more important as access to and transmission of the alternative perspective is obstructed.

In August 1985, the BBC, responding to government pressure, had to face the dilemma of whether or not to air the program "At the Edge of the Union," which contained interviews with two men with ties to violent organizations. In addressing the issue, Professor Paul Wilkinson stood firmly against the British government's intrusion into the BBC's affairs. As he noted, "[A]ny suggestion that an external body is bringing pressure to bear and altering editorial judgement as a result of political considerations undermines not only the credibility of the media, but the credibility of democratic government."[8]

Credibility certainly lost when the media becomes viewed less as a neutral observer of events than as a purveyor of government positions, and this is one of the costs of censorship to a democracy. A media subjected to government intrusion and restrained from pursuing certain subjects is also restricted from exposing injustice to the light of truth.

Such thoughts frequently are discussed in broad, abstract terms of political philosophy or policy. Yet the best illustration of the importance of such ideas, perhaps, is most clearly seen in how they affect individual lives. The case of the "Guildford Four" is a penetrating illustration of injustice swept away by truth and of a responsible free media refusing to permit a miscarriage of justice to persist. The case of the Guildford Four personifies the wisdom of Professor Wilkinson's comments and makes a strong case as to why capping the lens is not the solution to media excess.

From a personal perspective the case of the Guildford Four came down to one individual, Gerard Conlon; and as I walked toward Capitol Hill to interview him in March, 1990 there was the deep abiding realization that without a free media that interview itself would not be taking place, for Gerard Conlon would still be serving a sentence for a crime he did not commit.

THE GUILDFORD FOUR: A CASE STUDY

Gerard Conlon still looks young. From newspaper clips that are now nearly sixteen years old, I recognized the distinctive big, mournful eyes and the long thick mane of hair as I looked for him amid the lunch crowd in a Washington restaurant.[9] This man lost his youth to what two of Britain's law lords called one of the most serious miscarriages of justice of English law.[10] Gerard Conlon spent nearly fifteen years in a British prison for the Guildford pub bombing: a crime he did not commit. For the remainder of his life, Conlon always will be known as a member of the once infamous "Guildford Four."

The Guildford episode is about coerced and drug-induced confessions, suppressed and fabricated evidence, and of a society under siege rushing to judgement.[11] But it is also a story about the media—a responsible electronic media that refused to let the case die and exposed judicial inconsistencies to public scrutiny. In a sense, the electronic media in Britain served as a court of final judicial appeal long after the Court of Appeal, in its first hearing of the case, sent Gerard Conlon and three others back to prison, in 1977, for brutal crimes to which others had confessed in court.[12]

From an American perspective, the role of the electronic media in serious investigative journalism is somewhat unusual. In America, prestige newspapers traditionally have dominated this field by being willing to devote the time and the resources to pursue an important story. From the Pentagon Papers to Watergate to the Iran/Contra scandals, investigative reporting by newspaper reporters found and pursued these stories, and it was the electronic media that sat as spectators on the sidelines, transmitting what the newspapers uncovered. In the Guildford case, in contrast, this was decidedly not the situation.

In 1975, then age 20, Gerard Conlon, along with Paul Hill and Patrick Armstrong, all of Belfast, and Carole Richardson, Armstrong's seventeen-year-old English girlfriend, were convicted of the Guildford and Woolwich pub bombings in which seven died and forty-two were injured. The bombings, which took place in October and November 1974, were part of a larger bombing campaign conducted independently by active service units—as they choose to call themselves—of both the provisional and official Irish Republican Army operating across the Irish Sea in England. The campaign primarily, although certainly not exclusively, targeted pubs frequented by off-duty British soldiers.[13]

Paul Hill was the first arrested, and he named the others, who were part of a list of some sixty individuals he tried to implicate.[14] His confessions were contradictory and inconsistent. In going through Hill's list the police ran up against solid alibis of individuals without the least connection to the Republican movement.[15]

Conlon, Armstrong, and Richardson were vulnerable to suspicion. They were living an anti-social life style on the fringes of society. Richardson had been on drugs since she was eleven years old, and she and her boyfriend, Patrick Armstrong, lived in a "squat."[16]

The police had frequently raided their living quarters. During each raid, the young people gave their real names to the police. Ironically, the same factors that made them easy scapegoats made them unlikely bombers. IRA active service units adopted retiring life-styles that enabled them to blend into their surroundings without notice. Living in a situation that put one in contact with the police was not the way the IRA went about its business. In no event would a member of the IRA give his or her real name to the police—a name that could be crosschecked against computer files in both London and Belfast.

Except for Hill's allegations, the police had no evidence that the three other young people were involved in any IRA activity. Paul Hill was thought by police to have been involved on the periphery of the Republican movement, but Gerard Conlon, who was alleged to have been engaged in delinquent criminal activity in Belfast, had refused to acknowledge the Provisional IRA's control of the Catholic area of Belfast and, in turn, had been severely beaten by them.

Carole Richardson, alleged to be the woman in the "courting couple" that was presumed to have placed the Guildford bomb, was paraded through dozens of different police lineups and could not be identified by any of the survivors of the Guildford bombing.[17] Two of Richardson's girlfriends provided an unshaken alibi, putting her in the Elephant and Castle area of south London near the time of the Guildford bombing.[18]

From his parents' home in Belfast, Gerard Conlon watched as Paul Hill, with a blanket over his head, marched past the television cameras as the confessed Guildford bomber. Conlon says that if he really had been involved in the bombings, the first sight of Hill, or any other confederate that had been caught, would have sent him on his way to the border into the Republic of Ireland, where he would have been immune from British extradition. Little did Conlon realize as he watched the news reports that eventually Hill's confessions would ensnare not only Conlon but other members of his innocent family.[19]

The Royal Ulster Constabulary (RUC) picked up Conlon in Belfast and, according to Conlon, beat him so badly that his blood soaked through his clothing. The RUC sent the army back to his parents' home to retrieve clean clothing for the trip to England.

Transported back to England, Conlon says that he was beaten, made to stand naked in an unheated cell with open windows, and deprived of food for six days. He also experienced the sensory deprivation treatment that the British practiced at Castlereagh and Maze prisons and for which the Republic of Ireland took Britain before the European Commission on Human Rights in 1971.[20] Eventually Conlon signed a statement saying what the police wanted him to say.

Before her confession, the police drugged Carole Richardson with a combination of pethidine and barbiturates. Dr. Kamis Makos, the police surgeon, admitted that he administered an injection of pethidine to the seventeen-year-old Richardson before her confession.[21] Richardson made her confession without the presence of counsel representing her and without a single adult functioning in her behalf.

Armed with confessions from the four accused—and only the confessions—and without one shred of forensic or other evidence, the Crown proceeded to prosecute the young people. In Scotland, as well as in most American states, an indictment could not have been obtained on the basis of an uncorroborated confession.

Standing before the court, the accused repudiated the confessions. In court under oath, Conlon told how he had been brutalized by the police, an allegation the police strongly denied.

IRA terror had taken a terrible toll on Britain, and the Guildford case needs to be viewed against this backdrop. In the first ten months of 1974 there were ninety-nine bombings with deaths to nineteen people and injuries to 145 others. Spaced out as they were, the deaths and injuries might have been at a tolerable level. But on November 21, 1974, that all changed as two explosions ripped through two pubs in Birmingham, bringing death to twenty-one and injury to 180.[22]

In the aftermath, vengeful mobs attacked innocent Irish people in the streets of Birmingham, and Irish businesses in London were firebombed. Britain convulsed in anger. Public officials appealed for calm and for not making innocent Irish residents and subjects of England scapegoats for the IRA atrocities. Parliament responded by sitting through the night on November 27–28 to pass the Prevention of Terrorism Act. Mr. Roy Jenkins, the Home Secretary, stood in the Commons and called for the legislation's swift passage and then described it as "draconian" and "unprecedented in peace time" but a necessary response to the clear and present danger of the moment.[23] Unable to stop the bombings in the streets, Britain was searching for security in the symbolism and enforcement of harsh laws.

A sampling of headlines and sub-headlines from October through December 1974 provides a sense of the IRA's campaign against England: Coventry—Bomb explodes at telephone exchange, one killed; Two West End military clubs hit by bomb; Third club bombed; Three pillar box (post boxes) blasts hurt 21; Post office suspend collections; Post box bombed at Victoria; Two bombs in Chelsea injure police; Four people hurt in Belgravia bomb attack; Three hurt as car bomb explosions shatter West End shops; Bomb explodes at Harrods Newport—shopping centre blast shows similarities to other IRA bomb attacks; Northhampton—bomb explodes at RAF club; Tower of London bombed.[24]

In the midst of this state of siege, the Guildford Four were arrested and charged as were seven others named in the confessions that began with Paul Hill's attempts to implicate as a terrorist everyone he knew.

To this day, Hill's motives are not fully known. To some, he has spoken of being tortured, describing physical abuse almost identical to what Conlon says he experienced. But Gerard Conlon disputes Hill's torture. Conlon compares to his own experience how Hill looked and how the police treated Hill. Every time Conlon saw Hill in jail, he, unlike Conlon, had no marks from beatings. The police joked good-naturedly with Hill, and he always had an ample supply of cigarettes.

Despite the Crown's case standing on the uncorroborated confessions, now repudiated in court, the jury, by majority vote, accepted the police version of events and found the four guilty. In sentencing the four to life, the trial judge wished out loud that the law would have permitted him to send the four to the gallows.[25]

Even after the convictions, bombings with the identical signature continued. The IRA called the police and told them they had the wrong people and for proof they would leave an undetonated bomb identical to those used at Guildford, Woolwich, and other locations at a specified place in Mrs. Thatcher's parliamentary district.

In Aldershot, a town with a large military barracks, a time bomb was found awaiting troops coming and going for Christmas holiday at the local train station. This bomb, as the one left in Mrs. Thatcher's district, was identical to the ones used at Guildford and Woolwich.

A bomb's signature is virtually as distinctive as a human fingerprint, especially when an entire undetonated device is left for forensic examination. A bomb's wrapping, the amount of explosive, the manufacture's explosive lot, and the characteristics of the detonation device are distinctive to a bomb maker. Bombs, unlike fingerprints, can be duplicated but only by someone who has intimate knowledge of the original device. The continuation of the bombing campaign and the bomb signature should have cast doubt on the Guildford convictions.[26]

THE MAGUIRE CASE: AN ADDENDUM

Paul Hill's rambling confessions named other members of Gerard Conlon's family. First was Hugh Maguire, an uncle, but Maguire had an alibi that could not be shaken. Hill retracted and said he had the wrong Maguire and then named Conlon's Aunt, Annie Maguire. But Annie Maguire had been to the circus with her two children on the night of the bombings and could prove it. The police had to let her go. But the ever-loquacious and compliant Hill said he had misspoken. He meant, he said, that he had built the bombs in Annie Maguire's kitchen in her one-bedroom flat.

The police returned to the Maguire's home, arresting Patrick and Annie Maguire, their two sons (the youngest thirteen), a boarder, a neighbor from next door who stopped by to ask the Maguires to watch his children while he visited his sick wife in the hospital, and, ironically, Guiseppe Conlon, Gerard's invalid father, who had come from Belfast to stay with his sister, Annie Maguire, while he hired a lawyer for his son. Before departing from Belfast, Guiseppe Conlon had checked in with the Royal Ulster Constabulary to advise them of his trip.

No bombs were found. No bomb-making paraphernalia was found. No traces of explosive were found. The police alleged they had found traces of nitroglycerine in fingernail scrapings and cuttings taken from the Maguires and those caught with them. Ironically, the largest samples came from the fingernails of the invalid Guiseppe Conlon.[27] The samples were subjected to a TLC (Thin Layer Chromatography) test by an eighteen-year-old technician, who destroyed the samples, putting them beyond the reach of independent scientific analysis or reanalysis by the defense. (The test has been repudiated by its creator and is no longer in use.)[28] To the end the Maguires and the others protested their innocence. They were all convicted and sentenced to prison terms ranging from twelve years for Annie Maguire to four years for her thirteen-year-old son. On January 23, 1980, Guiseppe Conlon died in Wormwood Scrubs prison while serving his sentence. A short time before his death he met with Cardinal Basil Hume and appealed to the cardinal that he and all the others were innocent. After visiting the failing man in jail, Hume was so moved by what he saw and heard that he personally involved himself in the case.

As early as two years after the convictions of the Guildford Four and the Maguire group, the verdicts were dramatically called into question. In 1977 an IRA group attempted a strike in London's West End, an area that had been targeted frequently. In anticipation of yet another West End terrorist strike, Scotland Yard had deployed over a hundred men in the area. When the IRA gunmen attempted to shoot up a pub, the police were in position and gave chase. The IRA men took a married couple hostage and barricaded themselves in the couple's flat in London's Balcombe Street. After a siege that lasted five days, the Balcombe Street gang, as they became known, surrendered.

At their trial, the Balcombe Street gang not only adopted the traditional IRA stance of not recognizing the court's jurisdiction, but they added a new objection. They objected to not being tried for the Guildford and Woolwich bombings, events to which they had confessed and for which, they proclaimed, innocent people now sat in prison. They also had been quite willing to provide the police with detailed information on the bombings that only the bombers themselves could have known. Their confessions stood in contrast to those of the Guildford Four, which were laced with inconsistencies and contained only information the police themselves already knew.[29]

The trial proved strange, for the focus of the defense was not only to prove the IRA defendants involvement in the bombings for which they had been charged but also to show the forensic connection to the Guildford and Woolwich bombings for which the Crown refused to charge them—and for which they announced innocent people had been convicted.[30] During this unusual trial, the defense asked the police forensic expert under cross examination whether the series of bomb explosions for which the defendants were being tried fit the pattern of the Guildford and Woolwich bombings. When the forensic expert acknowledged the existence of such a pattern, which also included Guildford and Woolwich, he was then asked why he had omitted any reference to Guildford and Woolwich in his original list of similar bomb incidents for which the defendants were on trial. His response was that a bomb squad officer had directed him to omit these bombings from his evidence. When James Nevill, Scotland Yard's Bomb Squad Commander, was cross-examined by the defense, he was asked why the bomb squad had directed the forensic expert to omit Guildford and Woolwich from his evidence. Commander Nevill responded that he had been told by the Director of Public Prosecutions to tell the forensic expert to omit Guildford and Woolwich.[31]

The irony of the trial repeated itself when the defendants were cross-examined. As the defense tried to prove their clients guilty of Guildford and Woolwich, the prosecution in their cross-examinations tried to prove the defendants innocent of these two bombings.[32]

Based on these courtroom confessions, the Guildford Four requested the court of appeal for a new trial. In a stunning verdict, the Court of Appeal refused a new trial by taking it upon itself to act as if it could sit and decide what a jury would have decided in the case had the jury seen the same evidence in a retrial. The court of appeal's decision brought to the fore a legal principle that challenged the historic Anglo–Saxon tradition of trial by jury, prompting law lords Devlin and Scarman to write some years later in their review of the court's decision sustaining the conviction. "These convictions [of the Guildford Four] rest upon a fundamental error of law which threatens Britain's system of trial by jury."[33]

Alluding to Chief Justice Vaughan's decision in 1670 in the Bushell's case, lords Scarman and Devlin noted that the doctrine that Vaughan ridiculed—

that if a judge has no reasonable doubt about a verdict then the judge does not believe the jury has one either—

has been sharpened by Court of Appeal in the case of the Guildford Four as to pierce the heart of the trial by jury. The court refused to order a new trial of the new evidence. There could be no need for it, it implied, since if a judge disbelieves a witness, so must a jury—"a strange new found conclusion" [referring to Chief Justice Vaughan's original language] indeed.[34]

The issue was succinctly put by lords Devlin and Scarman when they noted, "Four new witnesses appeared who had committed twenty massacres of the same type. They said that they did this one and knew nothing of the Guildford Four. Were they lying when they said that? That was a question for juries as it certainly would have been if the evidence had been given at trial."[35]

THE ROLE OF THE MEDIA

There is a widely shared perception that the Guildford Four conviction would have been sealed after the Court of Appeal's verdict despite Cardinal Basil Hume's involvement. To some it was the inordinate power of television that kept the case alive when all other avenues of appeal seemed closed.[36] In a large sense television was playing the role Alexis de Tocqueville had depicted for the press more than a century ago when he said, "Nowadays the oppressed citizen has only one means of defense: he can appeal to the nation as a whole, and if it is deaf, to humanity at large. The press provides the only means of doing this." Tocqueville would have marveled at the ability of the electronic media—when responsibly used—to engage the hearts and minds of "humanity at large."[37]

Journalist Tom McGurk first got interested in the case as a television reporter with the Republic of Ireland's Radio Telefis Eireann (RTE). But RTE was restrained by minister of posts and telegraph Conor Cruise O'Brien's censorship legislation, which prohibited interviews with IRA members and any broadcasts that would remotely cast them in a favorable light. O'Brien, a journalist and respected man of letters, promulgated in the Republic censorship legislation that was far more draconian than anything the British had implemented in practice against the BBC or the IRA.[38] For O'Brien, television was a special medium that had been too frequently exploited to aid the terrorist cause and to serve as a reward for acts of horror. O'Brien saw no inconsistencies between his policy of censorship and his status in the international community as a man committed to the life of the mind. Inquiry was one thing. Terrorists on television had nothing to do with freedom of thought, expression, or even the public's right to know. To O'Brien, terrorists on television were simply the exploitation of the medium to further violence.

He vigorously and eloquently defended that position whenever he was called upon to do so.[39] His statement, "We in the Irish state regard the appearance of terrorists on television as an incitement to murder," is widely quoted in justification of censorship.[40] In this climate, McGurk saw the investigative reporting into a miscarriage of justice against alleged IRA activists as a high-risk undertaking that would be met with endless resistance.

McGurk left RTE and went to England, where he found, much to his dismay, that getting British TV interested in the Guildford Four was as difficult as it had proved in the Republic of Ireland. This occurred in the face of a trial record and an appellate decision that had all the earmarks of fabricated evidence sustained by a disinterested judiciary predisposed to let matters remain unchanged. Eventually, McGurk prevailed upon Jonathan Dimbleby of Yorkshire Television's "First Tuesday" and got him interested in the case.

Dimbleby produced a three-part series for Yorkshire television, which began in March 1984 with a program that took its name from a tabloid headline, "Aunt Annie's Bomb Factory." The program was about Annie Maguire and her family and how they had been caught in the net of Paul Hill's inconsistent confessions. Once British television ran the program, it became possible, ironically, for RTE of the Republic of Ireland to air it, adding momentum and further heightening the publicity of the episode.[41]

In February 1985, Annie Maguire, having served ten years for a crime she did not commit, was released from prison. David Frost put Annie Maguire, whom the tabloids had called "Evil Aunt Annie, the Kitchen Bomb Maker," on "breakfast television." Here was Annie Maguire, looking very much the housewife she was, protesting her innocence before the morning television audience composed largely of British housewives. She was hardly the image of evil aunt Annie of the tabloids.

On March 3, 1987, ITV presented its audience with "A Case That Won't Go Away." Now the powerful endless protests that Guiseppe Conlon had made on his death bed were being hammered by the medium of television to the British public. The penetrating and dramatic impact of television was helping Cardinal Hume pry open the door of justice that the court of appeal had slammed shut in 1977.

On July 3, 1987, capitalizing on the impact of the ITV program, Cardinal Hume, joined by Law lords Devlin and Scarman and former home secretaries Merlyn Rees and Lord Jenkins, met with Home Secretary Douglas Hurd. He agreed to look at the new evidence in the case. On August 14, 1987, Home Secretary Hurd announced that the police force of Avon and Somerset would reinvestigate the case of the Guildford Four. (A common British practice where the members of one police jurisdiction investigate another.) The investigators found that major sections of the alleged contemporaneous notes that police are supposed to take during interrogations, and which were presented at the original trial as such, had been fabricated. In fact, the Somerset police discovered the actual draft notes that the Surrey police used to falsify

Patrick Armstrong's "confession."[42] On October 19, 1989, Lord Lane, the lord chief justice of England, announced to a crowded courtroom, "These appeals are allowed and the convictions are quashed."[43] A photographer caught a triumphant Gerard Conlon, then thirty-four, on the courthouse steps with his clenched fist raised in the air and accompanied by his sisters. The long night of Guildford and Woolwich came to a momentary halt but not an end.

Annie Maguire and her husband, Patrick, their children, and those swept up in the raid on the Maguire home are still considered convicted terrorists. They have not been exonerated. And Gerard Conlon needs to see this blight wiped away and his father's name and reputation vindicated.

As is true of many "survivors," Gerard Conlon is a man who jumped from youth into middle age—psychologically as well as chronologically. The prison memories still haunt him, and he is as unsure of his future as he was once certain, during fifteen years of prison, that in the end his innocence would be recognized. The long nightmare of Guildford goes on, interspersed with the awakening moments of the present.

ANALYSIS AND CONCEPTUAL IMPLICATIONS

The dramatic episode is in many ways a natural experiment in miniature. It permits us to observe close up, unintruded upon by laboratory conditions, and in great depth the workings of a society's political and legal systems under actual conditions. Such a case also can be perceived as unrepresentative. We should remember, however, that the Guildford case ultimately involved eleven convictions (including the Maguire seven) and is only one of a number of cases that unobtrusively reflect on the resiliency of a liberal democratic society, even one with Britain's strong institutions and respect for the rule of law, to deal with terrorism on its own shores—a terrorism that threatens its own citizens on its own territory and that came very close in October 1984, with the devastating bomb attack in Brighton, to decapitating its government.

For Americans the decades of the 1960s and 1970s have receded into history. Comparatively speaking, the civil rights demonstrations, the urban riots, and the anti-war movement confrontations of that period were never as great a threat to human life and the functioning of government as IRA terrorism has been to Britain. Taken together, the American forms of civil strife and violence were far more likely to damage property than life and limb. Yet they exposed the inability of the system always to muster proportional responses to deal with violence and disorder. The Ohio National Guard shootings of unarmed students at Kent State University (1970), the shootings of unarmed black students, many of them in their dormitory rooms, by the Mississippi State Police at Jackson State University (1970), the 1968 Chicago police riot, and the scores of incidents documented by the National Commission on the Causes and Prevention of Violence stand as testimonials to the inability of American democracy to cope with its own experiences with political strife.[44]

The Guildford experience needs to be viewed in this larger context—not as an indictment of British justice but as a symptom of the stress violence places on the institutions of a democratic society trying to respond to the attacks on its very existence while balancing its commitments to the cherished rule of law.

Students of terrorism long have acknowledged that terrorism and free institutions do not mix well. Societies under siege frequently believe it is necessary to deal with self-preservation even in ways that trample civil liberties. Terrorism in Turkey led to a military coup in 1980. In Uruguay, once South America's oldest democracy, Tupamaro-spawned terrorism led to a military takeover. In Germany and Italy, terrorism has resulted in the passage of strong anti-terrorist legislation that leans on the side of order over liberty, as does Britain's Prevention of Terrorism Act.[45] In the U.S. Senate consideration is being given to granting broad and discretionary powers to American federal agencies to combat the war in the shadows on foreign soil, a proposal that potentially can raise profound and difficult issues of international law. Under the proposed legislation, "the President may take whatever measures may be necessary to enforce United States criminal jurisdiction over any offense committed as part of international terrorism or internal drug trafficking." "Whatever measures" includes crossing international boundaries to apprehend in those cases where a foreign government refuses to or is incapable of cooperating with the apprehension and prosecution of the offender.[46]

This proposed legislation reflects a problem confronted by many democracies as they are increasingly frustrated in dealing with terrorism and other forms of political violence as a criminal justice issue. That frustration is felt most keenly in police circles where the normal course of training, experience, and activity do not lend themselves to combat the war in the shadows. As terrorism mounts and police and civilian casualties reach serious proportions, terrorists become viewed as soldiers without uniforms engaged in combat and as something other than a normal criminal justice problem.

In that sense the case of the Guildford Four is an episode symptomatic of a society under siege, where the police were willing to short-circuit civil liberties in the mistaken belief that this was an effective way to combat terrorism. This response was not unlike that which occurred in many American police departments in the turbulent days of the 1960s.

Ultimately, however, such tactics contribute little to the preservation of democracy. Instead, they call into question the very legitimacy of the system and make it appear that the system has resorted to its own brand of violence to deal with its political frustrations, just as the terrorists have used violence to deal with their political grievances.

The tainted confessions of the Guildford Four and the questionable forensic evidence in the Maguire case are appearing to be symptomatic of Britain's democracy straining under the weight of terrorism. As the media once called Guildford "the case that won't go away," so, too, now emerges a similar case involving the convicted Birmingham bombers, who were thought responsible for the savage pub bombings that brought about an all night Parliamentary session that resulted in the passage of Britain's Prevention of Terrorism Act.

But were they? In February 1988, the Court of Appeal heard evidence from former police officers that the Birmingham Six had been beaten in jail, and new questions have arisen as to the accuracy and reliability of the forensic evidence that served as the basis for their convictions.[47] Although the court of appeal turned them down—as initially were the Guildford Four—a police investigation is looking into the case.[48]

When the Guildford convictions were quashed in Old Bailey on October 19, 1989, Father Paddy Smyth and Miss Nyala Kelly, observers from the Irish Commission on Prisoners Overseas, were sitting in the gallery. They had strong praise for the ability of the British system of justice to correct its error in the Guildford case. But for them, as for many others, there are still nineteen Irish prisoners sitting in British jails who were wrongfully convicted.[49] The Irish Commission will now focus its concerns on those cases, beginning with the Birmingham Six.[50]

Throughout these episodes, it has been the media that has served as a court of final appeal long after the judicial system seemed incapable of rendering justice. In 1985, Granada's "World in Action" hired two scientists to replicate the Griess tests used to discover nitroglycerine on the hands of the Birmingham Six. The tests showed positive for a wide range of substances that commonly exist and that the men were known to have handled: playing cards, train-table finishes, cigarette packets, and cigarettes. The Court of Appeal in 1988, nonetheless, refused to doubt the "scientific evidence" despite the tests' imprecision and contradictory testimony from the scientists who conducted the tests. The court of appeal also refused to believe the testimony of former police officers that the Birmingham Six were beaten in jail.[51]

These episodes—and others that do not emanate from terrorism—have produced far reaching public concern about the police. The police in democratic society are often the first line of defense against terrorism. But if the police overreact and seek to trample the democratic process underfoot, as they may be prone to do because police seldom have the training or resources to deal appropriately with a campaign of violence launched by political terrorists, then the robust existence of free institutions, especially a responsible media, is vital to the protection of liberty from those who would extinguish it in the name of order.

For those who seek to cap the media's lens, the lesson from the Guildford Four and from the chilling advocacy of prior restraint is that a free and responsible media is absolutely essential to the preservation of liberty. (And freedom is no guarantee that media excess and irresponsible behavior still will not occur.) Those who judge the media by its excesses—and only its excesses—have forgotten the functional role of the media in preserving and securing freedom. A democratic society under siege might well need a free and responsible media more than does a normally functioning democracy. For a free media can help cause restraint to be exercised so that freedom and legitimacy are not readily extinguished in the pursuit of a false sense of order.

In the early 1970s, Irish broadcasters fought to have their lenses uncapped and lost. Under Section 31 of the Irish Broadcasting Act, any interviews with members of the official or provisional wings of the IRA are forbidden. Even coverage of Sinn Fein (the political wing of the IRA) events is allowed only if the sound is squelched.[52]

In 1971, when Sean MacStiofain, the chief of staff of the IRA, was interviewed by RTE radio, the government of the Republic had the journalist arrested, Section 31 put into law, and the entire RTE Authority (the board of governors) fired.

Since its implementation, Section 31 has become a source of journalistic farcical comedy. Now that Sinn Fein contests elections in both the South and the North, Section 31 mutes the coverage of Sinn Fein candidates making election speeches, and the victory speeches of successful candidates are shown with a voiceless moving mouth. Even Britain's Prevention of Terrorism Act has not resulted in this kind of impenetrable censorship, and Sinn Fein voters in the Republic merely have to press a button changing the television station from RTE to BBC or ITV to hear the sound of their candidate's words. In fact, more viewers in the Republic watch the BBC than RTE. Consequently, the censorship only hinders those viewers who remain loyal to RTE.

The comical aspect of the Republic's Section 31 ceases to be amusing when one realizes the serious political implications of such censorship: RTE never could have kept alive before the public the case of the Guildford Four or any others wrongly accused of committing Republican violence. In Scotland, Gerard Conlon never could have been tried. In a besieged Britain, free institutions, underscored by a vital free media, could undo the mistake of having convicted him, but in the Republic of Ireland those who spoke in his behalf would have need of a nation of lip readers to understand their pleas over a muted sound track.

VALUE INCONGRUITY AND SOCIAL CHANGE: THEORETICAL CONSIDERATIONS

Social change theorists see a society's failure to adhere to its own primary values as a source of social disequilibrium. When espoused values become "dissynchronized" from a society's value practices, the institutional integrity of the social system is undermined. As credibility and legitimacy are necessary to sustain institutional integrity, any loss of credibility and legitimacy moves the system toward disharmony.[53]

Cast into the analytical framework of systems theory, social change theory sees the neglect or abuse of civil liberties in a democratic society as a force that exacerbates the loss of credibility and legitimacy. From this perspective, the mistaken belief that there are short cuts to justice that promote order at reasonable costs to civil liberties plays directly into terrorists' attempts to undermine society.

Terrorists seek to destabilize society by calling into question its legitimacy. If a society's primary values can be shown to be at variance with its actual practices—if justice and the rule of law are only social myths designed to promote political quiescence—then the terrorists have found a justification for their violence. The exposed clash between values and practice does more damage to the society than terrorist violence.

Chalmers Johnson's application of systems theory to revolutionary change proposes that the course of action taken by those in power—and not those in the streets—is most likely to determine the system's ability to respond to the forces that threaten it.[54] This formulation from systems theory follows the perspective of Alexis de Tocqueville, who saw the "Old Regime's" inability to respond appropriately to the dynamics of social change as an important factor in the prelude to the French Revolution.[55] Tocqueville wrote, "Most of all, I am struck, not by the genius of those who served the Revolution's cause, but by the stupidity of those, who without in the least wishing it, caused it to occur."[56] In much the same way, systems theorists see government policy as either restoring a system's value integration or accelerating its loss of legitimacy.

If the police do not fight terrorism through the rule of law, then they contribute to the acceleration of the system's delegitimation. This is the case regardless of whether the police are acting in behalf of government policy or on their own.

By exposing those policies that lead to the undermining of legitimacy, the media in liberal democracy can serve the institutional function of moving the system back into harmony. In a liberal democracy, competing institutions represent different loci of power, and when one institution succumbs to the stress of violence, others can move to rectify the society appealing to its primary values. In America this is precisely the role the media played in the early days of the civil rights movement as the camera captured the incongruity between racial segregation and America's espoused values.

In authoritarian and totalitarian societies, the absence of both institutional independence and competition can result in the governing elite awakening one day, as did Tocqueville's Old Regime, to discover the cracks in the system as if they developed overnight. They, of course, did not, but the nonexistence of competing institutions preempted all hope of warnings.

The media, of course, will not always behave responsibly and at times will itself, through its own disregard of basic ethics and its rush to capture a story, falsely undermine the credibility of democratic government. But the ultimate strength of democratic society is that competing free institutions will themselves correct such abuses in ways censorship never can or will.

If Americans and Britons are aware of their respective media's excesses and abuses, it is because the media in a free society is not only in competition with other institutions but with itself. The media is not a monolith but an aggregation of different modes of expression whose free competition with one another takes place both in the marketplace and in the realm of ideas. The media itself is frequently its own harshest critic. If we believe that a free people, given free access to ideas, will recognize truth over falsehood, then we have less to fear from media excess than from censorship. As the Guildford case was ultimately the belated triumph of justice in a free society, so, too, it was the triumph of a free media.

NOTES

1. House Subcommittee on Europe and the Middle East of the Committee on Foreign Affairs, *The Media, Diplomacy, and Terrorism in the Middle East*, 30 July 1985.

2. The original statement appeared in *TV Guide*, 22 December 1979 as an editorial.

3. For a discussion of the media's behavior in the Tehran hostage crisis, see Robert A. Friedlander, "Iran: The Hostage Seizure, the Media, and International Law," in *Terrorism, the Media, and the Law*, ed. Abraham H. Miller (Dobbs Ferry, N.Y.: Transnational Publishers, Inc., 1982), 51–68.

4. House Subcommittee, *Media, Diplomacy and Terrorism.*

5. House Subcommittee, *Media, Diplomacy and Terrorism*, 126.

6. Rt. Honorable Lord Shackleton, *Review of the Operation of the Prevention of Terrorism (Temporary Provisions) Acts 1974 and 1976* (London: Her Majesty's Stationery Office, 1978). For a discussion of the operation of the Prevention of Terrorism Act, see Abraham H. Miller, "Terrorism and the Media in the United Kingdom: Government Policy as Symbolic Ritual," in *Democratic Responses to International Terrorism*, ed. David Charters (Dobbs Ferry, N.Y.: Transnational Publishers, in press).

7. Tony Fleck, "Serving the Divided Province," *Airwaves* (Summer 1986).

8. BBC World Report (Transcript) 32/85 "The Media and Terrorism." Professor Paul Wilkinson (then of Aberdeen University) and *New York Post* columnist John O'Sullivan discussed for the BBC World Service the issue of whether journalists should talk to people who espouse violence.

9. Personal interview with Gerard Conlon, Washington, D.C., 16 March 1990. The author gratefully acknowledges the assistance of Rep. Joseph Kennedy's staff, especially Ms. Sarah Burns, in setting up this interview.

10. Lord Devlin and Lord Scarman, "Justice and the Guildford Four," *Times* (London), 30 November 1988, 16; "Guildford Appeal," *Times* (London), editorial, 17 January 1989.

11. "Guildford Pub Bomb Four Get Fresh Hearing," *Times* (London), 17 January 1989.

12. A generally accurate summary of the case can be found in "Guildford Pub

Bombings: Convictions Quashed," *Survey of Current Affairs* (New York: British Information Services), 19, no. 11, 405–406.

13. The Horse and Groom pub in Guildford was hit first. This attack occurred on October 5, 1974, resulting in six killed and thirty-five injured. In Woolwich, the Kings Arms pub was bombed on November 7, 1974, and two were killed.

14. The number sixty comes from my interview with Gerard Conlon. Press reports, before Hill's identity was made public, put the number at thirty. These reports, however, had numerous inconsistencies. The exact number might be in dispute, but the incontrovertible fact is that Paul Hill named a lot of people who had solid alibis and were subsequently released from police custody.

15. Interview with Gerard Conlon. See also Chris Mullin, "Caught for Life by Cruel Chance," *New Statesman*, 1 January 1982, 6.; "Pub Blast Killing: Three Freed with Costs," *Evening Standard* (London), 9 February 1975, 9.

16. These "squats" were raided by police looking for common criminals. See Mullin, "Caught for Life," 7 for other detail of Richardson's and Armstrong's lifestyles that made them unlikely members of the IRA active service.

17. Grant McKee, "The Other Innocent Victims of the Guildford Bombings," *Listener*, 26 June 1986.

18. Mullin, "Caught for Life," 7.

19. Interview with Gerard Conlon.

20. The case dragged out for five years. In 1976, the European Commission on Human Rights found Britain guilty of inhuman and degrading treatment and torture. In 1978, the European Court of Human Rights heard the verdict on appeal and dropped the torture conviction. Yet the European Court of Human Rights concluded that inhuman and degrading treatment was officially sanctioned. According to Peter Taylor, *Beating the Terrorists* (Middlesex, U.K.: Penguin, 1980), the use of coercive methods continued well into 1979.

21. "Bomb Four Get Fresh Hearing," *Times*.

22. Shackleton, *Review of the Prevention Acts*.

23. *Hansard Parliamentary Debates*, 5th series, vol. 882, House of Commons, Session 1974–75, 25th November to 6th December, 1974 (London: Her Majesty's Stationery Office, 1974), 35.

24. Headlines and sub-headlines are from the *Times* (London) from October to December 1974.

25. Interview with Gerard Conlon.

26. The unexploded bomb was found on December 20, 1974, and this provided valuable and clear forensic evidence that it matched the Guildford, Woolwich, and other bombings.

27. Christopher Price, "Aunt Annie's Bomb Kitchen," *New Statesman*, 9 March 1984, 12.

28. Price, "Bomb Kitchen," 12.

29. Queen's Counsel, Sir Michael Havers (later attorney general), who led the prosecution, claimed that the inconsistencies were part of a technique designed to thwart interrogation. See McKee, "The Other Victims," and Mullin, "Caught for Life," 6.

30. Not only did the Crown refuse to prosecute the Balcombe Street gang for the Guildford and Woolwich bombings, but it suppressed the forensic evidence that would

have linked these bombings to other bombings to which the Balcombe Street gang confessed. Mullin, "Caught for Life," 7; Interview with Gerard Conlon.

31. Mullin, "Caught for Life," 7.

32. Mullin, "Caught for Life," 8; Interview with Gerard Conlon.

33. Devlin and Scarman, "Justice and the Guildford Four," 16.

34. Devlin and Scarman, "Justice and the Guildford Four," 16.

35. Devlin and Scarman, "Justice and the Guildford Four," 16.

36. Gerard Conlon believes that television was important but that no one was as important as Cardinal Basil Hume, with his commitment to see justice triumph. Television itself might well have the last word on the subject. With John Hurt cast in the role of Labor MP Chris Mullin, British viewers (and later American viewers on HBO) will be treated to a forthcoming docudrama titled, "The Investigation: Inside a Terrorist Bombing" (American title), which deals with the Birmingham and Guildford cases through Mullin's own indefatigable efforts to find justice. *New York Times*, 19 April 1990, C–22.

37. Alexis de Tocqueville, *Democracy in America*, vol. 1, ed. Phillips Bradley (New York: Vintage Books), 189.

38. Tom McGurk, "A Second Look," *Listener*, 6 January 1989.

39. Tom McGurk, "A Second Look," and "Irish Cracked," *New Statesman*, 9 August 1985, 8.

40. See, for example, "Lost in the Terrorist Theater," *Harpers* (October 1984): 51.

41. McGurk, "A Second Look."

42. *Hansard Parliamentary Debates*, House of Commons, Session 1988–89 (London: Her Majesty's Stationery Office, 1989), vol. 158, no. 156, cols. 271–85 and "Five Officers Mislead Court. Q.C. Says," *Times* (London), 20 October 1989, 3.

43. *Times* (London), 20 October 1989, 1. Lord Lane concluded that the investigating Surrey police officers "must have lied" at the original trial. They are currently under investigation. Ibid., 2.

44. Most of these events are documented in National Commission on the Causes and Prevention of Violence, *The Report of the National Commission on the Causes and Prevention of Violence and Supplemental Studies* (Washington, D.C.: U.S. Government Printing Office, 1968).

45. Vittorfranco S. Pisano, *Contemporary Italian Terrorism: Analysis and Countermeasures* (Washington, D.C.: Law Library, Library of Congress, 1979); Miklos Radvany *Anti-terrorist Legislation in the Federal Republic of Germany* (Washington, D.C.: Law Library, Library of Congress, 1979).

46. Senator Connie Mack (R., Fla.) introduced this legislation in the 1st Session of the 101st Congress. The bill was co-sponsored by senators D'Amato, Helms, Gorton, Coats, and Cochran.

47. Paul Foot, "Come Forward, Tell the Truth and Be Maligned," *New Statesman* 5 (February 1988): 10–11.

48. On April 14, 1991, the court of appeals overturned the convictions of the Birmingham Six on similar grounds as the Maguire Seven and the Guildford Four. The police investigation was shown to be filled with falsified evidence. See Craig R. Whitney, "British Free 6 Jailed in '74 I.R.A. Blasts," *The New York Times*, 15 March 1991.

49. The number does not include the Maguire Seven, all of whom served their sentences.

50. "Victory Salute Heralds A New Life," *Times* (London), 20 October 1989, 3.

51. "Victory Salute," 3.

52. McGurk, "Irish Cracked," 8.

53. Chalmers Johnson, *Revolutionary Change* (Boston: Little, Brown and Co., 1966), especially chapters 4 and 5.

54. Johnson, *Revolutionary Change*, diagram, 106.

55. Alexis de Tocqueville, *The Old Regime and the French Revolution*, trans. and ed. Stuart Gilbert (New York: Anchor Doubleday, 1955), especially 97–107.

56. Tocqueville quoted in Melvin Richter, "Tocqueville's Contributions to the Theory of Revolution," in *Revolution*, ed. C. J. Friedrich (New York: Atherton Press, 1967), 97. This aspect of Tocqueville's thought is far less commonly referred to than his allusions to what modern theorists call "rising expectations." In the latter instance Tocqueville is speaking largely to the economic conditions of revolution, while in the former he is referring to the erosion of regime legitimacy, which is the issue germane to the argument of this paper.

8

Low-intensity Conflict: Terrorism and Guerrilla Warfare in the Coming Decades

Bruce Hoffman

INTRODUCTION

Today at least twenty-six conflicts are being fought in some thirty countries around the globe.[1] They include the protracted, low-level, mostly urban, terrorist campaign waged by the Provisional Irish Republican Army against British forces in Northern Ireland; the primarily rural insurrection prosecuted by communist insurgents against the Aquino government in the Philippines; the combination rural guerrilla/urban terrorism campaign of the left-wing FMLN (Farabundo Manti Liberation Front) in El Salvador; the Maoist revolution being forced on Peru by the Shining Path; the rural guerrilla wars being fought—often in league with narcotics traffickers—in Colombia by left-wing groups such as the FARC (Revolutionary Armed Forces of Colombia), ELN (National Liberation Army), and ELP (Popular Army of Liberation); the bitter civil war between Tamils and Sinhalese that is slowly exhausting itself in Sri Lanka; and the variety of independence, secessionist, and even counter-revolutionary struggles presently being fought in Nicaragua, Angola, Namibia, Mozambique, Chad, Liberia, Ethiopia, the Sudan, Burma, Cambodia (formerly Kampuchea), and Indonesia.

None of these contemporary conflicts conforms to the traditionally accepted notion of war as fighting between the armed forces of two or more established states. Instead, they all involve irregular forces—guerrilla armies, national liberation movements, terrorist groups, private militias, and narcotics traf-fickers—arrayed either individually or in various combinations against state military and police forces, international peacekeeping teams, and, in some cases, rival irregular forces.[2]

This trend toward a world of conflict involving mostly non-state actors is by no means evanescent. Since 1945, some 105 conflicts have been fought throughout the world; only thirty-one pitted the armed forces of one state against another.[3] Apart from the international legal and diplomatic ramifications of a world where non-state actors wield power and influence equal, if not superior, to many established nation-states, this development has far-reaching consequences for the nature and conduct of warfare.

As conflict throughout the closing decades of the twentieth century has become more "unconventional," it has become more indiscriminate as well. Clashes between standing armies on demarcated battlefields have been supplanted by terrorist bombings, guerrilla hit-and-run attacks, kidnappings of foreigners by private militias, and vengeance campaigns by narcotics traffickers. Innocent civilians—who find themselves in the wrong place at the wrong time when a terrorist bomb explodes, who are inextricably caught in the cross fire of a guerrilla assault, who are taken hostage because of the passport they carry, or who are victimized by government death squads—now account for the vast majority of persons killed in international conflict. Indeed, according to one estimate, four-fifths of the four million people killed in these conflicts during the first half of the 1980s were civilians.[4] Moreover, in 1989 alone conflict in Third World countries displaced approximately 15.1 million people—up from 14.4 million in 1988. Since 1985 fighting has forced an average of 2,700 persons a day to leave their homes and become refugees.[5]

Because virtually all this death and dislocation occurred in the third world, the crumbling barriers between Eastern and Western Europe, the nascent "democratization" of the communist bloc, the solidification of U.S.–U.S.S.R. relations and, as Francis Fukuyama describes it, "the end of history as such" (that is, "the end of mankind's ideological evolution and the universalization of Western liberal democracy as the final form of human government") will— as Fukuyama himself admitted—probably have little impact on the rest of the world, whose dirty wars, bloody power struggles, and endemic conflict accounted for the vast majority of the decade's civilian casualties.

This chapter assesses the implications of these trends in contemporary international conflict on low-intensity conflict (as these non-"wars" are often categorized) and, particularly, U.S. military policy in the coming decade.

INTERNATIONAL TERRORISM

One of the distinguishing features of international terrorism during the 1980s was the large number of fatalities that terrorists inflicted. Although the total volume of terrorist activity increased by only a third compared to the previous decade, terrorists killed twice as many people.[6] International terrorism's increasing lethality is reflected in the 75 percent increase in the number of individual terrorist incidents resulting in fatalities and, even more so, in the 135 percent rise in the number of incidents that caused ten or more fatalities.[7] These patterns, which have continued throughout most of the past decade, indicate that terrorist violence has become more indiscriminate, with attacks increasingly directed toward ordinary citizens who happen to be in the wrong place at the wrong time. Terrorists apparently have come to regard victims as an important ingredient of a successful attack. Unfortunately, the reasons that account for this phenomenon give little cause for hope that the above trends will reverse in the coming decade.

Indeed, given that the vast majority of the globe's terrorism is fueled by nationalism, irredentism, and religion rather than ideology, it seems unlikely that the evolving rapprochement between East and West will have a salutary impact on either the level or lethality of international terrorism.[8] On the contrary, as the once rigid, bi-polar international order loosens and super-power influence declines, regional nationalist and ethnic tensions—often combined with intercommunal religious antagonism—long held in check or kept dormant by the cold war may erupt to produce even greater levels of non-state violence than occurred during the 1980s.[9]

Aggrieved members of a variety of worldwide ethnic and religious groups are increasingly turning to violence in pursuit of their nationalist, irredentist, or religious aims. Only thirteen identifiable terrorist groups were active in 1969, for example, compared with seventy-four today. However, not only has the number of terrorist groups tripled during the past two decades, but nationalist/separatist (in many cases combined with a strong religious component) goals and causes, as opposed to ideological reasons, have emerged as the predominant motivation of contemporary terrorism. Of the seventy-four international terrorist organizations active today, fifty-eight can be classified as nationalist/separatist, including twelve for whom religious identification is a factor as well, while only fifteen are ideologically-motivated groups.[10]

Older terrorist organizations, such as the Palestine Liberation Organization (PLO), the Provisional Irish Republican Army (PIRA), and the Basque ETA, have demonstrated to this new generation of terrorist organizations how long-standing, often ignored or forgotten, causes or grievances can be resurrected and thrust onto the world's agenda through a series of well-orchestrated and attention-riveting acts. Although none of these older groups has attained its long-range aims, the attention that they have received and the stature they have been accorded in some sections of the international community send a powerful message to similarly aggrieved peoples throughout the world.

The premier example of terrorism's power to rocket a cause from obscurity to renown was the murder of eleven Israeli athletes seized by Palestinian terrorists at the 1972 Munich Olympic Games. Those who had not heard of or who had dismissed the Palestinians were neither as ignorant nor as complacent after the grisly denouement played out in front of the worldwide audience following the sporting event. It is probably not entirely coincidental that two years later PLO Chairman Yasir Arafat was invited to address the United Nations General Assembly, and shortly afterward the PLO was accorded observer status in that organization. The PLO—a non-state actor—now has diplomatic relations with more countries than Israel. This message is not lost on the Shi'a, Sikhs, Armenians, Azeris, Kashmiris, Tamils, Catalonians, Corsicans, Puerto Ricans, and other ethnic minorities prosecuting their own violent campaigns for publicity and recognition today.

An explanation for the increasing lethality of terrorist acts is that public attention is not as readily claimed as it was in the past.[11] The proliferation of terrorist movements and the consequent increase in terrorist incidents have created problems for both old and—especially—new groups who now must compete with others for a wider audience share. Terrorists have therefore been forced to undertake spectacular and, unfortunately, bloody deeds in order to achieve the same effect a small action would have had ten years ago.[12] Six of the ten international terrorist incidents that have caused the greatest number of fatalities, for example, have occurred since 1983. A Tamil separatist group in Sri Lanka, the Liberation Tigers of Tamil Eelam, is a specific case in point. Although the group was formed in 1972 and commenced terrorist operations three years later, the Liberation Tigers went largely unnoticed outside of Sri Lanka until 1986, when a bomb placed aboard a Sri Lankan airliner delayed at Colombo International Airport killed twenty-one persons and wounded forty others—many of whom were foreign nationals. The large number of fatalities compared to previous Tamil terrorist incidents, combined with the fact that several foreigners were among the bombing's victims, assured the terrorists the international attention that their previous, more discriminate, campaign exclusively against Sri Lankan targets had lacked.

Terrorism's trend toward increasing lethality, however, is not simply a product of more numerous groups that are competing for the attention of a world audience inured to terrorist violence and bloodshed. Terrorists are also more adept at killing.[13] Not only are their weapons smaller, more sophisticated,[14] and deadlier—as exemplified by the two-step, barometric, time-triggered bomb constructed from an estimated 300 grams of a Czech-manufactured plastic explosive[15] and hidden inside a radio cassette player that brought down Pan Am Flight 103 in December 1988—but terrorists have greater access to these weapons through their alliances with foreign governments.[16]

In addition to their standard arsenal of small arms and plastic explosives, "state-sponsored" terrorists, for example, used a truck carrying a bomb consisting of some 12,000 pounds of high explosives, whose power was enhanced by canisters of flammable gases, to kill 241 U.S. Marines in what has been described as the "largest non-nuclear blast ever detonated on the face of the earth";[17] deployed nearly 200 sophisticated, multifused, Soviet-manufactured acoustic mines to disrupt shipping entering the Suez Canal from the Red Sea; carried out a coordinated car-bomb attack in the Karachi commercial district that killed seventy-two persons and wounded more than 250 others; and fabricated the device that exploded aboard Pan Am Flight 103. It is not surprising, therefore, to find that state-sponsored terrorist incidents were eight times more lethal than those carried out by groups acting on their own.[18]

Admittedly, diminishing communist-bloc support and training of various international terrorist organizations will make it more difficult for those groups to operate.[19] However, recent reports that during the past decade Czechoslovakia shipped more than 1,000 tons of *Semtex* plastic explosive (the same type used against Pan Am Flight 103) to Libya ensure that at least those terrorist organizations favored by Colonel Qaddafi[20] will have ample supplies of that explosive for years to come.[21] Moreover, in addition to the Libyan shipments, Czechoslovakia is also thought to have exported some 40,000 tons of *Semtex* to Syria, North Korea, Iran, and Iraq—countries long cited by the U.S. Department of State as sponsors of international terrorist activity. Accordingly, irrespective of communist-bloc action, terrorists are assured an almost inexhaustible international stockpile of plastic explosives on which to draw for future operations.[22]

There is also the terrifying prospect that, as airport security and bomb detection technology improves, terrorists will increasingly turn to readily available shoulder-fired, precision-guided surface-to-air missiles as the only practical means to attack commercial aircraft. A single terrorist trained in the use of this weapon could position himself at the edge of any airport's runway and fire at incoming or departing passenger planes. Indeed, on the few occasions in the past when guerrillas have targeted non-military aircraft with surface-to-air missiles, they have had spectacularly devastating results. Guerrillas downed two Rhodesian passenger jets with SAM–7s in 1978 and 1979, killing a total of 107 persons. Sudanese rebels used a SAM–7 in 1986 to shoot down a Sudan Airways commercial jet, killing all sixty persons on board. And Polisario Front guerrillas in Morocco downed an American DC7 weather plane in 1988 with a Soviet missile, killing its five-man crew.[23] Given the proven effectiveness of such weapons, the British Army reportedly has responded to alleged PIRA possession of Libyan-supplied SAM–7s[24] by equipping its helicopters in Northern Ireland with infrared defensive systems—described as "the most sophisticated anti-missile systems in use by the North Atlantic Treaty Organization (NATO) forces in Europe"—to thwart missile attacks.[25]

Weapons aside, an almost Darwinian principle of natural selection seems to affect all terrorist groups so that every new terrorist generation appears to be tougher, smarter, and more ruthless than the last. A dedicated "hardcore" of some twenty to thirty terrorists, for example, now composes a fourth generation of Germany's Red Army Faction (RAF) terrorist organization. In contrast to their more idealistic predecessors, who more than twenty years ago embarked on an anti-establishment campaign of non-lethal bombings and arson attacks, the present generation has pursued a strategy of cold-blooded assassination. During the past three years the terrorist group has murdered five prominent—and heavily guarded—formerly West Germans.

In a most sophisticated incident involving the death of financier Alfred Herrhausen in December 1989, a state-of-the-art remote-control bomb, concealed in a parked bicycle, was triggered by a microscopic light-beam just as the car carrying Herrhausen passed.[26] Almost as disturbing, the perpetrators—and their fellow conspirators—have eluded what is perhaps the most sophisticated anti-terrorist machinery in the world. More recently, in April 1991, the director of the agency Treuhand (Public Trust), established to liquidate formerly state-run enterprises in East Germany, Detlev Karsten Rohwedder, was killed in his home by a sniper. The RAF claimed responsibility for the murder.[27]

Finally, a key reason for terrorism's increased lethality is the growing incidence of violence motivated by a religious, as well as a nationalist/separatist, imperative.[28] Certainly, the relationship between terrorism and religion is not new. In fact, as David Rapoport points out in his seminal study of what he terms "holy terror," until the nineteenth century "religion provided the only acceptable justifications for terror."[29] This form of terrorism has occurred throughout history, although in recent decades it has largely been overshadowed by nationalist/separatist or ideologically motivated terrorism.[30]

The record of terrorist acts by Shi'a Islamic groups reinforces, for example, the causal link between religion-motivated terrorism and terrorism's growing lethality. Although these groups have committed only 8 percent of all international terrorist incidents since 1982, those incidents are responsible for 30 percent of the total number of deaths.[31] Terrorism motivated by religion is by no means restricted to Islamic terrorist groups exclusively in the Middle East. Many of the characteristics of Shi'a terrorist groups—the legitimization of violence based on religious precepts, the sense of alienation, the existence of a terrorist movement in which the activists are the constituents, and preoccupation with the elimination of a broadly defined category of "enemies"—also are apparent among militant Christian White supremacists in the United States and radical Jewish messianic terrorist movements in Israel. The elimination of whole segments of society is, in fact, a major objective of the White supremacists and the Jewish zealots. Both groups view violence as morally justified and as an expedient toward the attainment of the religious and racial "purification" of their respective countries. In 1987, for example, fourteen American White supremacists were indicted on federal charges of plotting to engage in indiscriminate, mass killing through poisoning municipal water supplies in two major American cities.[32] Similarly, in 1984, two separate groups of Israeli religious fanatics were convicted of plotting to blow up the Dome of the Rock in Jerusalem, Islam's third holiest shrine, in order to provoke a cataclysmic holy war between Muslims and Jews that would force the Jewish Messiah to intervene.[33]

That terrorists motivated by a religious imperative can contemplate such massive acts of death is a reflection of their belief that violence is a sacramental act or a divine duty. Terrorism thus assumes a transcendental dimension,[34] and its perpetrators are unconstrained by the political, moral, or practical constraints that affect other terrorists. Whereas secular terrorists generally consider indiscriminate violence immoral and counterproductive,[35] religious terrorists regard such violence as both morally justified and expedient for the attainment of their goals.

Religious and secular terrorists also differ in their constituencies. Religious terrorists are at once activists and constituents engaged in what they regard as a "total war." They perform their terrorist acts for no audience but themselves. Thus the restraints on violence that are imposed on secular terrorists by the desire to appeal to an uncommitted constituency are not relevant to the religious terrorist. Finally, religious and secular terrorists have different perceptions of themselves and their violent acts. Secular terrorists regard violence as a means to an end—a way of instigating the correction of a flaw in a system that is basically good or to foment the creation of a new system.[36] Religious terrorists, on the other hand, regard themselves not as components of a system but as "outsiders" who seek vast changes in the existing order.[37] This sense of alienation enables the religious terrorist to contemplate far more destructive and deadly types of terrorist operations than secular terrorists would and, in fact, to view violence as an end in itself.

Meanwhile, as terrorists become more lethal and the targets of their struggles more indiscriminate, a new generation of terrorists is coming of age throughout the world. They have grown up in the refugee camps outside Beirut, the shanty towns ringing Lima, the sectarian ghettos in Belfast, and the slums of San Salvador. They eschew political compromise and negotiation and embrace violence and armed struggle as an ameliorating cathartic, if not the only solution to their plight.[38] They are Palestinians, aged only twelve or fourteen years, who receive their education as soldiers fighting for *al-Fatah* in southern Lebanon[39] before graduating to more extremist terrorist organizations and more desperate acts of violence. A typical product of this environment perhaps is the terrorist belonging to the Abu Nidal Organization who was the lone survivor of that group's December 1985 attack on the Rome airport. A nineteen-year old from a third generation exile family, Mahmoud Ibrahim Khaled grew up in Beirut surrounded by the squalor of refugee camps and the violence engulfing Lebanon. His home was in the Shatila refugee camp—the scene of the massacre carried out by Israeli-backed Christian militiamen in 1982. That incident, Khaled explained to his Italian interrogators, justified the terrorist attack on the airport four years later and the retribution heaped on a world insensitive to his people's plight.[40]

Joe, an eleven-year old growing up in Belfast, is Khaled's Irish Catholic equivalent. Like children throughout the world who play cops and robbers or cowboys and Indians, Joe and his friends play "Provos and coppers."[41] However, unlike the imaginary playmates other children have, Joe and his friends blaze away at actual British soldiers with their make-believe Kalishnakovs. Not surprisingly, Joe's central aim in life is to be able to throw a genuine Molotov cocktail at a passing security force patrol,[42] a goal reinforced by membership in the "junior IRA" and attendant political indoctrination classes.[43] Half a world away Mirko, a five-year veteran of Peru's *Sendero Luminoso* at age twenty-one, demonstrates the chilling effects of this type of terrorist indoctrination. Although his late father was a policeman, Mirko now has no compunction about killing policemen. "To tell you the truth," he explained in an interview, "I was uncomfortable about that part in the beginning. I didn't understand why. But they educated me, and they educated me well. Now I understand."[44]

As James LeMoyne recently observed in an article on the war in El Salvador, a "second generation of young fighters is entering rebel ranks, mostly teenage children of rebel families who have known only fighting."[45] They are only part of the estimated 200,000 children under the age of fifteen who the United Nations estimates are currently fighting in one conflict or another around the world.[46] When they reach adulthood—if they reach adulthood—it will surprise no one to find that this succeeding terrorist generation will be harder, more ruthless, and more bloodthirsty than its predecessor. As Mirko remarked, it has been educated well.

GUERRILLA WARFARE

Although the changes that have occurred in guerrilla warfare during the 1980s are less dramatic than those pertaining to international terrorism, many of the same trends toward the use of more sophisticated weapons and increased lethality are evident. Guerrillas, like their terrorist counterparts, are better armed and more proficient at killing. Indeed, throughout the past decade, guerrillas were given access to the sophisticated weapons in the arsenals of both superpowers and lesser military powers alike. In this respect, the gap between guerrilla armaments and those of government military forces narrowed considerably. Governments, perhaps, retained a clear superiority over guerrillas only in air power. But even this advantage has arguably been neutralized by the availability of shoulder-fired, precision-guided, surface-to-air missiles such as the American Stinger, the British Blowpipe, and the Soviet Strela.[47]

The potential for older, considerably less-sophisticated, surface-to-air missiles to alter fundamentally the insurgent–government balance of power was demonstrated in December 1989 when Salvadoran President Alfredo Christiani hastily convened a news conference to announce that FMLN guerrillas had fired two SAM–7s at government helicopters.[48] Given that the arsenals of more than forty countries now contain SAM–7s,[49] guerrilla use of these weapons is likely to increase and, consequently, become less "newsworthy."

A more significant point, however, and one that has received less attention is the increasing "urbanization" of insurgency. Today, low-intensity conflicts are increasingly fought in the crowded, built-up areas in and around third world cities. This development is partly a reflection of the vast demographic changes occurring throughout the undeveloped world as persons uprooted by rural conflict or simply seeking a better life leave the countryside and migrate to the cities and partly a product of a specific guerrilla strategy. Some 50 percent of Latin America's population, for example, is now urban—a figure expected to rise to 75 percent by the year 2010.[50] Following close behind this shifting population are the guerrillas.

Insurgent strategy long has been described in classic Maoist terms as that of the fish swimming within a friendly sea. Thus, effectively harried in largely depopulated rural war zones by numerically superior government forces, the guerrillas increasingly have been forced to adapt and apply their rural insurgent strategies to urban environments. "The common denominator of most insurgent groups," a Central Intelligence Agency (CIA) publication titled *Guide to the Analysis of Insurgency* has explained, "is their desire to control a particular area. This objective differentiates insurgent groups from purely terrorist organizations, whose objectives do not include the creation of an alternative government capable of controlling a given area or country."[51] Urban insurgents today similarly have seized control over defined geographic areas in the band of slums and shanty towns ringing cities such as Lima and San Salvador, establishing in some cases shadow, alternative forms of government and exercising a crude form of sovereignty while repulsing government efforts to reassert its control over these so-called "liberated zones."

Abimael Guzman, the founder and leader of Peru's Shining Path, for example, states that this group's strategy is to "lay the groundwork to ensure that the action of the People's Guerrilla Army converges with the insurrection in the cities.... Just as combatants and communists initially moved from the cities to the countryside [they must now begin] to move from the countryside to the cities."[52] Captured FMLN documents from 1988 similarly speak of "radical and violent actions ... [having] a growing role" in urban areas.[53] Given that nearly half the total populations of both Peru and El Salvador, for example, now live in and around those two countries' capitals, it is perhaps not surprising to find that roughly the same percentage of both Shining Path and FMLN operations has occurred, respectively, in those two cities.

A variety of hospitable conditions enables the guerrillas to adapt an ostensibly rural insurgency strategy to an urban environment. Guerrillas have not only the same benefits and advantages that they have traditionally enjoyed in rural areas—control over territory; the allegiance (whether voluntary or coerced) of a considerable part of a country's population; inaccessibility to security forces; and a reasonably secure base for operations around the very heart of the government and its administrative and commercial infrastructure—but also opportunities for media coverage and international attention that otherwise would be unobtainable in tortuously traveled jungles or isolated mountain areas of these countries.

Moreover, because of their warren-like alleys and unpaved roads, these slums become as impregnable to the security forces as rural insurgents' jungle or forest bases. The police are unable to enter these areas, much less exert control over them. The insurgents thus seek to sever the government's authority over its urban centers and thereby weaken both its resolve to govern and its support from the people, with the aim of eventually taking power first in the cities and then in the rest of the country.

This development has unfortunate consequences for a civilian populace that, as violence in the cities escalates, will increasingly be caught in the cross fire of guerrillas and government security forces. In addition to the guerrillas' often deliberate use of civilians as shields or screens, such as occurred during the FMLN's November 1989 offensive in San Salvador, the security forces themselves typically are neither specifically trained nor adequately prepared for operations in urban areas—a point driven home by the Salvadoran security forces' aerial bombardment of guerrilla positions in the slums surrounding the country's capital[54] as well as by the high casualty rates both suffered by U.S. special operations military forces in Panama and inflicted inadvertently upon the civilians during the December 1989 invasion of that country.[55]

Even the Israeli Army, arguably the world's most combat-hardened and experienced force, stopped short at the gates of Beirut in June 1982 rather than pursue PLO forces into the city's labyrinthian streets and alleys.[56] This reluctance is largely because armies generally are taught—and therefore prefer—to fight against a mostly discernible enemy on a more or less demarcated battlefield under rules of engagement where an army's might can be exercised fully. The "battlefield" in an urban area, however, frequently is not a neatly defined, open territory where opposing armies clash but a crowded city with narrow streets and alleyways affording readily exploitable sniper's lairs and ambush points. Moreover, the enemy typically is indistinguishable from the civilian populace and, as in many recent cases, may be the population itself. Accordingly, when inserted in this unfamiliar setting, armies often fall back on the massive use of firepower that, although appropriate to a large-scale conventional war, is wholly inapplicable to urban areas filled with civilians.[57]

CONCLUSION

Clearly, the United States faces a revolution in warfare for which it is unprepared. For more than forty years, American defense planning has been oriented primarily toward fighting a conventional war along the central front in Europe against the Soviet Union. The collapse of the Soviet government and the democratization of the regions of Eastern Europe make this, perhaps, the least likely conflict that the United States will face in the future. Instead, it seems likely that in the coming decades U.S. security concerns and overseas interests increasingly will be affected by a multiplicity of small-scale, low-intensity conflicts occurring around the globe that will require a variety of different resources and a range of innovative, flexible policy responses.

Concerning international terrorism, the United States must have a clear and consistent policy on responding to terrorist attacks and provocations. We should accept once and for all that no progress will be made in the struggle against terrorism until the terrorists' state-patrons are held accountable for their aid and encouragement. Given that most terrorist organizations have no known permanent bases for the United States to target, we have no choice but to focus our attention on the foreign governments that support their activities.

Military options, however, will succeed only when they are used in support of a coherent, overarching plan. Although dramatic reprisal operations without specific objectives may assuage the American public's frustration, they may have little, if any, effect on the terrorists. This is not to say that military force should not be used, but it should be applied carefully and with a clearly defined strategic purpose.

Attacks should be crafted in such a way as to send a powerful message, not to create martyrs and therefore prove counteproductive in the long run. Operations that strike at a terrorist state-patron's economic infrastructure— oil fields and refineries, for example—or that disrupt internal and external telecommunications or black out entire cities by damaging power transmitters and substations will have a more salutary impact than those that kill innocent civilians. They also will help the United States to escape at least some international criticism.

Finally, President Bush has a responsibility to educate the American public about what it can reasonably do and what gains reasonably can be expected in the fight against terrorism. He must shape public opinion on this issue rather than—as happened to his predecessors—be shaped by it. Some observers, for example, have likened international terrorism to organized crime: no one expects that we will eliminate it completely, but neither do we do nothing about it. This is a point that needs to be driven home to the American people so that the present administration and its successors can react coolly and calmly to terrorist incidents and not feel driven to dramatic—and possibly pointless—military reprisals.

The United States, however, faces its greatest challenge perhaps in adapting to the changing low-intensity conflict environment as it affects guerrilla warfare. Here, in contrast to international terrorism, the United States certainly has a more indirect role to play because of the unlikelihood of large-scale American troop commitments abroad. But in facing the challenges of better-equipped guerrillas, urban insurgencies that unfold in tandem with rural insurgencies and, indeed, the war against South American narcotics traffickers, the United States nonetheless has a critical advisory and support role to play

The problem, however, is that the U.S. military arguably lacks many of the specific skills and capabilities required to respond effectively to the spectrum of low-intensity conflicts. Because of the American military's long preoccupation with the Soviet threat, our forces are overwhelmingly "high-tech" and trained primarily to fight conventional wars as opposed to the often "low-tech," small-unit tactics and "special operations" required in counter-insurgency. Military planners, therefore, have paid scant attention to the essentially "low-tech" requirements of low-intensity conflicts, assuming as a matter of course that, by preparing for the largest (even though it may be the least likely) contingency, a range of responses could be sized downward to fit lesser contingencies. The American experience in Vietnam further vitiated any interest in low-intensity conflict, refocusing the military's attention on its conventional European defense role while firmly relegating low-intensity conflict to a secondary priority. U.S. training and advisory personnel therefore often reflect our conventional war-fighting orientation and, accordingly, third world armies are trained in our own image.

In sum, the United States faces a new era of conflict that will necessitate rethinking as well as rebudgeting if we are to respond effectively to these challenges.

NOTES

1. These figures are based on the author's interpretation and updating of data presented in "Turn South for the Killing Fields," *The Economist* (London), 12 March 1986: 19–22. See also "Wars Galore," *The Economist* (London), 21 April 1990; and, Patrick Brogan, *The Fighting Never Stopped: A Comprehensive Guide to World Conflict Since 1945* (New York: Vintage Books, 1990), vii–xvii.

2. This phenomenon forms the basis of the discussion in Brian Michael Jenkins, *New Modes of Conflict* (Santa Monica: The RAND Corporation, R–3009-DNA, June 1983).

3. This is a revised accounting of the figures presented in David Wood, *Conflict in the Twentieth Century, Adelphi Papers Number 48* (London: The Institute for Strategic Studies, June 1968). See also, "Turn South for the Killing Fields," 19.

4. "Turn South for the Killing Fields," 19.

5. Although the severest refugee problem by far is in Africa, only five of the ten countries with the most number of refugees are located in that region. Afghanistan heads the list, followed by the Palestinians, Mozambique, Ethiopia, Iraq, Angola, Sudan, Somalia, Kampuchea, and Iran. Source: U.S. Committee for Refugees, cited in Peter Grier, "Millions Uprooted by War," *Christian Science Monitor*, 25 April 1990. See also Brogan, *The Fighting Never Stopped*, vii, who observes that the number of refugees from conflicts today are "probably as many as there were during the mass movements of people after World War II."

6. According to *The RAND Corporation Chronology of International Terrorism* (Santa Monica: The RAND Corporation, 1968, 1989), 2,536 incidents occurred between 1970 and 1979 as compared to 3,658 between 1980 and 1989; a total of 4,077 persons were killed by terrorists between 1980 and 1989 as compared with the 1,975 killed between 1970 and 1979.

7. Unless otherwise noted the statistics presented in this chapter are taken from *The RAND Corporation Chronology of International Terrorism*.

8. Israeli intelligence sources, for example, estimate that 20,000 terrorists are currently receiving salaries from fifteen Palestinian organizations. See Joshua Brilliant, "'Terrorism will Increase,'" *Jerusalem Post* (International Edition), 30 June 1990.

9. For example, the same nationalist/separatist and religious fervor that drives terrorism throughout the world eventually may threaten the former Soviet Union's internal cohesion. Ethnic and/or nationalist-inspired unrest—in some instances mixed with sectarian animosity—already has been reported in at least thirteen Soviet republics, including: Estonia, Latvia, Lithuania, the Ukraine, Moldavia, Byelorussia, Georgia, Armenia, Azerbaijan, Turkmenia, Uzbekistan, Kazakhstan, Kirghizia, and Tadzhikistan. See Craig R. Whitney, "Riots Involving Ethinc Rivalries Erupt in Another Soviet Republic," *The New York Times*, 13 February 1990, and Associated Press, "Ethnic Warfare Grows in Soviet Asia, with 48 Killed in One City," *New York Times*, 8 June 1990.

10. All the ideological terrorist groups are left-wing in political orientation. The terrorist organization not accounted for in the above total is one run by Colombian narcotics traffickers.

11. David Hearst, "Publicity Key Element of Strategy," *The Guardian* (London), 31 July 1990.

12. See, for example, David Pallister, "Provos Seek to 'Play Havoc with British Nerves and Lifestyles,'" *The Guardian* (London), 31 July 1990.

13. The PIRA, for example, has been described by one senior British security official as "Without doubt . . . the most professional terrorist organization in the world today." James Adams and Liam Clarke, "War Without End," *The Sunday Times* (London), 17 June 1990.

14. See, for example, David Rose, "Devices Reveal IRA Know-how," *The Guardian* (London), 18 May 1990.

15. Discussion with U.S. airline official with particular knowledge of the Pan Am Flight 103 bombing. Eight ounces (249 grams), on the other hand, is the amount of plastic explosive that the new thermal neutron analysis devices are calibrated to detect. See "Explosive Detection Systems Boosted, Blasted at Hearing," *Counter-Terrorism and Security Intelligence*, 12 February 1990.

16. Even those terrorist organizations lacking a foreign patron or sponsor can obtain a range of sophisticated weapons, including *Semtex* and other plastic explosives, from the international black market. See James Adams, *Engines of War* (Cambridge, Mass.: Atlantic Monthly Press, 1990), and, John W. Soule, "Problems in Applying Counterterrorism to Prevent Terrorism: Two Decades of Violence in Northern Ireland Reconsidered," *Terrorism* 121 (1989): 38.

17. Eric Hammel, *The Root: The Marines in Beirut, August 1982–February 1984* (San Diego: Harcourt Brace Jovanovich, 1985), 303.

18. Statistic deduced based on information from *The RAND Chronology of International Terrorism*.

19. For example, according to Amos Gilboa, a former deputy head of Israeli military intelligence, some 5,000 members of various Palestinian terrorist organizations have been trained since 1973 in east-bloc countries such as East Germany, Romania, Poland, Hungary, and Czechoslovakia. See Ian Black, "East European reforms cut off sources of aid to PLO," *The Guardian*, 22 January 1990. In addition, the arrests in East Germany and extradition to West Germany of nine leading Red Army Faction (RAF) terrorists,

based on information apparently furnished by a disgruntled former agent in the East German state security organization, provides further evidence that the sanctuary previously enjoyed by terrorists behind the Iron Curtain has ended—even before reunification! See "East Germans Seize 4 Tied to Terror in West," *New York Times*, 16 June 1990; "Bonn Links Woman Held in East to Killings of G.I.'s," *New York Times*, 17 June 1990; "Terrorists Left Without a Curtain," *Washington Times*, 18 June 1990; and, "East Germans Hold Two More Suspects in Terrorist Attacks," *New York Times*, 20 June 1990.

20. Among the groups believed already to have benefitted from Libya's largesse are PIRA, the Popular Front for the Liberation of Palestine-General Command (the terrorist organization credited by many with the bombing of Pan Am Flight 103), the Lebanese Armed Revolutionary Faction (LARF), the Armenian Secret Army for the Liberation of Armenia (ASALA), the Palestinian May 15th Organization, the elite Force–17 unit of al-Fatah, the renegade Palestinian Abu Nidal Organization, and the Italian Red Brigades. See "Czechoslovakia and the Middle East: A New Ball Game," *MEDNEWS* (*Middle Eastern Defense News*) 3, no. 14, 30 April 1990: 5, and Glenn Frankel, "Sale of Explosive to Libya Detailed," *Washington Post*, 23 March 1990. The PIRA allegedly received five to ten tons of *Semtex* from Libya in addition to another 120 tons of arms and explosives, including 12 SAM–7 ground-to-air missiles. "IRA: The Libyan Connection," *The Economist* (London), 31 March 1990.

21. As Czechoslovakian President Vaclav Havel observed on a recent official visit to Britain, "If you consider that 200 grams is enough to blow up an aircraft … this means world terrorism has enough *Semtex* to last 150 years." Quoted in Glenn Frankel, "Sale of Explosive to Libya Detailed," *Washington Post*, 23 March 1990.

22. Frankel, "Sale of Explosive to Libya Detailed."

23. Margaret L. Rogg, "Sudanese Airliner With 60 On Board Downed By Missile," *New York Times*, 18 August 1986, and Brogan, *The Fighting Never Stopped*, xiii. UNITA (the National Union for Total Independence of Angola) claims to have shot down at least three civilian aircraft. In 1985 the Afghani government reported that mujahedeen shot down a civilian airliner killing its fifty-two passengers. See David Isby, "Sons of SAM," *Soldier of Fortune*, March 1989, 30–31.

24. James Adams and David Leppard, "IRA Set to Use SAM–7 Missiles in Terror Drive," *Sunday Times* (London), 19 February 1989.

25. Howell Raines, "Machine Guns Due on Ulster Copters," *New York Times*, 7 January 1988.

26. The Red Army Faction is believed to have used a similar device in its attempt to assassinate West Germany's senior adviser on terrorism, Hans Neusel, in July 1990. See "Bonn's Top Terror Expert Survives Bomb," *The Independent* (London), 28 July 1990, and Ian Murray, "German Police Chief Survives Car Bomb," *The Times* (London), 28 July 1990.

27. Steven Kinzer, "German Far Left Dogs New Agency," *The New York Times*, 5 April 1991.

28. For a more detailed discussion of these distinctions, see the author's "The Contrasting Ethical Foundations of Terrorism in the 1980s," in *Terrorism and Political Violence* 1, no. 3 (July 1989): 361–77. This article also was published, under the same title, in January 1988 by the RAND Corporation Paper series as P–7416.

29. David C. Rapoport, "Fear and Trembling: Terrorism in Three Religious Traditions," *American Political Science Review* 78, no. 3 (September 1984): 659.

30. For example, none of the identifiable terrorist groups active in 1969 could be classified as "religious." By 1989, however, at least twelve groups had a dominant religious component. Admittedly, many "secular" terrorist groups have a strong religious element as well—the PIRA, the Armenians, and perhaps the PLO as well. However, the political aspect is the predominant characteristic of these groups, as evinced by their nationalist or irredentist aims.

31. According to *The RAND Corporation Chronology of International Terrorism*, between 1982 and 1989 Shi'a terrorist groups committed 247 terrorist incidents but were responsible for 1,057 deaths.

32. See *Arkansas Gazette*, 27 April 1987, cited in Bruce Hoffman, *Recent Trends and Future Prospects of Terrorism in the United States* (Santa Monica: The RAND Corporation, R–3618, May 1988), 61.

33. Thomas L. Friedman, "Jewish Terrorists Freed by Israel," *The New York Times*, 9 December 1984. See also Grace Halsell, "Why Bobby Brown of Brooklyn Wants to Blow Up Al Aqsa," *Arabia* (London: August 1984); Martin Merzer, "Justice for All in Israel?" *Miami Herald*, 17 May 1985; and, "Jail Term of Jewish Terrorist Reduced," *Jerusalem Post* (International Edition), 12 October 1985.

34. See, for example, Rapoport, "Fear and Trembling: Terrorism in Three Religious Traditions," 674.

35. Brian M. Jenkins, *The Likelihood of Nuclear Terrorism* (Santa Monica: The RAND Corporation, P–7119, July 1985), 4–5.

36. See Rapoport, "Fear and Trembling: Terrorism in Three Religious Traditions," 659.

37. See, for example, Amir Taheri, *Holy Terror: The Inside Story of Islamic Terrorism* (London: Sphere Books, Ltd., 1987), 7–8.

38. Psychological studies of children in Lebanon, Northern Ireland, and South Africa, for example, reveal a strong connection between growing up in a world of violence and later becoming terrorists, arising out of a sense of hopelessness that is gradually transformed into violent rage. See the research conducted for more then twenty years by Dr. Rona Fields of Alexandria, Virginia, cited in Daniel Goldman, "The Roots of Terrorism Are Found in Brutality of Shattered Childhood," *The New York Times*, 2 September 1986.

39. See Lamai Lahoud, "Lebanon: Who Can We Take on Next?" *The Middle East* March 1990, 14. In 1989, for example, Reuters reported that the PLO was planning to hold a month-long military training exercise in Yemen for 1,000 Palestinian children from throughout the Middle East. See "PLO Plans Military Training for Children," *Los Angeles Times*, 28 July 1989.

40. See Bruce Hoffman, *The Other Terrorist War: Palestinian versus Palestinian* (Santa Monica: The RAND Corporation, P–7175, January 1986), 4.

41. "Provos" being slang for Provisional, as in the Provisional Irish Republican Army.

42. David Sapsted, "Fall Road War Games of Joe, Aged 11," *The Times* (London), 30 August 1988.

43. See Soule, "Problems in Applying Counterterrorism to Prevent Terrorism," 36. Indeed, as Soule observes,

Political socialization of young Catholics is also assisted by the constant presence of British soldiers patrolling their streets, doorways, and backyards. Squads of armed soldiers in Catholic communities, running doorway to doorway in full combat gear, pointing their Sterlings at phantom snipers, jostling the passerby, often exchanging bitter and crude remarks with neighborhood women, cannot but have powerful socialization effects on potential PIRA recruits. Young boys often learn hate from the ways their mothers and sisters are treated on the street.

See also, Allesandra Stanley, "Northern Ireland: Death After School," *Time,* 18 June 1990.

44. Quoted in Tina Rosenberg, "Thesis Disperuvian," *The New Republic,* 9 October 1989.

45. James LeMoyne, "El Salvador's Forgotten War," *Foreign Affairs* 68, no. 3 (Summer 1989): 120.

46. Alessandra Stanley, "Child Warriors," *Time,* 18 June 1990.

47. The Stinger, one of the more technologically advanced hand-held missiles, has, in fact, been credited with almost singlehandedly turning the tide of battle in Afghanistan away from the high-tech, numerically superior, Soviet forces to the simple mujahidin ("holy warrior"). See, for example, "Weapons, Deadly Weapons," *The Economist* (London), 18 February 1989: 18.

48. *The New York Times,* 2 December 1989.

49. James Adams and David Leppard, "IRA Set to Use SAM–7 Missiles in Terror Drive," *Sunday Times* (London), 19 February 1989.

50. Report by the Regional Conflict Working Group submitted to the Commission on Integrated Long-Term Strategy, *Supporting U.S. Strategy For Third World Conflict* (Washington, D.C.: The Pentagon, June 1988), 12.

51. Central Intelligence Agency, *Guide to the Analysis of Insurgency* (Washington, D.C.: U.S. Government Printing Office, no date), 2.

52. Quoted in Gordon McCormick, *The Shining Path and the Future of Peru* (Santa Monica: The RAND Corporation, R–3781-DOS/OSD, March 1990), 24.

53. Quoted in James LeMoyne, "The Guns of Salvador," *The New York Times Magazine,* 5 February 1989, 53.

54. According to the Associated Press, at least 3,360 persons—civilian, soldiers, and guerrillas—were killed or injured during the FMLN's offensive in November 1989. See America's Watch, *Carnage Again: Preliminary Report on Violations of the Laws of War by Both Sides in the November 1989 Offensive in El Salvador* (Washington, D.C.: America's Watch, 24 November 1989), 56. In addition, *The New York Times* reported that relief officials in El Salvador claim that the "great majority of wounded people treated thus far received their injuries from the Government's aerial bombardments. And the officials assert that at least four-fifths of the casualties processed so far have been civilians." See Mark A. Uhlig, "Salvadoran Army Continues Attack," *The New York Times,* 19 November 1989.

55. According to one observer, U.S. special operations forces "suffered 10 killed and 93 wounded, easily the highest rate of any of the conventional units in the 12,000-man force sent to do the fighting." An estimated 400 civilians were killed and 2,000 wounded in the invasion, and another 13,000 were displaced from their homes. See Bernard E. Trainor, "Flaws in Panama Attack," *The New York Times,* 31 December 1989.

56. See, for example, the accounts in Richard Gabriel, *Operation Peace For Galilee* (New York: Hill and Wang, 1984), 128–29, 132–39, 159, and Ze'ev Schiff and Ehud Ya'ari, *Israel's Lebanon War* (New York: Simon and Schuster, 1984), 210–19.

57. See, for example, Edward Luttwak, " 'Just Cause'—A Military Score Sheet," *The Washington Post,* 31 December 1989.

9

Observations on the Relationship of Freedom and Terrorism

Paul Wilkinson

One of the needs in this day is for a greater public awareness of the problems of terrorism. It is a particularly characteristic mode of conflict in our time. We don't like it, and we don't want to look at it too closely because it is a particularly grim and often gruesome subject. Yet we need to understand the roots of the problem and the dilemmas it poses for the liberal democratic system and international society as a whole.

Justice Oliver Wendell Holmes often used to lose his train ticket when traveling on suburban railroads. Once after furiously patting down his pockets to no avail, he said in desperation to the disapproving conductor, "My problem is not the whereabouts of my ticket. My problem is knowing where I'm going." One of the problems in peace studies, in international relations, and in particular in the study of terrorism is knowing where we are going, having something of a map to guide us through the complex field. While I cannot in this chapter provide a complete map of the field, I can point out some of the main landmarks of the domain.

The first landmark is to establish a working definition of terrorism, a term abused by academics as well as journalists—and certainly by politicians—as a general term of reproach for anything disapproved. Some governments label any sort of political opposition, even those using the most peaceful and rational means of opposition, as terrorist. This is an illegitimate use, but we should not be surprised by it. Concepts, after all, are weapons that are constantly used and abused. The concepts of democracy, war, revolution, and imperialism all have been subject to propagandist abuse. We must ensure as serious students of the subject that we can recognize these propagandistic abuses when they emerge.

There is now a substantial and rigorous body of literature on terrorism.

There are a set of conditions or criteria accepted by all serious workers in the field, most of which were studied by Schmid and Jongeman in their systematic review of the literature on terrorism.[1] Terrorism is quite clearly not a synonym for violence in general; it is not a synonym for war; nor is it a synonym for insurgency. One can discern important differences between violence that takes place in conventional conflict, in criminal violence, in crimes of passion, and terrorism, whether of groups or of states.

It is, first of all, the systematic and premeditated use of violence to create a climate of extreme fear for political purposes. Second, it is violence directed at a wider audience—a wider target—than the immediate victim of the violence. Third, as a consequence of this wider targeting, it inevitably involves random and symbolic targets that include civilians. Fourth, it involves extra-normal means in a quite literal sense, which is to say, a deliberate violation of the norms of society regarding conflicts and disputes and political behavior to create the impact of fear and the exploitation of that fear for the terrorists' ends. Indeed, one of the major characteristics of terrorism, as stated by Raymond Aron, is that it involves a degree of violence totally disproportionate to the numbers of people actually involved: "An action of violence is labelled 'terrorist' when its psychological effects are out of proportion to its purely physical result. . . . The lack of discrimination helps to spread fear, for if no one in particular is a target, no one can be safe."[2]

There is an unlimited number of ways this might be done: by seeking publicity for atrocities; by trying to wreak concessions from a government or some powerful groups in society; by trying to raise huge sums of ransom; by attempting to secure the release of political prisoners from jail; or by suppressing and controlling large numbers of people. States use terror in this latter way, even exporting terror overseas to suppress dissent further afield or to export revolution. While I will not attempt to draw a complete list of terrorist acts, I will add to this list of characteristics of terrorism by Schmid and Jongeman an important addition. We need to broaden their concept of politics to include the acts of groups that are motivated in part by religious aspirations. Some of these groups believe that terror is a justifiable weapon to rid the religious order of systems that are inherently evil or corrupt and to replace them with a superior one. One can say that their objectives are interwoven with politics, but it would be wrong to neglect that element of religious fanaticism present within it.[3] We must broaden our concept of politics to include, for instance, religious fundamentalism—not just Muslim fundamentalists, who have gotten all the press. In America there are dangerous groups that have welded together crude near-Nazi ideas of racial superiority with select ideas of fundamentalist Christianity.[4] Although fundamentalism is not unique to Islam, internationally Muslim fundamentalism in its various forms does constitute a major problem because of the prominence of some of these groups in terrible atrocities and the willingness to condone terrorism as an instrument of holy war.[5]

It is important to notice that these defining criteria are broad enough to encompass state terrorism as well as that performed by groups. States historically have been the greatest perpetrators of terror by far. They have had the means and the instruments of terror, and they are still the worst agents of repression and tyranny.

Typologically, it is useful to distinguish state from factional terror. Normally, in the literature a state's use of terror is referred to as terror, while sub-state terror is referred to as terrorism. I shall employ this distinction throughout this chapter.

One also must recall that terrorism is a weapon that can be used for both just and unjust ends. However one might define justice, it is clear that the cause of a terrorist may well turn out to be one toward which a liberal democratic person might find himself in moral sympathy. But, of course, that does not justify the use of unjust means to strive toward a just end. And there are unfortunately a vast number of cases where terrorism is used for unjust ends, where the claim to be a legitimate representative of a religious or national group or some class of society is wholly spurious. They do not represent even a large minority of the group they claim to represent. ETA (*Euskadi ta Askatasuna* or Basque Fatherland and Liberty Movement), the military faction of the Basque movement in Spain, enjoys the political support of between 6 to 7.5 percent of the Basque population. The largest political demonstrations in Europe in the post-war era have not been by the European disarmament movement protesting the dual-track decision of NATO, but they have been by Basques in Basque regions—places like Bilbao and San Sebastian—protesting the terrorism of ETA.

Freedom of the will is another important concept in the study of political violence and terrorism. Unless you are an out-and-out determinist (which I am not), you would assume that individuals are capable of free choice of their actions, of the choice of methods of political struggle to battle evils and remedy injustices; therefore, the conscious choice of individuals is an important element in this concept of freedom.

It is important to contrast freedom as the result and consequence of collective and individual acts of self-determination with the above sense. Freedom as self-determination is a characteristic concept of the twentieth century. Some suggest that self-determination is a full expression of freedom when, in truth, self-determination in the sense of achieving national independence may indeed create independence from foreign rule but may fail to bring about a condition of personal freedom for those living within the borders of the new nation. It is, therefore, important to distinguish freedom in the sense of a collective national self-determination; a freedom from foreign rule; and the condition of freedom in the sense of achieving democratic rights for the individual, civil liberties, toleration, and justice within the society that is thus created.

With these distinctions in hand, I first will examine the relationship of state terror and the struggle for freedom; second, terrorism and freedom in the third world; third, terrorism in liberal democracies; and fourth, terrorism in the international order.

STATE TERROR AND FREEDOM

It is an appropriate time to reflect on the relationship of these ideas after the remarkable events of 1989 and 1990. In Eastern Europe and the Soviet Union this was an amazing period. The Soviets abandoned Article 6 of the Soviet Constitution to introduce for the first time multi-party politics into the Soviet Union. Drawn up by Brezhnev in 1977, Article 6, which guaranteed the Communist Party a preeminent role in virtually all aspects of Soviet life, was discarded at the Congress of People's Deputies in the spring of 1990 and ratified by the 28th Party Congress in the summer. United States Attorney General Richard Thornburgh considered this a momentous act:

Gorbachev's willingness to amend Article 6 and to subject the party to electoral competition amounts to nothing less than a repudiation of the major tenant of Leninism—namely, that the party, as vanguard of the proletariat, has the right to hold power irrespective of the actual wishes of the populace.[6]

Eastern Europe heralded this pattern. Poland, Czechoslovakia, and Hungary now have elected non-communist governments, as has the Russian Republic. Germany has been unified on a Western model. The Warsaw Treaty Organization has abandoned its military structure. And now in South Africa the loathsome system of apartheid is at last in retreat. There are still strongholds of severe repression (for example, in Iran, China, North Korea, Albania, and many other countries). But the general trend world-wide is the overthrow of communist and one-party regimes and dictatorships in favor of regimes that favor some form of liberal democracy.

Is this reform in Eastern Europe all the result of the activities of Mr. Gorbachev? I think we have to give him credit where it is his due. He has brought about enormous changes. He has proved a remarkably adroit politician, he is a revolutionary in a whole new sense. But he is not nor does he claim to be a superman. He often has had to react very quickly to events in order to keep up with the pace of change, as he is having to do with the ethnic disturbance in the Soviet Union, and as he did for the growing demand for a multi-party system in the Soviet Union. But one of the reasons Mr. Gorbachev found himself and his advisors in the position of wanting a program of reform was because of the pressure being exerted from the grass roots. It has taken a lot of hard, patient, and dangerous work by groups protesting the injustices of these regimes. I think we must pay tribute to these courageous, non-violent groups and the leaders involved and acknowledge the limitations of even powerful modern states using the modern technologies of control. George Orwell's nightmare vision of *1984* has not shown that it can succeed over the determined will of the people seeking democratic change. This is one of the most wonderful outcomes to emerge from the clash of terror and freedom we have been observing.

Nor let us neglect the moral and intellectual resistance of churches in Poland, Lithuania, Romania, and many parts of the old Soviet Union. These churches have remained brave islands of dissent against stubborn regimes. The churches played the role of sustaining the underlying values of national independence, pride in national culture, freedom, the sanctity of the individual, and justice.

But none of these victories would have been possible without the continuing strength and commitment of democracies outside of the tyrannized world of Eastern Europe, the evident capabilities of the democracies to defend themselves, and the evident economic success enjoyed by the democracies in meeting the demands of their citizens so much more effectively than the bureaucratic systems and state planning organs of Eastern Europe. Above all, without the attractive power of free, open, pluralistic societies of the Western democracies, as evidenced by the constant flood of people pouring through the wall in 1989 and 1990, this transformation would not have occurred.

For all the popularity of terrorism elsewhere in the world, factional terrorism played no role in bringing freedom to Eastern Europe. Solidarity, New Forum, and the other resistance groups knew that terrorism would give the totalitarian regimes an excuse for mass repression. They always resisted terrorism on moral grounds, and this was always supported by their popular movements. Their studious avoidance of terrorism only enhanced their normal legitimacy, power, and influence among their populations. And it is clear that in Eastern Europe terror has been for decades the monopoly, not of subnational groups but of regimes that have resorted to it to stamp out dissent.

It seems to me there are two other major implications of these dramatic changes in Eastern Europe for the future development of terrorism. First, as the constituents of the former Soviet Union and Eastern European countries generally become more open and pluralistic and we see an intensification of internal, ethnic, religious, and possibly ideological conflict, these countries paradoxically will become vulnerable to one of the features we associate with the freedoms of open societies of the West: sub-national terrorism.

Those groups that choose to abuse the freedoms that they gain in order to use terrorism as a means of achieving their ends will find themselves able to do so to the extent that the governmental systems of Eastern Europe become more relaxed and more liberal. I believe that is a price the peoples of Eastern Europe are willing to pay. If we lived in Eastern Europe, we would be prepared to pay it.

For this reason, however, in order to avoid endangering their political and economic relations with the West, these countries, as they become democratized, will want increasingly to distance themselves from the state sponsorship of terrorism, from involvement in helping terrorist movements abroad. Why should they help something that might end up endangering their own people and their own society? This has made the Kremlin and the political systems of Eastern Europe generally think afresh about the desirability of terrorism as a political weapon, even internationally.[7]

There is a very strong possibility of East–West cooperation internationally on terrorism. Newly democratized Eastern European states and the former Soviet Union will be prepared as never before to lend some practical cooperation to the problems of preventing and countering the terrorist acts against the innocent that have been a distressing feature of the Eastern Bloc for the past twenty years. There have been actual professional meetings of American and Soviet experts on terrorism.[8] The Americans were particularly impressed that, although they had academic differences with the Soviet specialists, they did agree about many aspects of policy. They agreed that some forms of terrorism were a particular danger and deserved high priority of attention. The bombing of airliners was one. The Soviets were interested in exchanging information about technology to prevent terrorism and in exchanging data on the movements of terrorists. They also wish to cooperate on the tagging of explosives and the tracing of weapons that might be used by terrorists. These ideas are not just academic but have a real chance of being translated into policy.

The early stages of the reformist challenge in Eastern Europe are in many ways the most dangerous ones. Often embittered members of old guard groups, such as the *Securitati* in Romania, will try ruthlessly to use terror in a last-ditch effort to destroy the reform process or at least to provide themselves with a breathing space. Sometimes they will act out of blind obedience because they feel that they have nowhere to go when a change occurs in the system. The more adroit figures in the one-party systems are trying to learn to ride the wave of change before they are swept away by it. The most appropriate model of response to ethnic rebellion in the recently collapsed Soviet Union should not be Stalin's empire ruled by terror but the model provided by the astonishing wind-down of empire by Britain and France in the 1950s and 1960s.

While it is true in some cases that France and Britain became locked in bloody conflict, in most cases Britain and France did succeed in negotiating with their former dependencies. This proved a remarkably successful means of dealing with the problem of empire because it left a spirit of reasonable willingness to cooperate after independence had been granted. Indeed, quite amicable relations exist between France and the majority of nations that were formerly her colonies in Africa and elsewhere. The same could be said for many of the nations that were formerly under British rule. This model should be examined in facing Armenia, the Baltic republics, Georgia, and the half-dozen Muslim republics that sought independence or autonomy. Creating a real federal system, rather than the wholly cosmetic federalism now present in the Soviet Union up to the end, may have preserved some goodwill between Moscow and these ethnic regions and possibly avoid total secession.

There is a final observation on the relationship of freedom and state terror. It is crucial to avoid equating the achievement of national self-determinism in Eastern Europe and the former Soviet Union with the state of freedom in the broadest sense, a condition of genuine freedom, justice, and democratic participation. Will these states be prepared to live at peace with their neighbors when independence is obtained? Or is there a danger that they will be striking out at their neighbor's territory to resolve old ethnic boundary disputes? That sort of aggressive nationalism in the inter-war period and in the nineteenth century was a source of great strife that plunged Europe into terrible wars. We must not look upon the emergence of nationalism as itself a magical solution to the problem of peaceful international relations in the strife-prone region of Eastern Europe.

THE PROBLEM OF FREEDOM AND TERRORISM IN THE THIRD WORLD

Only a small minority of the states established in the post-war period, the period of massive decolonization, have succeeded in establishing truly viable liberal democracies. The majority of people in these states live under some form of dictatorship. Professor Richard Falk and others have argued that the international community still has precious little power to influence those situations of massive violations of human rights.[9] What could be done if another Pol Pot regime were to be established in Cambodia or another Idi Amin appears in Uganda? Saddam Hussein is a more contemporary example. With the fall of the one-party regimes in Eastern Europe, terror and terrorism as instruments of human repression in the third world are the most significant problems in the international system. These problems are ubiquitous in that part of the world for a number of reasons.

First there is the inheritance of colonization itself. Colonization was an arbitrary system imposed upon these peoples by the colonial powers. Ethnic and religious groups were caught astride the boundaries drawn along rivers or at lines of latitude according to the treaties signed in Berlin, London, or Paris. It should be no wonder that this division would create problems that come back to haunt the world in the period of decolonization. Many groups during decolonization felt that they were left outside the consideration of true self-determination, which their neighbors had gained. Peoples with grievances against the colonial power transferred those grievances to the new states almost as they were born. Thus countries like Sudan, Ethiopia, India, and Pakistan may have dozens of ethnic groups directing violence against the system because they believe it to be fundamentally illegitimate. They do not recognize it as a lawful government of their ethnic group. This is one basic reason why we have such endemic conflict in those parts of the world.

Second there is the fact that these third world governments are the most fragile, the most indebted to foreign sources of capital, and the most weighted down by poverty of regimes anywhere in the world. And these same governments are the ones least able to cope with these high levels of conflict. Tragically, many new nationalities in the third world have manifested aggressive designs toward their rival ethnic group, often becoming locked in bitter inter-ethnic conflict—conflict that historically has tended to beget terrorism and civil wars. All too often these conflicts are further complicated by foreign intervention.

In some cases these conflicts have raised the concept of *ungovernability*. Sri Lanka is tragically in this state;[10] Lebanon, too, has been in this state now for years, struggling to find a constitutional formula to escape the worst form of anarchy. Only the impositon of order from Syria seems to have ended the strife. As Richard Falk and others remind us, we have no machinery, no means of humanitarian intervention through the United Nations or any other agency to address such extreme cases of ungovernability and crises as these. We are so wedded to the notions of domestic sovereignty and the norms of non-intervention—for obvious historical reasons—that we have not yet devised a means of coping with that particular anarchistic breakdown of order and the explosion of terror that marks these situations.

TERRORISM AND LIBERAL DEMOCRACIES

In any truly operative liberal democracy terrorism must, by definition, be a totally illegitimate means of pursuing political ends. For liberal democracy inherently provides the channels of peaceful protest and opposition. The political party systems, the electoral systems, the mass media, the freedom of opinion, and the expression of public debate all serve to give expression to opposition and dissent. Of course it is true that some of the small fanatical groups that have plagued liberal democracies since the late 1960s have claimed to be fighting for freedom and justice. They much prefer to see themselves as soldiers or freedom fighters than portray themselves as terrorists. One is reminded of the observation of one of the salon leaders during the French revolutionary period: "O Liberte! O Liberte! que de crimes on commet en ton nom."[11] It is easy to use the term liberty to justify the shooting down of people in the streets or the bombing of people who are "legitimate targets" for terrorists. But when one thinks of the actual claims of legitimacy of groups like the Red Brigades, the Red Army Faction, the IRA, or ETA, and one realizes how spurious are their claims to be the "true voice of the people," it becomes obvious that terrorism in such contexts is the enemy of freedom. Terrorism is a threat to human rights not on the massive scale found in warfare but on a tragic scale for those individuals killed or injured or whose lives are ruined. What these tiny groups have been doing is using their freedoms within the democratic society to choose methods to kill and maim their fellow citizens. These are petty tyrannies of the bomb and the gun trying to impose demands by coercion that they know they cannot achieve through the ballot box. When surveying the victims of their crimes, one must conclude they are enemies of liberty.

But although terrorists can and do inflict tragedies of this kind, so long as liberal democracies themselves remain true to their principles of democracy, they can always ultimately defeat the terrorist. This is another paradox worthy of emphasis.

The price of a pluralistic and open society is that some people will exploit those freedoms to attack others in the name of some cause they believe to be just. But this does not mean that a liberal democracy is as inherently fragile and vulnerable as the impoverished and weak states in the third world.[12] The more serious problems of liberal democracies occur in a context wider than pure terrorism. The most dangerous of all threats to liberal democracies is a situation in which the liberal government is failing to meet the widely perceived basic expectations and needs of its citizens. It is a more insidious problem because it cannot be seen and measured easily or represented dramatically. When a liberal democracy begins to lose its basic legitimacy by failing to meet the basic needs of the populace, then it is placed in jeopardy. Such conditions of major social and economic crisis are the classic setting for the rise of totalitarian and authoritarian movements. And these sorts of movements often use terror as a weapon. Lenin's dictatorial Bolshevik Party hijacked the control of the Russian system at precisely such a time of economic crisis following the enormous destruction in the first world war. Hitler, too, rode to power on the back of a massive economic depression in Germany in the inter-war period. Bismarck once said, "Fools say they learn from experience; I prefer to learn by others' experience." Faced with such historical examples from the very recent past, liberal democracies must learn from others' experience. Let us hope that we do.

TERRORISM AND FREEDOM IN THE INTERNATIONAL ORDER

The central lesson to be drawn from the twentieth-century experience of the relationship of terror and freedom is that terror is the child of tyrannies, of hatred, of ideological dogmatism. Strong and vigorous liberal, open societies are the best protection against terrorist challenges to democratic politics. The best policy toward terrorism and other major violations of human rights is, therefore, to greatly strengthen the forces of liberal democracy in the contemporary world. It has been a good couple of years for democracy. However, there is no iron law guaranteeing that this process toward greater democracy, peace, harmony, and stability will continue. These victories must be worked for because of the nature of the problems that still confront us.

The Arab–Israeli problem has shown little sign of resolution yet. That tragic conflict looms like a shadow not only over the whole Middle East; it also presents a danger to the stability and peace of the world. There are other sources of conflict in the Middle East. The Iran–Iraq war has ended after claiming a million casualties. With the victorious prosecution of the war against Iraq we still have the huge problems of winning a just and lasting peace in the Middle East. During the hostilities between the coalition and Iraq, the U.S. State Department recorded 166 terrorist incidents against the United States and other coalition targets around the world.[13] Most of these were of a low-level nature and highly amateur in execution, and the majority of the attacks appear to have been carried out by groups sympathizing with Saddam Hussein and seizing the opportunity to hit American and other Western targets. Experienced observers had expected rather more spectacular attacks within the coalition countries. It is likely that these were forestalled by the swift action of Western security services in expelling Iraqi "diplomats" and others[14] and by the stunning effect of the allied bombardment of the Iraqi command and communication centers in Baghdad and elsewhere.

The task of creating a viable, long-term security framework for the Middle East should primarily lie with the United Nations. After all, the liberation of Kuwait was carried out under Security Council Resolutions. Part of the U.N. effort must be directed at resolving the deep underlying conflicts that spawn violence and terrorism, particularly the Arab–Israeli conflict. But the U.N. also must take a central role in preventing the massive state terror of Saddam Hussein against the Kurds and the Shi'ites in Iraq. Some have tried to argue that these are purely internal matters for Iraq. The threat of genocide can never be allowed to become merely a domestic issue. It is a matter for the conscience and the moral responsibility of mankind to prevent such outrages against humanity from occurring. What hope is there for a "new world order" if such a system proves unwilling even to attempt the prevention and punishment of genocide? A useful precedent for U.N. intervention in Iraq to prevent the horrors of internal strife can be found in the U.N. peacekeeping mission to the Congo in the 1960s. This was successful in its mission, and it was carried out without Soviet cooperation with the U.N., which is a striking feature of the current crisis.

These are examples of conflicts that have nothing to do with the East–West divide that preoccupied us for so long in the cold war and that still presents challenges to the stability and security of the international order.

In North America, the European Community, and Japan we can witness the undoubted success of liberal democratic states in delivering on the promise of freedom to their citizens—not that they have delivered this in full. One needs only go out into certain parts of Philadelphia, New York, Washington, London, or Birmingham to realize that we have still a long way to go. But at least some of the conditions of freedom and justice have been attained in those liberal democratic states.

The greatest challenge for the international community of democracies is to ensure that the transition from the kind of hegemonies that we lived under in a world dominated by a bloc system to a more multi-polar world is free of serious conflict that could engulf whole regions. This is going to be a difficult period for the management of international relations. It is going to involve a far more radical and imaginative use of the United Nations' machinery. And for the first time we have a chance of breathing life into that machinery once again. The Soviet Union recognized that that machinery has not been used adequately but that it is there on the drawing board. This view has been repeated by Mr. Yeltsin. The Security Council for years was hardly able to reform its key functions because of the cold war clash. Now you have the Soviet Union issuing papers from high-level officials calling for enhanced peacekeeping enhancement of U.N. machinery and greater cooperation.[15] We see the Russian Republic, in a time of economic distress, paying their U.N. dues and arguing that other countries ought to do so as well.

We ought to think seriously through the possibilities of using the machineries of the United Nations properly as they were originally envisioned. There was a Military Staff Committee for the enforcement of peace written into the original U.N. Charter. Let us revive it because the U.N. secretary general has pathetic resources to call upon to help him with these security problems. Let us provide the expertise the founding fathers of the U.N. intended but which was never actually forthcoming because of the occurrence of the cold war.

In the third world the most daunting challenge is to find ways by which the fragile economies of countries submerged by debt can be strengthened, thereby nurturing the democratic institutions. To do this, far more is needed than unilateral measures by the United States or the richer European states. The machineries of the U.N. must be revivified so it may become an engine of freedom and the growth of human rights as it was intended. It is only these long-term political, social, and economic reforms in the noble project of the global enlargement of freedom, justice, and peace that carry the hope of moving from a world still highly vulnerable to war, terror, and tyranny to a world of greater harmony and stability. Let us not be afraid of this ideal. The heart and call of liberal democratic political thought is not the idea that the triumph of reason and progress will occur automatically but the crucial ideal that by harnessing collective will and reason man can create a world characterized by freedom, justice, and peace. Our generation inherits this great challenge. Let us work together internationally to achieve it.

NOTES

1. Alex P. Schmid (with Albert J. Jongeman), *Political Terrorism: A New Guide to Actors, Authors, Concepts, Theories, Data Bases and Literature*, rev. ed. (Amsterdam: North Holland Publishing, 1988).

2. Raymond Aaron, *Peace and War* (London: Weidenfeld & Nicholson, 1966), 170.

3. See Leo Kuper's chilling piece, "Theological Warrants for Genocide: Judaism,

Islam and Christianity," *Terrorism and Political Violence* 2, no. 3 (Autumn 1990): 351–79. He argues that genocides often are motivated by religious differences that find a one-sided theological justification in sacred texts.

4. See Bruce Hoffman's chapter in this volume and his *Recent Trends and Future Prospects of Terrorism in the United States* (Santa Monica: The RAND Corporation, R–3618, May 1988). For a journalistic account of the campaign against violent White/supremacist groups see Kevin Flynn and Gary Gerhardt, *The Silent Brotherhood: Inside America's Racist Underground* (New York: The Free Press, 1989).

5. See the chapter by Khalid Duran, this volume.

6. Richard Thornburg, "The Soviet Union and the Rule of Law," *Foreign Affairs* 69, no. 2 (Spring 1990): 18.

7. The Jaffee Center for Strategic Studies in Tel Aviv reports a significant drop in Palestinian terrorism in 1989, reflecting both an emphasis on the intifada and strong pressure from the Soviet Union and Eastern Europe. See Kim Murphy, "Decline in Support, Havens Cuts Palestinian Terrorism," *Los Angeles Times*, 11 December 1989.

8. Brian Michael Jenkins, *The Possibilities of Soviet–American Cooperation Against Terrorism* (Santa Monica: The RAND Corporation, P–7541, March 1989).

9. This is a theme in Richard Falk, *The End of World Order: Essays on Normative International Relations* (New York: Holmes and Meier, 1983).

10. The head of the Sri Lankan government's anti-Tamil separatist campaign was recently killed by a car bomb. "Car Bomb Kills Top Official and 18 Others in Sri Lanka," *The New York Times*, 3 March 1991.

11. "Liberty, Liberty, what crimes are committed in your name!" These are the words of Mme Roland (1754–1793), on passing the Statue of Liberty in Paris on the way to the scaffold.

12. The RAND Corporation in Santa Monica, California, reports that terrorism has caused 3,000 deaths world-wide since 1968. By contrast, Amnesty International reports that there were 15,000 deaths in Guatamala alone between 1980 and 1984. Reported in Gerard Chaliand, "Terrorism: A Means of Liberation," *Terrorism and Political Violence* 1, no. 1 (January 1989): 21.

13. Briefing paper produced by the U.S. Department of State, Bureau of Security, March 1991.

14. See Bob Drogin and Charles P. Wallace, "As Terrorist Acts Multiply, Iraqis Are Expelled," *Los Angeles Times*, 22 January 1991.

15. In 1987 General Secretary Gorbachev called for a renewed use of the U.N. and other regional organizations:

We are arriving at the conclusion that wider use should be made of the institution of UN military observers and UN peace-keeping forces in disengaging the troops of warring sides, observing ceasefire and armistice agreements. . . . The Security Council's permanent members should become guarantors of regional security. "Secure World," printed in *FBIS–SOV* (Moscow) 17 September 1987, 25.

10

Can the European Community Develop a Concerted Policy on Terrorism?

Paul Wilkinson

Because the institutions of the European Community (EC) have a supra-national character, they often are mistakenly perceived as being federal. It is true that they possess autonomous powers of legislation and decision-making on Community matters and that within their specialized areas of competence they can make laws on individuals throughout the Community. But so far the pooling of sovereignty among member states has been mainly limited to "low politics," economic and technical matters. Foreign policy, security, law and order, and macro-economic policy still are regarded as the sole province of national governments and legislatures. Moreover, the supreme Community policy and legislative body, the Council of Ministers, directly represents national governments, and on key issues it has to act unanimously. For these reasons the Community still resembles a particularly durable and close alliance or a confederation more than a federation.

However, the current debate within the Community suggests that the pace of the integration effort is heating up. Jacques Delors, the president of the European Commission, has urged the Community's leaders to regard January 1994 as the target date for stage two of his plan for economic and monetary union. And despite the strains and stresses of German reunification, Chancellor Kohl has given his full backing to this target date. The effect of German reunification on the other Community members has been to make them all the more anxious to bind Germany tightly into the fabric of European integration.

With 1992 now looming closer and the prospect of a single European market for the movement of capital goods and services and people, there has been a flurry of proposals backed by continental member states designed to shift the Community in the direction of increased federalism. Among the ideas being discussed in inter-governmental committees are: a strengthening of the powers of the European Parliament; a common European foreign policy; and a common European security policy. Some wish to give the European Parliament the power of co-decision with the Council of Ministers. The implications of such a move are that MEPs (Members of the European Parliament) would have the power to reject the Council's decisions. This idea has revolutionary implications, but a more feasible proposal is to reduce the number of policy areas in which the Council of Ministers is subject to unanimous voting while retaining the unanimity requirements in more sensitive policy areas. Another proposal is that MEPs should have a direct role in approving agreements with non-EC states and in the selection of the president of the Commission.

Some of these ideas may well get dropped or greatly diluted during the EC's complex processes of decision and consultation. However, there is no mistaking the strong mood of support among the majority of EC governments for a substantial strengthening of the powers of the EC's supra-national institutions.

Yet despite these growing signs of a more rapid move toward greater political union, the Community appears curiously bereft of any genuine Europe-wide policy to deal with terrorism following the dismantling of internal borders in 1992. According to an old legal maxim *"De non apparentibus et de non existendibus eadem est ratio"* (It is presumed that what does not appear does not exist). But few can doubt that the threat of terrorism really does exist and that it will become far more dangerous when terrorists are free to move at will throughout the Community. Every European Community state has experienced some degree of domestic and international terrorism over the past twenty years. The IRA is still highly active and has demonstrated its ability to stage its murderous attacks on the continent as well as in Northern Ireland and the British mainland. It claimed responsibility for a mortar attack upon Number 10 Downing Street and two bombings of crowded railway stations during the Gulf War. The stubborn rump of ETA continues to take its toll of life in Spain, and the tiny residue of the Red Army Faction in Germany has proved its continuing capacity to commit brutal assassinations of major German business leaders. Italian juridical experts have warned that, given half a chance, in a Europe without internal borders organizations such as Mafia will exploit the opportunities of an "open market" throughout Europe. Police and drug enforcement agencies throughout Europe naturally are extremely concerned at the prospect of an increase in drug trafficking throughout the Community. While it is true that drug smugglers, like terrorists, currently are able to slip unobserved across frontiers, the existence of border controls, customs, and passport checks does at least provide some minimal means of monitoring the movements of criminals and even, in some cases, helping to prevent crimes from being committed. There are numerous cases of suspect terrorists being detained at ports and airports, for example, throughout Community countries.[1] Britain and Ireland have a particular interest in preserving their advantage as island countries, where it is inherently more practicable to maintain secure borders. In short, many security experts, police, and intelligence officers would agree with the comments of Hans-Ludwig Zachert, president of BKA (Federal Criminal Office) in Germany, who recently stated, "I support the European vision, but it means that we will all have to accept a loss of security. The main thing is that the price we end up paying is not too high."[2]

When one considers that the projected dismantling of Community borders has been known to all member-states for many years, it is remarkable that so little progress has been made in developing an effective Community-wide criminal justice system to serve Europe after 1992. It took five years before the "Schengen" group of countries in the Community (Belgium, the Netherlands, Luxembourg, France, and Germany) delivered on their 1985 pledge that they would get rid of all their mutual border controls, thus establishing a model for the wider Community. Even as late as December 1989, Luxembourg and Holland were arguing over the former's refusal to agree on tax fraud investigations. Then the whole agreement was held up by Chancellor Kohl's request for time to reexamine the terms in light of the problems arising from reunification with East Germany. It is true that reunified Germany has now signed the agreement, and there is now a zone at the heart of Europe where internal frontier controls have been scrapped. Yet it would be dishonest to claim that the Schengen group agreement provides the necessary standard of criminal justice coordination to offset the dangers of abandoning internal frontiers.

Hot pursuit is severely limited in terms of distance (ten kilometers). Plans for a computerized intelligence exchange between member-states will take nearly two years to implement, and there is no plan for a common court or law enforcement structure. Above all, there is no commonly agreed policy as yet on external frontier policy issues such as immigration, visas, political asylum, and the treatment of refugees. Without a concerted policy on these key issues at the Community level, the implications for counter-terrorism of a Europe without internal frontiers are very worrying.

Why has the collective response of democracies been so ineffective? It is inherently difficult in a world of sovereign states to secure effective international cooperation. Despite the fact that Western states cooperate in such organizations as the OECD and NATO, it is extremely hard for them to cooperate in the sensitive area of internal security and law and order. On such matters of acute sensitivity, nation states have traditionally taken the view that national governments have total sovereign control. Western politicians and judiciaries are as chauvinistic in this respect as other states despite the many moral and legal values they have in common with fellow Western governments.

A major practical difficulty in cooperating against terrorism is the lack of a clear single forum for Western democratic cooperation. The European Community does not include all the major Western states and in any case is primarily concerned with economic matters. NATO, although it has a larger membership, is by no means comprehensive and essentially remains an inter-governmental organization in which member states jealously guard their national sovereignty. It has been left to the Council of Europe to mount the most serious effort at Western European legal cooperation against terrorism, The European Convention for the Suppression of Terrorism (ECST). However the Council lacks political weight and influence, and its convention is in practice unenforceable.

Some Western democracies have little or no direct experience of terrorism and thus cannot see the importance of the problem. Enthusiasm for action often dissipates rapidly once shock at a specific outrage has died away. Some Western governments are unwilling to sacrifice or endanger commercial outlets, possible markets, trade links, sources of oil, or raw materials by taking really tough action against pro-terrorist states like Libya. Some states are also afraid of attracting revenge attacks from terrorist states and thus hope to buy security by appeasement. Some have a double standard and insist on re-garding some terrorists as "freedom fighters" who need not be condemned. Worst of all is the widespread defeatist illusion (assiduously cultivated by terrorist movements' propaganda) and there is nothing democracies can do to defeat terrorism. This is dangerous rubbish. Look at the success of countries like Canada (against the FLQ) and Italy (against the Red Brigades).

A far more radical approach involving major innovation and reform in Community institutions is required if the challenges of post–1992 Europe are going to be met adequately. It is surely time for the European Commission, the Council of Ministers, the European Parliament, and the legislatures of all member states to consider the possibilities of establishing a European Crim-inal Court to augment the existing structures of the European Court of Justice and the Council of Europe's Court of Human Rights. In a way, it is rather odd that Europe's legal framework should have grown in such a lopsided way, without any Europe-wide criminal law statute, court, and police enforce-ment system. The new court would be empowered to investigate, try, and sentence in cases of terrorism and other serious crimes, such as drug trafficking.

French jurists were discussing such a scheme as early as the 1930s. President Giscard D'Estaing spoke of his idea of a European judicial zone. It is surely time Community leaders revived this idea and set up at least a high-level working group to study preliminary proposals for a draft criminal law statute and court. It would have some enormous practical benefits. The confusion, red tape, and political abuse of the extradition process would be bypassed in the case of these major international crimes. Small countries would not need to feel so intimidated by fear of retaliation. And terrorists would know with certainty that the whole Community was no longer a safe area for them to base themselves and plan their acts of murder.

I was encouraged to see that the British Labour Party's front-bench spokesman on Northern Ireland, Mr. Kevin McNamara, took up this idea and wrote in favor of a European Community Court in an article in the London *Times*.[3]

Lastly, and most important of all, let us remember that the primary causes of the bitter ethnic and ideological conflicts that spawn terrorism are political. It is not enough simply for the European Community to address legal procedures to staunch violence. The Community should be urgently and actively promoting measures of conflict prevention, conflict avoidance, and mediation, both in the troubled situations such as the volatile conflicts of Eastern Europe and in areas such as the Middle East. Strengthening the rule of law for its own sake is useless unless it is done in harness with efforts to enhance human rights.

NOTES

1. To cite a single example, Kikumuru Yu, a high-ranking Japanese Red Army member, was apprehended at the Schiphol Airport in Amsterdam on May 1, 1986, carrying a kilogram of high explosive and detonators. Following the American bombing of Libya, Dutch customs officials had been warned to watch for Palestinian and Japanese travelers carrying transistor radios. William R. Farrell, *Blood and Rage: The Story of the Japanese Red Army* (Lexington, Mass.: Lexington Books, 1990), 211.

2. Interview reported in John Eisenhammer, "Risk of Crime Knows No Borders," *Independent* (London), 14 April 1990.

3. Kevin McNamara, "How Europe Must Block the Terrorist Bolt-holes," *The Times* (London), 20 June 1990.

Selected Bibliography

Clutterbuck, Richard. *Guerrillas and Terrorists*. London: Faber and Faber, 1977.

Crenshaw, Martha, ed. *Terrorism, Legitimacy, and Power: The Consequences of Political Violence*. Middletown, CT: Wesleyan University Press, 1983.

Hamnett, Brian R. *Roots of Insurgency: Mexican Regions, 1750–1824*. Cambridge: Cambridge University Press, 1986.

Heggoy, Alf Andrew. *Insurgency and Counterinsurgency in Algeria*. Bloomington: Indiana University Press, 1972.

Hermann, Margaret G., ed. *Political Psychology*. San Francisco: Jossey–Bass, 1986.

Horne, Alistair. *A Savage War of Peace, Algeria, 1954–1962*. London: Macmillan, 1977.

Jenkins, Brian Michael. *International Terrorism: A New Mode of Conflict*. Los Angeles: Crescent Publications, 1975.

Katz, Frederich, ed. *Riot, Rebellion, Revolution: Rural Social Conflict in Mexico*. Princeton: Princeton University Press, 1988.

Kupperman, Robert and Jeff Kamen, *Final Warning: Averting Disaster in the New Age of Terrorism* (New York: Doubleday, 1989).

Laquer, Walter. *Terrorism*. Boston: Little, Brown and Company, 1977.

Merkl, Peter H. *Political Violence and Terror: Motifs and Motivations*. Berkeley: University of California Press, 1986.

Miller, Abraham H., ed. *Terrorism, The Media and The Law*. Dobbs Ferry, New York: Transnational Publishers, 1982.

Morgan, Robin. *The Demon Lover: On the Sexuality of Terrorism*. New York: W. W. Norton & Company, 1989.

Rapoport, David D. *Inside Terrorist Organizations*. New York: Columbia University Press, 1988.

Reich, Walter, ed. *Origins of Terrorism: Psychologies, Ideologies, Theologies, States of Mind*. New York: Cambridge University Press, 1990.

Schmid, Alex P., and de Graff, Janny. *Violence as Communication*. Beverly Hills: Sage Publishers, 1982.

Schmid, Alex P. (with Albert J. Jongman). *Political Terrorism: A New Guide to Actors, Authors, Concepts, Data Bases, Theories and Literature*. Amsterdam: North-Holland Publishing, 1988.

Wardlow, Grant. *Political Terrorism: Theory, Tactics, and Counter-measures*. 2d ed. New York: Cambridge University Press, 1989.

Wilkinson, Paul. *Terroism and the Liberal State*. 2d ed. New York: New York University Press, 1986.

Wilkinson, Paul. *The New Fascists*. London: Grant McIntyre, 1981.

Index

Apodaca, Juan Ruiz de, 40–41, 42
Arab-Israeli conflict, 164
Arabs, 52
Arab states, 58
Arafat, Yasir, 53, 141
Archer, Christon, 3
Arendt, Hannah, 87
Argentina, 55
Armenians, 17
Armenian Secret Army for the
    Liberation of Armenia (ASALA), 152
    n.20
Arms trade, 5, 7, 15, 21, 26 n.17, 59
Armstrong, Patrick, 121, 122, 129. *See
    also* Guildford Four case
Aron, Raymond, 156
Artemis temple destruction, 5, 99, 114
Article 19, 111
Asia, 17
Asia Watch, 68 n.55
Assassinations, 52, 58, 60–63, 66 n.19;
    attempt on Reagan, 99; of caliphs, 54;
    derivation from hashish user, 54–55;
    Israeli mistake, 79; in Persia and Iran,
    55; Red Army Faction strategy on,
    143–44, 152 n.26, 168; of Sadat, 49;
    U.S. policy on, 78–79
Associated Press, 154 n.54
"At the Edge of the Union" (TV
    program), 120
Atlacomulco mob attack, 33
"Aunt Annie's Bomb Factory" (TV
    program), 128
Australia, 114
Authority, attitude toward, 89
Avon police, 128
Azerbaijanis, 17, 18

Baader-Meinhof group (Germany), 108
Bagdikian, Ben, 100
Baghdad, 164
Bahrain, 55
Balcombe Street gang, 125–26, 135–36
    n.30
Banditry, 35, 41, 42
al-Banna, Hasan, 65 n.13
Bases, 3

Basque separatists, 4, 5, 17, 72, 75, 84,
    107
Bassiouni, Cherif, 115
Ba'thism, 64 n.2
Ba'th Party, 66 n.22
Baumann, Bommi, 84, 98
BBC (British Broadcasting Corporation),
    110, 120, 132, 134 n.8
Begin, Menachem, 53, 101
Behavioral norms, 4
Beirut, 145, 148
Belfast, 98, 121, 122, 123, 145
Berger, Peter, 82
Berkowitz, Leonard, 85
Berlin, 84
Berri, Nabih, 55, 103
Bhutto, Benazir, 60, 61
Bhutto, Zulfikir Ali, 58, 68 n.47
Billig, Michael, 86
Bin Sabah, Hasan, 55, 66 n.24
Biological weapons, 19
Birmingham Six, 10 n.6, 123, 131, 136
    n.48
Bismarck, 163
BKA (Federal Criminal Office),
    Germany, 169
Black September, 57, 78, 79
Bloch, Jochanan, 66 n.19
Blood and fire policies, 35, 37
Bolshevik Party, 163
Bomb detection devices, 19–20
Bombings, 6, 10 n.6, 18, 19, 20, 26
    nn.15, 18, 30, 129; of airlines, 2, 11
    n.20, 18, 20, 30, 67 n.39; of Baghdad
    "command post," 8; as favored tactic,
    77; Greiss tests, 131; by IRA, 123, 124,
    125–26, 135 n.13; of King David
    Hotel, 66 n.18; of Libya, 9; of Marine
    Barracks in Beirut, 53, 66 n.18, 142;
    of refugee camps, 52; of Shi'ite
    villages, 52; signature of bombs, 124;
    of Suez Canal, 142; and suicide, 64;
    thin-layer-chromatography test, 125;
    using cars in Karachi, 142; using cars
    in Lebanon, 53; using transistor
    radios, 171 n.1. *See also* Guildford
    Four case; Pan Am Flight 103; Plastic
    explosives

European Commission of Human
Rights, 123, 135 n.l20
European Community, 9, 61–62; border
controls in, 169; computerized
intelligence exchange, 169; Council of
Ministers of, 167, 168, 169, 170;
criminal justice system in, 169;
European Criminal Court proposed,
170–71; and German reunification,
167, 169; hot pursuit, 169; policy on
terrorism, 167–71; and Schengen
group, 169; threat of terrorism, 168
European Convention for the
Supression of Terrorism, 170
European Court of Human Rights, 9,
135 n.20, 170
European Court of Justice, 170
European Parliament, 168, 170
Europeans, 51
Evening Telegraph (Belfast), 98

Factional terrorism, 159
Falk, Richard, 161, 162
False imprisonment, 6
Family Liaison and Action Group
(FLAG), 102
Fascism, 4, 51
al-Fatah, 145, 152 n.20
Fatah Revolutionary Council, 75
FMLN (Farabundo Marti National
Liberation Front), 26 n.17, 146, 147,
148; deaths in offensive, 154 n.54
Federal Aviation Administration, 20
Fenyvesi, Charles, 113
Ferracuti, Franco, 84
Fields, Rona, 153 n.38
Fighters for Israel's Freedom, 66 n.18
First Amendment, 6, 95, 110, 115, 130.
See also Censorship
"First Tuesday" (TV program), 128
Flórez, Cristóval, 41
Florida, 10 n.6
FLQ (Front de Liberation Quebecois),
Canada, 170
Flying detachments, 36–38
Foreign Policy Research Institute, 3
France, 3, 17, 32, 36, 56, 61, 84, 103, 160
France Inter (radio station), 103

Franco regime, 4, 72
Frank, Robert, 82
Free choice, 157
Free speech. *See* First Amendment
Freedom and terror, 157–65
French counterinsurgency model, 36, 38
French intelligence service, 60
Friedland, Nehemia, 5
Friedrich-Ebert-Stiftung, 62
Front de la Liberation National (France),
98
Frost, David, 128
Frustration-aggression models. *See*
Psychological factors
Fukuyama, Francis, 140

Galula, David, 31
Geneva Convention, 14
Geneva Protocol, 26 n.20
Genocide, 32, 33, 60–63, 164
Gerbner, George, 108
Germany, 8, 11 n.18, 17, 23, 26 nn.12,
15, 56, 60, 68–69 n.60, 84, 97, 98, 99–
100, 106, 116 n.30, 158; assassinations
in, 143–44, 152 n.26, 168; economic
depression in, 163; end of sanctuary
in East, 151–52 n.19; news blackout,
108; repressive legislation, 130;
reunification, 167, 169. *See also* Red
Army Faction (Germany)
Gilboa, Amos, 151 n.19
Giscard d'Estaing, Valéry, 170
Goebbels, Joseph, 98
Gorbachev, Mikhail, 158, 166 n.15
Gorton, Slade, 136 n.46
Granada (TV), 131
Great power patronage, 53
Grievances, 7, 15
Group behavior, 5, 82; clear group
identity, 82; frustrations suffered by
perpetrators, 86; group disintegration,
80; group maintenance or solidarity,
75, 82; group or peer pressure, 75,
77; group processes in selection of
targets, 82; group violence
explanations, 85–86; joining of group,
84, 86. *See also* Psychological factors;
Social psychological factors

About the Contributors

CHRISTON I. ARCHER is professor of history and the chair of the Department of History at the University of Calgary, where he has taught since 1969. He is the author of *The Army in Bourbon Mexico, 1760–1810* and the editor (with T.H.E. Travers) of *Men at War, 1914–1976*. He has written extensively on the Spanish military presence in Mexico and the causes of the Mexican revolution. Professor Archer has received social science research grants and fellowships and the Herbert E. Bolton Prize for the best book in English on Latin American history.

MARTHA CRENSHAW is professor of government at Wesleyan University, where she has taught international politics and foreign policy since 1974. She is the author of *Revolutionary Terrorism: The FLN in Algeria, 1954–1962* and the editor of *Terrorism, Legitimacy and Power: The Consequences of Political Violence*. Her most recent research has been on the psychology of terrorism, the internal politics of terrorist organizations, the development of terrorist strategies, and the effects of terrorism. Professor Crenshaw has held fellowships from the National Endowment for the Humanities, the Russell Sage Foundation, and the Harry Frank Guggenheim Foundation. She has been a consultant for the U.S. Department of State and the U.S. Department of Defense.

KHALID DURAN is an Associate Scholar at the Foreign Policy Research Institute in Philadelphia. He serves on the editorial board of the *Journal of Ecumenical Studies*. He is the author of *Die Politiche Rolle des Islam in Vorderen Orient*, "Religious Liberty and Human Rights in Sudan" in L. Swidler, *Religious Liberty and Human Rights in Nations and in Religions*, and numerous articles on

Islamic thought and history, Islamic resurgence, and Islam in the West. He has held the Ibn Khaldun Chair of Islamic Studies, Department of Philosophy and Religion, the American University, Washington, D.C., and has been a Visiting Professor in the Program of Comparative Culture, University of California, Irvine and at numerous academic institutions.

NEHEMIA FRIEDLAND is associate professor of psychology at Tel Aviv University. His principal research interests involve political terrorism and decision-making in stressful environments. His publications include "Hostage Negotiations: Dilemmas about Policy" in L. Z. Freedman and Y. Alexander (eds.), *Perspectives on Terrorism*, and "Political Terrorism: A Social Psychological Perspective" in W. Stroebe, et al. (eds.), *The Social Psychology of Intergroup and International Conflict*.

BRUCE HOFFMAN is an Associate Social Scientist in the Behavioral Sciences Department of the RAND Corporation, Santa Monica, California, where he has conducted research since 1981. He is the author of *"Only Thus": Jewish Terrorism and the End of the Palestine Mandate; The Future of British Military Policy Within Palestine, 1939–1947*; and numerous contracted RAND publications, including *Recent Trends and Future Prospects of Iranian Sponsored International Terrorism* and *The Contrasting Ethical Foundations of Terrorism in the 1980s*. His areas of research are low-intensity conflict, terrorism, and the Middle East. He has been a consultant to the United States and the Israel government.

LAWRENCE HOWARD received his training as a cognitive and developmental psychologist from the University of California at Irvine, where he is currently a research associate in the Global Peace and Conflict Studies Program and a lecturer in politics and society. His research is in the psychological basis of deterrence and the cultural roots of violence and terrorism. He is currently working on a paper on religious violence in Buddhist societies.

BRIAN MICHAEL JENKINS is Managing Director of Kroll Associates, Inc. Mr. Jenkins was Chairman of The RAND Corporation's Political Science Department from 1986 to 1989 and directed RAND's research program on political violence. A former captain in the Green Berets, Mr. Jenkins served in the Dominican Republic and in Vietnam, being decorated for valor in combat. He is the author of *A Hundred Wars* and *International Terrorism: A New Mode Of Conflict*, as well as contributing chapters to several volumes on political violence and authoring more than a hundred RAND reports and papers. He is the editor-in-chief of *TVI Report* and an associate editor of the journals *Terrorism* and *Conflict*.

ABRAHAM H. MILLER is a professor of political science at the University of Cincinnati. A specialist on the subject of political violence, he is the author of *Terrorism and Hostage Negotiations* and editor of *Terrorism, the Media and the Law*. His work has appeared in numerous scholarly and popular journals and his "Evolution of Terrorism" is standard reading for NATO forces. He has lectured extensively both here and abroad to the International Red Cross, Geneva, Switzerland; the Anglo-American Ditchly Foundation, Oxford, England; and the United States Military Academy, West Point. He has taught on the faculties of the University of Illinois, Urbana, and the University of California, Davis. He recently was the Bradley Resident Scholar at the Heritage Foundation, Washington, D.C.

ALEX P. SCHMID received his training as a historian at the University of Zurich, Switzerland. He is an associate professor in the Department of Political Science and a Senior Researcher at the Center for the Study of Social Conflicts (COMPT) at the University of Leiden, where he is the Research Director for the Program for the Interdisciplinary Study of Root Causes of Violence (PIOOM). He is the author (with J. de Graaf) of *Violence as Communication* (with A. J. Jongman), *Political Terrorism: A Research Guide to Concepts, Data Bases, Theories, and Literature and Research on Gross Human Rights Violations: A Programme*, as well as articles and monographs on terrorism, military affairs, and human rights.

PAUL WILKINSON is the Chairman of the Department of International Relations and Director of The Research Institute for the Study of Conflict and Terrorism at the University of St. Andrews, Scotland. He is the author of *Terrorism Versus Liberal Democracy, British Perspectives on Terrorism* and multiple chapters and articles on terrorism, airport security, and international relations. He is the co-editor of *Terrorism and Political Violence*.